THE POLITICAL SUBLIME

THOUGHT IN THE ACT *A series edited by Erin Manning and Brian Massumi*

THE POLITICAL SUBLIME MICHAEL J. SHAPIRO

Duke University Press   Durham and London   2018

© 2018 Duke University Press
All rights reserved
Printed in the United States of America on acid-free paper ∞
Designed by Courtney Leigh Baker
Typeset in Whitman by Graphic Composition, Inc.,
Bogart, GA.
Library of Congress Cataloging-in-Publication Data
Names: Shapiro, Michael J., author.
Title: The political sublime / Michael J. Shapiro.
Description: Durham : Duke University Press, 2018. | Series:
    Thought in the act | Includes bibliographical references
    and index. |
Identifiers: LCCN 2017035993 (print)
LCCN 2017045061 (ebook)
ISBN 9780822372059 (ebook)
ISBN 9780822370338 (hardcover : alk. paper)
ISBN 9780822370529 (pbk. : alk. paper)
Subjects: LCSH: Sublime, The—Political aspects. | Aesthetics
    —Political aspects. | Political science—Philosophy.
Classification: LCC BH301.S7 (ebook) | LCC BH301.S7 S537 2018
    (print) | DDC 111/.85—dc23
LC record available at https://lccn.loc.gov/2017035993

Cover art: David Maisel, *Terminal Mirage I*, 2003. Courtesy
the artist / www.davidmaisel.com. © David Maisel.

Duke University Press gratefully acknowledges the University
of Hawaii at Manoa, Department of Political Science, which
provided funds toward the publication of this book.

For Hannah

CONTENTS

I am grateful for the support of many who welcomed my investigation of the political aspects of the sublime in its initial stages and subsequently in draft form. Thanks are owed to the series editors, Brian Massumi and Erin Manning, and Duke University Press's Editorial Director, Ken Wissoker, who welcomed the project enthusiastically when it was in its inchoate form. Thereafter my editor Courtney Berger managed an outstanding review process and provided important editing suggestions that helped me reshape my introduction. The two reviewers (one of whom was Davide Panagia and one who remained anonymous) provided suggestions that were cogent and helped me clarify my project and make the text's intentions more intelligible to the reader (as well as to me). I couldn't have had better reviewers.

Some of the chapters' drafts have been presented at colloquia and professional conferences. For the invitations and acceptances that made that possible I am grateful to Yehonatan Abramson, Libby Anker, Marieke de Goede, Brad Evans, Caroline Holmqvist, Sankaran Krishna, Joao Nogueira, Nandita Sharma, Lars Toender, Roberto Yamato, and Andreja Zevnik. Thanks also to Sam Opondo and Andreja Zevnik for their suggestions that helped me reshape chapter 1. And finally, special thanks are owed to my students in the University of Hawai'i's Political Science program and in the Pontifical Catholic University of Rio de Janeiro's Institute for International Relations, who heard and reacted generously to chapter drafts delivered in lectures.

Finally, I want to express my appreciation to the Duke personnel who helped manage the production process—Sandra Korn, Bonnie Perkel, Lisa Bintrim, and Christi Stanforth—and freelance copyeditor Stephanie Sakson.

This investigation is my second engagement with Immanuel Kant's Analytic of the Sublime. In my first analysis of that analytic, I was intrigued by Kant's ambivalence. While Kant saw an encounter with an object of beauty (in his Analytic of the Beautiful) as an event that yields harmonious universalizing accord among the subject's diverse mental faculties, promising a consensus among subjects, a "subjective necessity," his confidence in the possibility of such a consensus was shaken when he explored the experience of the sublime. Influenced by Edmund Burke's account of the terror of the sublime, an object or event so vast and/or sudden that one's imagination is immobilized and attempts to make sense and verbalize the feeling are stymied, Kant recognized that in the experience of the sublime one's mind is in disarray. He admitted that in this kind of experience, where pain and discord reigns (at least initially), it's hard to be convinced that subjective necessity can result. Although Kant was ultimately unwilling to abandon his commitment to a *sensus communis* and accept the enduring fragility and singularity of subjectivity he had discovered when he turned to the sublime (he purported to rescue subjective necessity by recurring to his Critique of Practical Reason, where he proffers a universalizing moral consensus), others have pursued the radical political implications he refused to accept. As I put it in my original engagement with his argument, "[Kant's] inability to establish the subjective necessity he sought when he evoked the encounter with the sublime opens up the possibility of a plurality of loci of enunciation and . . . challenges . . . those reigning political discourses that depend for the cogency on naturalizing or rendering necessary contingent modes of facticity."[1]

My return to the sublime in this investigation engages Kant's Analytic of the Sublime from a somewhat different angle, prompted by the way the sublime kept coming up in my recent investigation of political temporalities, in which, as I moved from example to example, I found myself being ambushed by the sublime. It's a concept that manifests a high degree of insistence (albeit it with the help of astute commentators).[2] Relevant to many political concerns, the concept of the sublime tends to flash up as soon as one contemplates the extent to which there is a challenge to one's imagination because of an experience's immense and difficult to comprehend scope.

The persistent relevance of the concept of the sublime is owed in no small measure to Kant's enduring influence. He wasn't exaggerating when he characterized his philosophical intervention as a Copernican Revolution in philosophy. His three critiques are a revolutionary event in the history of thought. The attention they summon is owed primarily to Kant's elaboration of the subject's active role in constituting experience, which continues to provoke and nourish critical thinking. In particular, Kant's Third Critique, concerned with aesthetic judgment, still inspires politically oriented investigation in a wide variety of disciplines. After centuries of scholarly engagement, its implications have not been exhausted, even though it has attracted strong criticism from thinkers who have convincingly resisted Kant's pious hope for a universal sensibility, a piety that Kant himself undermined (even as he sought to rescue it) when he saw it imperiled as he proceeded to his Analytic of the Sublime.

In this investigation I again contest Kant's commitment to a universalizing *sensus communis*. However, the pluralization to which I turn (an assumption that there exist multiple, often oppositional communities of sense that pre- and remediate events) derives from the way artistic and cultural texts intervene and mediate the experience of the sublime. Heeding the implications of those interventions enables the primary contribution I hope to make: the articulation of a politics of aesthetics that can capture the political implications of catastrophic events. Crucially, the textual hopscotch that moves my analysis along in each chapter (a writing method I address below) presumes a revision of the temporal process that Kant attributed to the sublime experience. Where Kantian temporality is constituted as a dynamic of mentality—a rapid and wholly cognitive movement from one's initial (and painful) apprehension of the sublime to a pleasurable comprehension, as one recognizes that one's reasoning mind is greater than anything nature can dish out—I side with those who defer that dynamic and displace mentality with textuality, focusing on a negotiation among diverse mediations that keep events from achieving definitive consensual closure. The alteration in the temporal frame with which the sublime is thought provides an opening to an analysis of how sublime experiences activate diverse sense-making communities within the body politic. And most significantly for purposes of my investigations throughout my various chapters, it provides for a political apprehension of the way events endure as subjects of ongoing political engagements in which they are recovered and reinterpreted.

A Political Sublime?

What then is the "political sublime"? Some have seen a turn to the sublime as politically conservative. For example, Donald Pease insists, "Despite all the *revolutionary* rhetoric invested in the term, the sublime has, in what we could call the politics of historical formation, always served conservative purposes."[3] Pease's "always" is now dated. He is correct in applying that insistence to Kant: "the sublime, instead of disclosing a revolutionary way of being other than the ethical, in Kant's rendition, is reduced to strictly ethical duties. . . . the [Kantian] sublime makes the formation of an ethical character *sound as* if it is a rebellious task."[4] And he may be right about the various other approaches to the sublime that he identifies, those who—operating within a variety of disciplines, such as literature and history, among others—view the sublime as disruptive of traditional normativities, only to recuperate them or posit durational shifts with no political consequences.

However, the influence of critical philosophical approaches—notably those of Gilles Deleuze, J.-F. Lyotard, and Jacques Rancière—have since encouraged versions of a politics of aesthetics within which disruptions (those of sublime experiences among others) yield critical political challenges to sense making.[5] While Deleuze and Lyotard develop their politically oriented aesthetics with an emphasis on Kant's Analytic of the Sublime, Rancière favors Kant's Analytic of the Beautiful as a starting point.[6] Nevertheless, in Rancière's appropriation of Kant's Third Critique, it's fair to say that for him "politics *is* sublime" (my emphasis); it is sublime in the sense that politics is an event based on an "aesthetic break."[7] Rancière's political focus on the disparities that emerge as new voices make political claims is in accord with the way I want to conceive a sublime politics. For me (as for Rancière among other post-Kantians), the crucial political initiatives that challenge authoritative and institutionalized modes of power and authority are precipitated by disruptive events that provoke the formation of oppositional communities of sense, which register the existence of multiple experiential and thought worlds. The political sensibility that emerges from the revisions of Kant's exploration of the aesthetic faculty is well summarized in Rancière's remark that "the aesthetic nature of politics" directs our attention not to "a specific single world" but to "a world of competing worlds."[8] The attention-grabbing experience of the sublime therefore leads not (as Kant had hoped) toward a shared moral sensibility but to an ethico-political sensibility that recognizes the fragilities of our grasp of experience and enjoins engagement with a pluralist world in which the in-common must be continually negotiated.

How then can we characterize the narrative trajectory in which the concept of the sublime has emerged to facilitate such an aesthetics of politics? Deleuze provides a model. He suggests that concepts are historical dramas.[9] Heeding that suggestion, much of chapter 1 records the historical drama of the concept of the sublime as I track it from Longinus to Kant and thereafter to contributions of post-Kantian thinking, with an emphasis on how revisions of Kant's temporal account of the sublime experience open analysis to renegotiations of the meanings and implications of catastrophic events. Here I want to invoke the beginning of that drama with attention to the way Longinus's textual practice inspires the way my analyses are composed.

Writing, Method, and the Sublime

Longinus, whose attributed treatises inaugurate the concept of the sublime, addressed the question of the organizing principle of a compelling treatise. Putting the matter simply (deceivingly so), he wrote, "In every systematic treatise two things are required. The first is a statement of the subject; the other, which although second in order ranks higher in importance, is an indication of the methods by which we may attain our end."[10] Given those injunctions, it's surprising how elliptical Longinus's treatises seem to be. They are distinguishable more for their poesis than for their explicit theoretical argumentation. Nevertheless, as Neil Hertz points out, in the case of Longinus's treatise on Homer's Battle of the Gods, "Longinus' admirers, struck by the force of the treatise, are usually willing to release him from the strictures of theoretical discourse and allow him the license of a poet; they are likely to appreciate his transgressions of conventional limits without ever calling them into question . . . It has been left to more skeptical readers, wary of Longinus' 'transports,' to draw attention to his odd movements of thought." Among the critical responses to which Hertz refers is W. K. Wimsatt's complaint about Longinus's "'sliding' from one theoretical distinction to another, a slide 'which seems to harbor a certain duplicity and invalidity.'" Hertz grants that "a 'slide' is observable again and again in the treatise, and not merely from one theoretical distinction to another [so that one finds] oneself attending to a quotation, a fragment of analysis, a metaphor—some interestingly resonant bit of language that draws one into quite another system of relationships," but he goes on to rescue the value of Longinus's style.[11]

I want to dwell briefly on Hertz's rescue of Longinus's "sliding" because it helps account for my style of analysis/writing, *its* "odd movements." What Hertz shows convincingly is that the "movement" of Longinus's treatise "is clearly not linear; it does not run in tandem with the progress of rhetorical argument from topic to topic but is in some ways cumulative—that is, at certain points one becomes aware of a thickening of texture." And he adds, "Longinus seems to be working . . . at locating his discourse close to the energies of his authors . . . [that for example while approaching what he regards as sublime writing] . . . he too is drawn into a sublime turning, and what he is moved to produce is not merely an analysis illustrative of the sublime but further figures for it."[12] In short, Hertz suggests that Longinus's sliding evokes a flow of textual fragments that are impressively adequate to (even expressive of) his subject; Longinus (as Hertz makes evident) informs through form rather than through conventional linear explication. He doesn't, as his above quoted remarks imply, begin with a simple statement of his subject and go on to explicate his method. To borrow from an approach described by Walter Benjamin about *his* mode of analysis, "literary montage," Longinus "shows" rather than tells.[13] Without suggesting that my text bears favorable comparison with those of Longinus (whose immense learning and lyricism are daunting), I am moved nevertheless to try to achieve an instructive account of the compositions that constitute the investigations in this book, which proceed through a series of textual engagements.

To figure my approach to writing-as-method, we can assume that metaphorically the writer is standing on the bank of a river whose rapidly moving current would render perilous an attempt at wading to get across to the other side (the consummation of the analysis). However, there are many large stones that break the surface and lead in various patterns across the river, making possible a dry and safe crossing if one can leap from stone to stone. If we imagine that each stone is a text and that although there is more than one configuration of stones that affords a safe navigation of the crossing, only some (textual) configurations provide an effective thickening of the argument (one could find oneself leaping onto a stone from which no subsequent leaps will work to make an effective crossing, i.e., to amplify the analysis). Although there is more than one workable configuration, there have to be compelling reasons for the trajectory of leaps, which become evident when each stone—each textual choice—makes its own case by adding to the analysis without requiring extensive meta-textual justification. Presuming such a writing method, the narrative in each of my chapters is a textual hopscotch in which each leap adds an encounter with a text to thicken the analysis. However, before moving to an elaboration of some of the specifics of the textual analyses in each chapter, I want to address the critical implications of textual engagement.

Textuality

Attentive to Roland Barthes's theoretically pregnant remarks on the historical movement from work to text, I treat a text as a "methodological field" rather than simply as an object or a "fragment of substance, occupying part of the space of books."[14] For Barthes a text "cannot be contained in a hierarchy, even in a simple division of genres . . . What constitutes it is . . . its subversive force in respect to old classifications."[15] And crucially with respect to my concern with deferring the movement from apprehension to comprehension, for Barthes a "work . . . functions as a general sign . . . [which] should represent an institutional category of the civilization of the Sign. The Text, on the contrary, practices the infinite deferment of the signified . . . [although] its field is that of the signifier [it] must not be conceived as 'the first stage of meaning' . . . [but] as its *deferred action*."[16]

Taking up Barthes's distinction and playing it into a challenge to disciplinary allegiances, John Mowitt sees textuality as succeeding where discursive practices fail their critical mission. For example, looking at the historical discourse on sexuality, he notes that (as Foucault points out in his *History of Sexuality*), "Freud remained ensnared with the apparatus of sexuality."[17] Seeing such discursive formations as caught within the confines of disciplinary fields, Mowitt treats the text as an "antidisciplinary field" rather than an intra-disciplinary object: "the text is divided against itself—not only in terms of the way it straddles the domain of examples and models, but also in terms of the way it links the constitution of examples to the utopic, to the not yet integrated," resulting I would add in an opening of the spaces that the discursive practices of disciplinary orthodoxies have closed.[18]

Moreover and importantly for the sense that I derive from texts, for Mowitt, "the 'plural' character of the text (cf. Barthes) has less to do with some bland notion of multiple meanings, than with the empowerment that enables our constructions to be ceaselessly challenged—not merely contested at the level of conclusions, but subverted at the level of disciplinary legitimation."[19] Jacques Rancière has a similar take on the closural aspects of disciplinary knowledge. Disciplinary sensibility (for example in the case of sociology) has historically reconstituted "the social fabric such that individuals and groups at a given place would have their *ethos*, the ways of feeling and thinking . . . correspond to their place and to a collective harmony." Like other disciplines, it is part of a "scientific war against the allodoxy of judgments . . . [and against the] 'anomie of behavior.'"[20] Rancière privileges "indisciplinary thought . . . thought which recalls the context of the war . . . In order to do so, it must practice a certain ignorance. It must ignore disciplinary boundaries to thereby restore their status as weapons in a dispute."[21]

Reviewing Mowitt's and Rancière's versions of resisting the closural institution-supporting effects of disciplinary practices takes me back to why I have been intrigued by the ambivalence that emerged when Kant confronted the problem of the sublime-subjective finality problem. As I noted in my first encounter with Kant's texts, in the discipline of political science (as practiced by both international relations and political theory scholars) the focus has been on Kant's political essays. In pursuit of his ideological positions, they have sought to draw Kant into their disciplinary concerns by sifting through the treatises for content with which they can describe Kant's politics. Finding myself taking a different direction, I treated the political implications that come from an encounter with Kant's treatise on aesthetic judgment. The question I raised was about how to think the political after Kant.[22]

Mowitt comes to a similar conclusion with respect to literary disciplines. Examining the manifesto of the *Tel Quel* declaration (in the late 1970s), which called for a separation of literature from ideology, he asks, "What is at stake in the separation of literature and ideology called for in the declaration?" "Obviously a great deal," he responds, "but at a certain rudimentary level what is implied concerns one's ability to read a literary text without rifling its content for statements illustrating the text's adherence to prevalent ideological positions."[23] Similarly, witnessing the struggle within the text of the Third Critique, which for Kant recalled his philosophical project as a whole, helped me to see the text as a philosophically engendered methodological field with implications for political analysis. Encouraged to seek realization of those implications, in my earlier engagement with Kant's sublime I staged an encounter with a cinematic text, Stephen Frears's film *Dirty Pretty Things* (2002), which shows subjects in disarray, caught up in a very concrete, contemporary global economic sublime—a vast field of exchange that brings together those desperate enough to sell their organs, those precarious enough to be forced to assist in the process, those predatory enough to run the business, and those privileged enough to be buyers. The film's spatial trajectory maps some of the spaces of those different types, revealing a radically divided London, differentiated by alternative trajectories of arrival and subsequent habitation (which has created an abyss between the temporary population of well-off tourists and the desperate, recently arriving, mostly illegal refugees). And its narrative trajectory, within which the encounters among different lifeworlds display the contingencies of global forces, provides a text that opens itself to a wide variety of critical interpretations that disrupt traditional ways of reading the city of London. I take a similar approach to the texts to which I turn in this investigation.

The Chapters

As was the case in my original iteration of a politics of the sublime, in this investigation I deploy a philosophical analytic derived from post-Kantian versions of the implications of sublime experiences on artistic and cultural texts, this time with a more extensive set of applications and with a more elaborated set of reflections on sublimity.

My applications in the various chapters treat both immediate and longer-term catastrophes. Among the former are the earthquakes that constitute the bookends of chapter 1 (a reaction to the 1989 San Francisco earthquake inaugurates the chapter and reactions to the 1995 Kobe earthquake, fictionally rendered in Haruki Murakami's stories in his *After the Quake*, end the chapter). The last chapter, "The 9/11 Terror Sublime," is also about an immediate catastrophe, the destruction of the World Trade Center and the loss of thousands of lives.

The middle three chapters—"the racial sublime," "the nuclear sublime," and the "industrial sublime"—treat longer-term catastrophes (associated with the violence of the color line, nuclear poisoning in the American West and the Pacific, and the damage to land- and peoplescapes from the machine age onward, respectively). In all the chapters, my emphasis is on the way the meanings and implications of events are mediated in diverse cultural and artistic texts. Within each of those investigations, I enlist philosophical frames that "interfere" with the texts that constitute the trajectory of my politically oriented textual mediations of the apprehension–comprehension temporal gap.[24]

Chapter 1, which as I noted, focuses on the "natural sublime" (specifically earthquakes), articulates theorizations of the sublime—both Kantian and Freudian (where the latter is framed by Freud's concept of the uncanny)—with a progression of illustrative texts. In confrontation with those texts, I elaborate a series of conceptual strategies while foregrounding a substantive theme, the role of mediating authorities who purport to enable the filling of the apprehension–comprehension gap. The authority on which I focus much of the attention is the "father" (in both actual and symbolic versions), with special attention to the father function in Ingmar Bergman's film *Winter Light* (a text to which I return in subsequent chapters). In the film the "father" is a church pastor whose paternal function is impaired because he has lost his faith. And thematically as well as analytically, the chapter is shaped by my primary "aesthetic subjects"—small girls (one actual and one fictional)—who are confronted with the very large, imagination-challenging natural events, the above-mentioned San Francisco and Kobe earthquakes.[25]

In chapter 2, on the "racial sublime," my analysis is articulated through the writings of what I refer to as African American organic intellectuals (a long list in which the key texts are by James Baldwin and Ta-Nehisi Coates). Treating the trajectory of the racial sublime from the plantation era to the present, my emphasis is on the perils that black parents have faced in keeping their children and young relatives alive. That problem is the main focus of Spike Lee's film *Clockers* (1995), which I contrast with Paul Brickman's *Risky Business* (1983), in which a white family's problem is getting their son into an Ivy League college so that he can be sure to achieve their level of affluence.

To characterize the contemporary "racial sublime," the still vast oppressive structure that imperils black lives, I note the extent to which contemporary broadcast and social media have made that peril evident to white America, quoting Michael Eric Dyson's and Clyde Woods's remarks on how images of Hurricane Katrina disproportionately affect black lives—Dyson: "[It] has become evident in a way not previously appreciated by white America, 'the lived experience of race feels like terror for black folk.'" Woods: "The disasters surrounding Hurricane Katrina revealed the impaired contemporary social vision of every segment of society. Despite mountains of communication and surveillance devices, America was still shocked by the revelation of impoverishment, racism, brutality, corruption, and official neglect in a place it thought it knew intimately." In this chapter, as in the case in chapter 1, I also turn to musical texts to indicate the divisions (as well as the convergences) between white and black communities of sense. I note the way musical reception of blues has onto-political significance for much of black America—for example Bessie Smith's song "Crazy Blues" (1920), which while seemingly politically innocent to white Americans, "has consistently registered itself among much of the African American assemblage as 'an insurrectionary social text.'" However, I also treat the way music has in some cases attenuated the color line, a line subject to the historical "turbulences" that I address.

In chapter 3, on the "nuclear sublime," my main focus is on the way the imagining-challenging apprehension of the overwhelmingly sublime experience of the first nuclear explosions was turned into a purposive, government-sponsored militarized mode of comprehension in which the victims (after those killed in the bombing of Hiroshima and Nagasaki) have been sickened by radiation poisoning (from mining, nuclear storage dumps, and testing): army personnel from the testing, nearby resident Native Americans from all three, and Pacific Islanders from the testing and residual radiation since. As many have pointed out, the geography of nuclear poisoning was constituted as "sacrifice zones," where the peoples affected were regarded as lives less worthy of protection. The chapter proceeds with texts and counter-texts—for example the Euro-American landscape paintings that erased Indianness as they pictured the "first American sublime," followed by the texts of Native American artists and writers who, with images and narratives, described the lethal effects of nuclearization on the American West (the "second American sublime"). And I enlist texts by and about Pacific Islanders that counter the official verdict that the remoteness of the Pacific justified its selection for atomic testing.

The chapter closes with a reading of Terrence Malick's film *The Thin Red Line*, which juxtaposes a landscape-attuned, peaceful Pacific Island lifeworld to the devastating violence of the military advances on the Pacific Islands during World War II. I treat the film as an encounter of technologies of perception—those that failed to discern worthy life in the spaces selected for nuclear poisoning versus those, such as Malick's cinematic rendering of Pacific Islanders, which permit a devalued world "to emerge from the shadows that other technologies of perception have created" and as a result allow those people and their world to emerge from the shadows, become objects of empathy, and achieve the "ethical weight" to which they are entitled.

Chapter 4, on the "industrial sublime," is shaped by the imagery of the "machine in the garden" (Leo Marx's title in a monograph about how industrialization displaced Jefferson's pastoral ideal). Beginning with a discussion of the paintings of urban scenes that register large industrial development, I move on to an extended reading of a film that features a train journey westward, Jim Jarmusch's film *Dead Man*, to treat the westward spread of industrial technology, mainly steel manufacturing, which provided the railway system (tracks and locomotives) and the weapons that facilitated the assault on Native America. The subsequent textual trajectory involves texts that register the development and decline of factories with an examination of U.S. ruins and an extended reading of Michelangelo Antonioni's film *Red Desert*, which through the imposition of color, creates a chromatic dissonance that articulates an ambivalence toward the consequences of industrialization in the vicinity of the city of Ravenna. The chapter ends with readings of texts that visualize and comment on sweatshops, which constitute the contemporary stage in the historical narrative of industrial demise and its subsequent restoration, as the factory has moved from the former centers of industrialization to the third world, with its exploitable labor pools. The last text receiving extended commentary in the chapter is a documentary focused on a sweatshop in Indonesia that manufactures Nike shoes and sports clothing.

Chapter 5, on the "9/11 terror sublime," begins with focus on Stan Douglas's installation *The Secret Agent* (2015), in which he remediates Joseph Conrad's novel *The Secret Agent* (1907) by switching the venue from early twentieth-century London to Lisbon in the 1970s at a revolutionary moment and by decentering the perceptual perspectives on the event by displaying the action on multiple screens so that what constitutes "terror" becomes radically contestable. After a discussion of organic versus contemporary textual communities and the texts to which they are allegiant, the chapter turns to an extensive engagement with Don DeLillo's novel *Falling Man* (2005), whose many aesthetic subjects are on different temporal trajectories, pulling in diverse ideational directions, as they either perpetrate or seek to come to terms with the destruction of the World Trade Center towers.

The analysis of DeLillo's text is followed by a turn to Art Spiegelman's commix version of the event, *In the Shadow of No Towers*, whose graphic form creates a narrative space with no commanding center. With many repetitions of the images from the event, the text undermines any totalizing frame with which the event can be captured. What Spiegelman's text provides is akin to the contribution of DeLillo's novel. It issues a political challenge to the dominant narratives created by the mainstream media and U.S. government. It is therefore fitting that I follow that text with an analysis of a video film that precedes the 9/11 event and effectively premediates it, Johan Grimonprez's *Dial H-I-S-T-O-R-Y* (1997), a montage of archive footage of the history of plane hijacking within a nonlinear narrative aimed at displaying and challenging the way broadcast media have hijacked the hijackings.

Finally, because both the target of the attack and the city of New York's memorial response to the event are architectural, I close the chapter with a focus on the difference between monumental architecture, which tends to close off alternative historical narratives while stifling practices of memory, and architectural forms that feature transparency and ambiguity to resist narrative closure and open a space for contention among alternative communities of sense. Providing the bridge to the afterword, which focuses on the critical effect of interventions in duration, the chapter ends with a reiteration of what is central to the political significance of the texts I have engaged throughout the investigation, the art–community of sense relationship that informs what I mean by the "political sublime."

A father's no shield for his child.—Robert Lowell, "Fall 1961"

1. **WHEN THE EARTH MOVES**   TOWARD A POLITICAL SUBLIME

Reading this line from Immanuel Kant's Analytic of the Sublime, "*that is sublime in comparison with which all else is small*," I recalled a conversation I had with my (very small) three-year-old niece, Hannah.[1] When the (very large) San Francisco earthquake hit during an October 17, 1989, World Series game between the San Francisco Giants and Oakland Athletics, suspending play temporarily (and wreaking havoc on much of the city, e.g., collapsing a large section of the Bay Bridge), I turned away from the television broadcast to pick up the phone and call my sister in San Francisco to make sure that she and her family were okay. When Hannah got on the phone, I asked her what the earthquake was like. "Very big," she said. "How big?" I asked. "Too big for my daddy to hold," she replied.

Hannah's remarks accord with Kant's explication of the feeling of the sublime. In his discussion of the interplay between apprehension and comprehension that an encounter with the sublime precipitates, he refers to a breakdown that imperils comprehension. The first moments in one's apprehension of a "sublime" (an "*absolutely great*") object or event attenuate because "apprehension has reached a point beyond which the representation of sensuous intuition in the case of the parts first apprehended begin to disappear from the imagination as this advances to the apprehension of yet others . . . and for comprehension we get a maximum which the imagination cannot exceed."[2] However, little Hannah was undaunted. As Kant would have it, "The end to be attained by the presentation of a concept [i.e., the task of moving from apprehension to comprehension] is made harder to realize by the intuition of the object being almost too great for our faculty of apprehension [so that] . . . our faculty of imagination breaks down in presenting the concept of a magnitude and proves unequal to the task."[3] Hannah's imagination, although challenged, was in a way "equal to the task" of estimation. For her the earthquake exceeded her estimation of size when she submitted it to her primary unit of measure—that which her "daddy" is able to hold. Whereas for Kant, the unit of measure for subjective judgments "is always our body"; as Hannah's case suggests, it can be another body.[4]

So much for what Kant calls "the mathematically sublime," which provides an initial analysis of what happens when something of vast magnitude challenges the imagination and sets the mind in motion. Turning to Kant's subsequent section, the "dynamically sublime," we find him evoking fear. He suggests that an encounter with the sublime (e.g., "ravages of nature") "strikes the untutored man as terrifying."[5] Doubtless, anything too big for her daddy to hold was momentarily frightening for Hannah. However (according to Kant), once contemplation of the sublime proceeds, one achieves a level of satisfaction in the realization that however fearful nature can be, there is a "sphere of the mind which altogether exceeds the realm of nature."[6] Although she had apparently become satisfied about her safety after the quake hit, it is doubtful that the motions of Hannah's mind (which summoned her primary mediating authority, "Daddy") led to such a realization (which would have fulfilled Kant's suggestion that the ultimate effect of the sublime is a recognition of one's freedom and thus capacity for morality). That said, I want to consider what we can surmise about her subsequent encounters with the sublime, in the period beyond childhood when in the transition to adolescence and adulthood *everything* becomes too big for her daddy to hold. When the insulation of the traditional patriarchal household loses its hold on the scope of a child's imagination, and the emerging adult must manage a world outside the home, one whose normative codes exceed the contained moral universe of the household, the interplay of apprehension and comprehension set off by sublime moments presents challenges that one cannot manage by turning to one's parents for reassurance. Reviewing Walter Benjamin's childhood writings, Burkhardt Lindner makes that case: "From the child's point of view, the world of adults appears to be as infinite as impenetrable."[7]

Just as the aging child is effectively thrust into a different world with different implications for managing the daunting forms of vastness that

Figure 1.1 Albrecht
Dürer's father at age
seventy

challenge comprehension, the same goes for aging fathers who had once felt secure in their command of the moral spaces both within and outside the household (at least for the purposes of managing the traditional family's domestic and social worlds). They begin to lose their command capabilities as their mental agility and accordingly their ability to manage change (both practically and ideationally) attenuates. Such seems to be the case with the painter, Albrecht Dürer's seventy-year-old father (figure 1.1).

As Gilles Deleuze and Félix Guattari suggest, "the face is a veritable megaphone."[8] A quick look at *this* face suggests that what is being broadcast is anger. However, a longer look yields a different impression. If we abide for a while with the image, we can see the fearfulness (and the related querulous suspicion) behind the anger of a man who is losing his grip and likely his moral authority as well.

Extending Fatherhood

Certainly, the father function endures outside the household, at least as it is symbolically reproduced in a variety of ways by other figures, once the ties to a biological father are cut or attenuated. One version of that cutting is rendered as the concept of "foreclosure," which Jacques Lacan develops as a radical version of Freudian transference. Foreclosure is a form of cutting that speaks to instances in which the place formerly occupied by an inadequate father has been left empty and leads to a psychosis. As Lacan puts it, "When the Name-of-the-Father is foreclosed for a particular subject, it leaves a hole in the symbolic order which can never be filled."[9] Nevertheless, a filling effort takes place. Bracketing the issue of psychosis and pursuing what Lacan identifies as a subsequent search to fill the void, I turn to the place where Lacan asks, "How can the name-of the Father be called by the subject to the only place in which it could have reached him and in which it has never been?" He answers, "Simply by a real father, not necessarily by the subject's own father, but by A-father," i.e., by an Other who serves as a substitute that can legislate and can thus provide normative reassurance or solace for the subject.[10] It can well be a mother rather than a father (as Lacan points out, in Shakespeare's *Hamlet*, "the play is dominated by the Mother as Other [*Autre*]").[11] And the authority import of much of Pedro Almodovar's films is captured in the title of one of them: *All about My Mother* (1999).

Focused on the situations in which "the father really has the function of a legislator," Lacan provides an example of a father who makes the laws, a "pillar of faith as a paragon of integrity and devotion, as virtuous or as a virtuoso, by serving a work of salvation, or of whatever object or lack of object, of nation or of birth of safeguard or salubrity, of legacy or legality . . . all ideals that provide him with many opportunities of being in a posture of undeserving inadequacy, even of fraud."[12] One of Lacan's examples, "the pillar of faith," resonates with a scenario in Ingmar Bergman's film *Winter Light* (1962), especially if we also heed the last part of the quotation that refers to "being in a posture of undeserving inadequacy, even of fraud."

The protagonist in the film is a Lutheran minister, who carries on with his liturgical and guidance functions even though he has lost his faith and is unable as a result to offer solace to a parishioner traumatized by what can best be described as the nuclear sublime. Tobias Wolff's summary captures the essence of the moment:

> Tomas, a Lutheran pastor and widower, is suffering a crisis of faith, barely going through the motions of his ministry. . . . One of his parishioners has become obsessed with the prospect of nuclear annihilation. At his wife's urging, this man, a fisherman, comes to the pastor for reassurance, some blessed word of hope that he can grasp as a lifeline, but Tomas can offer nothing but the bleakness of his own despair. The fisherman commits suicide.[13]

The conversation of Tomas Ericsson (Gunnar Björnstrand) with his parishioner, Jonas Perrson (Max von Sydow), who is traumatized because he's heard that they are so hate filled that when the Chinese get the bomb, they'll destroy the planet, is an encounter of sublimes—Christian and nuclear, respectively—both of which challenge comprehension. Both Tomas and Jonas are confronted with what Michel Foucault (in a reinflection of Lacan's concept of foreclosure) calls "The Father's No."[14] The pastor, who is no longer able to take his role seriously, cannot function as an adequate father because *he* has experienced a father's no; "God-the-father" does not function as father for him because of "his" silence. Tomas is therefore as afflicted as Jonas. His god (a figure in a Lutheran version of the Christian sublime) will not reveal himself. After asking Jonas about his work, his health, and his marriage in a search for what afflicts him, he turns the focus on himself. Telling Jonas that he will be frank with him, he proceeds to ramble on about his own despair. He says that he can no longer presume the world he thought he shared with his paternal deity. As he puts it, "My God and I resided in an organized world where everything made sense. . . . I put my faith in an improbable private image of a fatherly god . . . an echo god who gave benign answers and reassuring blessings." Recalling that his (late) wife had helped him to "patch the holes," it had nevertheless become clear to him that what there is in the place of that "fatherly god" is a void. He concludes that "suffering is incomprehensible, so it needs no explanation," and ends with the remark, "Jonas, there is no creator" (see figure 1.2).

Figure 1.2 Tomas and Jonas in Bergman's *Winter Light*

Other Figures

Certainly, there have been other father surrogates to whom people have turned in the face of the nuclear sublime. For example, Edward Teller (1908–2003), the scientist who became known for his advocacy of American nuclear domination (and for designing a superior nuclear weapon, the hydrogen bomb), was frequently referred to as "the father of the H bomb." Many in the United States found his policy advocacy and design accomplishment reassuring. However, the father figure is but one among a wide variety of authorities—cultural, political, religious, and scientific—to which people have turned as they have learned to "live with the Bomb" (and other sublime objects and events).[15] A variety of presumptive authority structures are resorted to in sublime moments when, contrary to Kant's model, the result is not recognition of one's freedom but rather failed attempts to manage disruption and unease, prompting individuals to seek affirmation or reassurance from authority figures. Allucquére Rosanne Stone supplies a conceptual frame for such structures in her analysis of the contemporary technological sublime, which among other things involves the emergence of a "prosthetic sociality" in which a gap exists between one's physical body and one's "disembodied subjectivity . . . [in] cyberspace [where] you are everywhere and somewhere and nowhere."[16] When for example communication prosthetics "disrupt so thoroughly" that which constitutes "a socially apprehensible citizen," the form of reassurance, she suggests, is an act of "warranting" through which "the political apparatus of government is able to guarantee the production of stable concepts of citizenry." Although alternative cultural authorities weigh in to provide warrants for the coherence of the self for subjects who have technological extensions, it is primarily governmental authority according to Stone that answers calls for reassurance in the face of a technological sublime that challenges a subject's sociopolitical presence to itself and at the same time warrants the existence of "community" in light of the contemporary shift in the nature of civic space: "from a predominantly public space to a congeries of spaces increasingly privatized."[17] Stone's reflections on the technological sublime provide an opening to a consideration of the political context of sublime objects and events, suggesting that sublime episodes occasion turbulence among communities of sense, which can either reveal or reorient authority structures. I return to that implication of the sublime after a review and analysis of the development of the concept.

The Sublime: Language and the Critique of Representation

The appearance of a sustained speculation on the sublime precedes the well-known Kantian version by many centuries. It originates with Longinus (likely writing in the first century B.C.E.), for whom the sublime is articulated through language: "Sublimity," he writes, "is a kind of height and conspicuous excellence in speeches and writings," an excellence he adds that manifests itself not through mere persuasion but through an "originality" that "makes everything different, like lightning and directly shows the 'all at once' capability of the speaker."[18] For Longinus, the sublime inheres in the extraordinary adequacy of words and rhetorical structures, which provoke amazement and wonder as well as influence. Functioning to prompt the hearer to think beyond what is heard, sublime expressions in speech and writing linger; they "leave deep [in one's] mind more to theorize than what was actually said."[19]

However, eloquence has its perils. Longinus cautions against making one's figuration unconcealed lest the effect be dangerous. If one's "figures [are] too obvious," they imply "insinuation" and "deception," which might make "somebody who is to make a decision (e.g., a king or tyrant) angry," for "such a man" may regard them as an "insult" and go "completely wild" or, if able to "prevail over his rage, firm himself entirely against the persuasiveness of the speech and writings."[20] Centuries later, Jean-Paul Sartre offered another view of the dangerously powerful effect of words. They can "wreak havoc when they happen to name something that is experienced but is not yet named."[21] The danger to which Sartre was referring was occasioned by the word "love" in Stendhal's novel *The Charter House of Parma*, which if mentioned in a relationship between a young man and his aunt—the character Count Mosca, the Prime Minister of Parma, says, "If the word *love* is pronounced between them, I am lost"—would provoke a censorious community of sense.[22]

The concept of a community of sense looms large in my analysis of the political implications of the sublime throughout this investigation. Here I want to note that the contemporary approach to words in analyses of the sublime contrasts with the approach of Longinus. For Longinus, words are either adequate to inspiring awe or inadequate because of a failed use of figures and or "selections" (i.e., composition). The contemporary post-Burkean, post-Kantian word–sublime relationship is quite the reverse. After Burke and Kant, rather than being awe-inspiring, words *fail* in the face of the sublime. They become inadequate rather than *being* sublime. As one commentator puts it, "In broad terms, whenever experience slips out of conventional understanding, whenever the power of an object or event is such that words fail and points of comparison disappear, *then* we resort to the feeling of the sublime."[23] As is the case for Longinus, sublime experiences for Kant are ultimately thought provoking, but they "arouse more thought than can be expressed in a concept determined by words."[24]

Nevertheless, despite the considerable distance between Longinus's location of the sublime in lofty language rather than (as in the post-Kantian view) blocked or disabled language, aspects of his analysis of the sublime comport well with critically oriented post-Kantian thinking. Especially notable is the seeming prescience of Longinus's remark that sublimity has "first and most powerful . . . a solid thrust of conception."[25] At one point he even suggests that "sublimity often subsists even in a single concept."[26] That perspective accords well with Deleuze and Guattari's emphasis on the critical effects of inventing concepts. For them, what are sublime are the contributions of "great philosophers," who "create concepts for problems that necessarily change."[27] Moreover, Deleuze and Guattari share an aspect of Longinus's view of an effectively critical aesthetic. Longinus uses the concept of selection; sublimity for him derives from a capability of recognizing that "there are certain parts which are by nature fundamentally in session together with their material [so that] . . . we must be capable over and over again . . . of selecting them from all that brings itself out to our attention [and] setting it together so as to make a unity, a kind of body."[28] Similarly, Deleuze and Guattari identify the importance of "composition," which is essential to the effectiveness of the work of art, which must operate between "technical and aesthetic planes of composition."[29]

However, perhaps what Longinus's analyses of sublime expressions best preview are the complications of representation. Where Longinus refers to sublime expressions that (as noted) "leave deep [in one's] mind more to theorize than what was actually said," he anticipates contemporary reflections on sublime experience that identify not "an object *beyond* reason and expression, but rather 'that within representation which nonetheless *exceeds* the possibility of representation.'"[30] Whether resident in Longinus's observations or in contemporary post-Kantian ones, what is shared by sublime experiences and disruptions to representation is a provocation to think critically about subjectivity. For purposes of illustration, I engage two examples, one art historical and the other cinematic. The former is Georges Didi-Huberman's analysis of a disruption of representation in an anti-iconographic analysis of Vermeer paintings. Pointing to patches of color that disrupt depiction and thus disturb representation by being an "intrusion," he refers to a "catastrophic commotion" in the canvases that turns the viewer away from an image's reference and toward the artist/subject and thereby to the act of painting.[31] Similarly, in an analysis of Gus Van Sant's recreation of Alfred Hitchcock's film *Psycho* (his *Psycho*, 1998), Chelsey Crawford suggests that cinematic "quotation interrupts the linearity of the text . . . [and that the] break with mimesis" constitutes an "interruption" that "fractures the mind of the viewer" turning her/his attention to the director/subject's cinematic production, "the mechanical sources within the diegesis," instead of toward the "material objects captured in the image itself."[32]

From Object to Subject

The shift in perspectives that Didi-Huberman's analysis of Vermeer's canvases—from the paintings' reference (what is depicted) to the paintings' production (to the painting subject)—and Crawford's analysis of Van Sant's cinematic quotation—from the materiality of the image to the director's filming mechanism—aligns itself with Kant's primary contribution in his Analytic of the Sublime, a frame for thinking about the dynamics of a disrupted subjectivity (which has since been rendered even more dislocated and divided in post-Kantian analyses). As Heidegger famously puts it in his identification of Kant's philosophical contribution, Kant changed the question from what is a thing to who is "man," i.e., to the subject.[33] And by the time Kant gets to his Analytic of the Sublime, that subject is in disarray, so much so that the Kantian aim of illustrating subject finality is threatened. However, already in Longinus's treatise *On the Sublime*, subjectivity was rendered critically divided. As John Milbank points out, "With Longinus, the discourse on the sublime was concerned not only with the manifestation of the singular individual, but with the elevation of this individual above himself, often in circumstances which pose a threat to his own survival."[34]

Crucially, the threat of the sublime for Kant involves a tension between faculties *within* the subject, between the faculty of imagination and the faculty of reason. In an encounter with the sublime, which is "boundless" (unlike objects of beauty, which have definite boundaries), there's "a momentary check to the vital forces followed at once by a discharge of the more powerful, and so it is an emotion that seems to be no sport, but dead earnest in the affairs of the imagination."[35] Importantly, what is evoked is a more intense emotion than earnestness: "The feeling of the sublime is . . . at once a feeling of displeasure, arising from the inadequacy of imagination in the aesthetical estimation of magnitude to attain to its estimation by reason."[36]

Ultimately, the sublime threatens Kant's ethico-political project of warranting a *sensus communis*. He notes that unlike the case of judgments of taste, for which we can expect "subjective necessity" (i.e., judgmental consensus), sublime experiences threaten such an "accordance":

> BEAUTIFUL nature contains countless things as to which we at once take every one as in their judgement concurring with our own, and as to which we may further expect this concurrence without facts finding us far astray. But in respect of our judgement upon the sublime in nature we cannot so easily vouch ready acceptance by others.[37]

Unlike the effect of encounters with the beautiful, which occasion a feeling of satisfaction that one's mind participates in a universality of sense, in the case of the sublime the mind experiences a negative pleasure; initially confounded, it quickly experiences an *inner* accord, achieving the modest pleasure of agreement among faculties, having thus coped with displeasure. Deleuze effectively characterizes the discordance that Kant attributes to sublime experience. It is "explained by the free agreement of reason and imagination. But this new 'spontaneous' agreement occurs under very special conditions: pain, opposition, constrain, and discord."[38]

Saving the *Sensus Communis*

How does Kant seek to save the subjective necessity he sees occurring so easily in the case of the Beautiful but potentially fugitive with the sublime? If we heed an extension of the passage above, beginning with "Beautiful nature" and ending with Kant's admission that we cannot "easily vouch ready acceptance by others," in the case of the sublime, we find him turning to a concept of culture: "a far higher degree of culture, not merely aesthetic judgment, but also of the faculties of cognition [operating in the "realm" of the "practical"] which lie at the basis, seems to be requisite to enable us to lay down a judgement upon this high distinction of natural objects," and thence (a few lines further along in the text) to a culturally induced morality, to the "development of moral ideas" derived from "preparatory culture" which relies on "a dominion which reason exercises over sensibility" in the minds of all but the "untutored" and "simple-minded."[39]

Kant's evocation of the "practical" is the key to his strategy for rescuing the inevitability of a *sensus communis*. To restore the subjective necessity that he sees as threatened by the sublime, he recurs to his Second Critique, the *Critique of Practical Reason*, in which he posits the existence of a "culture" (the above-noted "preparatory culture") that consists in a "natural moral sense." As I have put it elsewhere, "To finesse the seeming recalcitrance of the sublime to the 'subjective necessity' that [his *Critique of Judgment*] is designed to establish, Kant turns to the concept of culture . . . which for Kant turns out to consist in the sharing of a natural moral sensibility which can unite those with a refined and those with a vulgar cultural sensibility."[40]

For Kant, the overcoming of the initial fear occasioned by the sublime, which he details in his section on "The Dynamically Sublime," is doubtless influenced by Edmund Burke's emphasis on the terror produced by the sublime: "Whatever is fitted in any sort to excite the ideas of pain, and danger . . . whatever is in any sort terrible, or is conversant about terrible objects, or operates in a manner analogous to terror is a source of the *sublime*."[41] Burke also precedes Kant in reflecting on negative pleasure, "the pleasure of pain" in his terms, so that the "pleasure of the sublime is our delight at pain threatened but avoided."[42] While Burke and Kant are very much in accord with respect to the emotions occasioned by the experience of the sublime, they depart in their approach to how what is occasioned in individual encounters with the sublime can contribute to a *sensus communis*. For Burke, among what people share is a passion for self-preservation, which he deems "the strongest of all the passions."[43] As a result, insofar as a community of sense emerges from the terror of the sublime for Burke, it is Hobbesian; it is based on the like-mindedness (the collective resonances) of the security-seeking passion, the drive to avoid danger (although Burke also sides with Scottish Enlightenment thinkers in seeing "sympathy" at the distress of others as also constitutive of the social bond).[44] Ultimately, "in Kant's analysis of the sublime, Burke's self-preservation is replaced by the awareness of our transcendent freedom and moral vocation."[45] Although that replacement seemingly constitutes a "move from the empirical to the a priori level,"[46] its effects can be empirically illustrated (as many post-Kantians have shown).

From the Ethical to the Political: Post-Kantian Political Philosophy

Kant's contemporary, Friedrich Schiller, is among those who have sought to extend Kant's analytic of the sublime into an ethico-political perspective. Absorbing both Kant's and Burke's analyses of the sublime, Schiller's emphasis is on "the political unconscious of the aesthetic of terror, which he presumes had to be suppressed for subjects to be able to "achieve active mastery over it rather than allowing ourselves to be passively overcome by it."[47] In his earlier essay on the sublime, he modifies Kant's distinction between the mathematical and dynamical sublimes (and heeds Burke's emphasis on the drive to self-preservation), referring instead to the theoretical and practical sublimes, respectively: "with the theoretical-sublime nature stands as *an object of cognition* in opposition to the conceptual drive. With the practical-sublime, it stands as an *object of feeling* in opposition to the preservation drive."[48] He adds, "The theoretical sublime contradicts the conceptual drive, the practical-sublime contradicts the preservation drive."[49] Insofar as there are political moments in those contradictions (which for Schiller involve minds realizing themselves in their capacity and independence), they involve an epistemological epiphany, a grasp that overcomes initial lack of comprehension and a more active posture, which

Schiller deems as resistance to fear. In both cases (as Schiller does a second take on the sublime, eight years after his initial commentary), "The sublime . . . procures for us an exit from the sensuous world . . . rather suddenly and through a shock."[50] Summoning a historical example and a mythological one—he refers to Hannibal's Alps-crossing feat and Prometheus's lack of regret for his deed—Schiller constructs the *subject* as sublime. Sublimity inheres in the individual subject that overcomes mere instinctual fear ("in a practical sense") by managing "misfortune."[51] In effect sublime subjects evince the moral person within.

Ultimately, Schiller's historically attuned reflections on the sublime, in which he reviews moments of violent conflict, fashion what Hayden White refers to as a "historical sublime," which White sees as "authoriz[ing] a totally different politics," one which promotes Schiller's account of "aesthetic education" to allow for "mastery over the deeply indifferent energy of the historical process."[52] Apart from his resistance to Kant's formalistic abstractions—Schiller turns from mere structures of apprehension and the cognitive dynamic that moves from apprehension to comprehension to historically attuned examples of sublime subjective enactments—his most significant contribution to a politics of the sublime lies in his turn to the role of the arts in "aesthetic education." His last gloss on the sublime articulates the position developed in his extended neo-Kantian turn to the arts in his *Letters on the Aesthetic Education of Man* (1794). For Schiller, the arts—for example, the Greek tragedies—provide "pathetical portraits of humanity wrestling with fate, of the irresistible flight of good fortune, of deceived security, . . . [which] the tragic art through imitation brings before our eyes."[53] In addition to providing an opening to the way the arts can instruct about sublime experience, Schiller introduces historical contingency, which both undermines the Kantian pursuit of subjective harmony and anticipates the analyses of contemporary post-Kantians who emphasize the contingencies of relations between subjects and communities of sense.

Contemporary Post-Kantian Critique

Much of critically oriented post-Kantian thinking resists Burke's, Kant's, and even Schiller's meta-political versions of a *sensus communis* (notions of shared sensibilities, whether empirical or a priori/noumenal) as bases for a threshold to thinking about the conditions of possibility for political community. The tendency instead has been to focus on discord or "dissensus" (to evoke Jacques Rancière's term), framed by a thoroughgoing rejection of perspectives that essentialize human sensibilities. That rejection is perhaps best epitomized by Foucault's remark, "Nothing in Man—not even his body—is sufficiently stable to serve as the basis for self-recognition or for understanding other men."[54] And Deleuze further destabilizes subjectivity by rejecting the transcendental version of a "preformed or prefigured" subject, displacing it with a dynamic process of subjectivity that is historically contingent, a series of subject formations in response to events.[55] Nevertheless, the legacies of late eighteenth-century versions of the sublime continue their relevance. For example, Rancière, despite his steadfast resistance to Kant's and Schiller's commitments to subjective harmony, shares Schiller's view of the political efficacy of the arts. Like Hegel (however in a wholly different way), Rancière renders the implications of the sublime by allocating its effects to artistic compositions and texts. However, in contrast to Hegel, who located the sublime effect in spiritual arts, Rancière turns to secular artistic texts whose effects he sees in reallocations of sensation.[56] He notes for example that "literature does not 'do' politics by providing messages or framing representations. It does so by triggering passions."[57] In accord with that strategy, as I proceed with my analyses of contemporary post-Kantian positions on the sublime, my emphasis will be on artistic genres that reference the sublime and/or provoke sublime experiences, as they inspire ways to shape a political comprehension that is negotiated within the events in which communities of sense emerge. As Deleuze points out, for Kant, it is the imagination, "which is not itself a legislative faculty," that "embodies the mediation [and thereby] brings about the synthesis which relates phenomena to the understanding."[58]

In my analysis throughout the investigations in the chapters that follow, rather than an aspect of mentality, the mediations I reference are textually situated discourses and images with varying degrees of cultural authority, especially those articulated in artistic genres. Among those who have also engaged and revised the philosophical basis of Kant's sublime and have foregrounded the role of artistic genres is Jean-Francois Lyotard. However, the political (or perhaps meta-political) contribution that Lyotard's thinking lends to a politics of the sublime inheres as much in the poesis of his writing as in his explicit (and quite equivocal) attitudes toward the sublime–politics relationship. For example, he figures Kant's transition from the analytic of the beautiful to the analytic of the sublime as a disrupted economy and broken betrothal: "the beautiful is a sentiment that proceeds from a 'fit' between nature and mind, i.e., when transcribed into Kant's economy of faculties, between the imagination and the understanding. This marriage or, at least this betrothal proper to the beautiful is broken by the sublime."[59] With that figuration, Lyotard opens a space of deferment. In his analytic of the sublime, Kant ultimately reduces experience of the sublime to a brief moment in which the failure of the imagination is overcome by the engagement of the faculty of reason, and this "negative pleasure" of having overcome discordance creates the conditions of possibility for a moral consensus.

In contrast, Lyotard, like many philosophical contemporaries, "affirm[s] the first moment, but defer[s] or avoid[s] the second," substituting ongoing discordance for Kant's reason-enabling resolution.[60] As I have put it elsewhere, evoking Lyotard's marriage metaphor, "Reason, which is the dominant faculty in this analytic, derives moral concepts through imitation: it 'takes from sensible nature nothing more than what pure reason can think on its own' [as a result] although the mind-nature marriage may be temporarily annulled in the encounter with the sublime . . . with Kant's summoning of culture-as-moral sensibility (from his Second Critique), a remarriage takes place as Kant retreats from the most radical implication of the sublime, its challenge to the idea of a naturally engendered common sense."[61] Thus Kant's retreat from the disruption occasioned by a sublime experience recurs to a shared morality that halts the process of sense making, bringing it to a conclusion. In contrast, by turning to the arts as mediators Lyotard defers that Kantian closure, presuming instead that something is "still in play for the mind," which turns out to be "matter, by which [he] means matter in the arts."[62] By positing the arts as mediators in the gap between apprehension and comprehension, Lyotard substitutes a nonclosural process for Kant's precipitous resting place in a moral/culture-imposed consensus. As he puts it, "The matter thus invoked is something that is not finalized, not destined [and which] . . . does not *address* itself *to the mind* [and eschews] . . . teleological destination."[63] Yet despite his resistance to the mode of finality that Kant imposes on the sublime experience, Lyotard derives a nonclosure from Kant as well. His politicization of the sublime draws inspiration from what he sees as a temporal deferral that Kant offers—Kant's suggestion that "central to the feeling of the sublime is the limitlessness of its determination," which opens up the possibility of linking the moments of sublime experience with inquiry into the "historical political" as "an unending critical process."[64]

Lyotard's primary reinflection of Kant involves the substitution of the "matter" of art for Kant's transcendental structures of mentality in order to show how the nuances of the arts, the "non-sense: of thought" (e.g., "timbres and nuances") that "are always being born," extend the sublime moment by taking it beyond both language and mentality. I want to extend that substitution into a way of conceiving a politics of the sublime event by focusing on the way various artistic texts turn events into historical negotiations. The historicity of those negotiations becomes evident if one heeds Deleuzian temporality. Deleuze like Kant privileges the instant; however, that privileging is not in the service of moral closure; it is rather in the service of an imagination of a different future. For Deleuze an event is an "instant" that articulates the "minimum time" of the instant with the "maximum time" of unlimited duration in order to "make the instant all the more intense, taut, and instantaneous since it expresses an unlimited future and an unlimited past, the pure instant grasped at the point at which it divides itself into the future and past."[65] Thus rather than moral closure, Deleuze theorizes an ethics of the event. In focusing on ethics rather than morality (where the morality involves rules for making judgments while ethics involves embracing uncertainty in order to exit from what is habitually recognized within one's milieu), Deleuze's aim is to liberate thinking, thus enabling an imagination of a different world. Deleuzian duration, as among other things a look toward the future, requires "the perpetual 'ungrounding' of the present."[66] Inspired in part by Deleuze's version of the duration of events, I have suggested elsewhere that events and experiences (sublime or otherwise) never conclude; they belong to evolving future anteriors (will-have-beens) which are constituted as continuing reinflections to which artistic texts contribute (for example the way the Marguerite Duras–Alain Resnais film *Hiroshima mon amour* alters how the atomic bombing of Hiroshima will-have-been).[67] When artistic texts remediate events, bringing them back for rethinking, they constitute an "event, a temporalizing occurrence and transformative rupture"[68] with ethico-political effects.

Heeding Deleuze's ethics of the event, particularly his suggestion that an event is a "pure instant grasped at the point at which it divides itself into the future and past," I turn briefly here to the writer Don DeLillo's responses to the 9/11 attack on the World Trade Center because his accounts are comparable to (and illustrative of) the temporality that Deleuze attributes to events. In an essay published roughly two months after the attack, DeLillo gives the event a simultaneous future and past. He suggests that on the one hand the old "world narrative" of the domination of capital markets and "uncontrolled investment potential" has been overcoded by what happened on 9/11: "Today, the world narrative belongs to terrorists [and as a result] . . . this catastrophic event changes the way we think and act, moment to moment, week to week, for unknown weeks and months to come, and steely years."[69] On the other hand, inasmuch as the "terrorists of September 11 want to bring back the past," we have to ask what grievances have been brewing—to which he answers, "It was America that drew their fury. It was the high gloss of our modernity. It was the thrust of our technology. It was our perceived godlessness. It was the blunt force of our foreign policy."[70] In response to the world-shaking effect of the 9/11 event DeLillo fashions two accounts. First, in his *Harper's* essay, he urges "us" to invent a new future: "The narrative ends in the rubble and it is left to us to create a counternarrative" (in Deleuze's terms, the suggestion is that we need to create a "counter-actualization" of the event).[71] However, DeLillo recognizes that the discursive frames with which we figure such a sublime event are inadequate; 9/11 confronts the author with the need to go beyond "figurative givens."[72] As DeLillo expresses it, "The event itself has no purchase in the mercies of analogy or simile."[73] And DeLillo also appreciates the (Kant-conceived) process involved in moving from apprehension to perception. In his *Falling Man*, his subsequent novel version of the event, his character Keith, watching the video of the attack with his estranged wife, Florence, lends the event an experiential duration as he describes the difference between the initial attack by the first plane and the follow-up by the second: "It still looks like an accident, the first one. . . . The second plane, by the time the second plane appears, we're all a little older and wiser."[74]

Throughout *Falling Man*, DeLillo expands that duration as he fills in the gap between the apprehension and comprehension of 9/11 through the perspectives of his characters. And because as an "event," it is an "effect that seems to exceed its causes . . . a change in the way reality appears to us . . . a shattering transformation of reality itself," he undertakes the creation of new languages and images, avoiding the "framework of other people's words."[75] As a result his novel "open[s] up new perspectives beyond the exhausted mainstream comparisons, a new unconsumed realm of images and language."[76] DeLillo's *Falling Man* receives extended commentary in chapter 5. Here I want to note that confrontations with the sublimity of the 9/11 event are not confined to U.S. literatures. For example, there is a set of eleven, eleven-minute feature films (by eleven filmmakers from eleven different countries) that respond to the event, each providing alternative (and oblique) modes of comprehension that evoke alternative communities of sense.

Treating the relevance of the films to the (Kantian) interplay between apprehension and comprehension first, we can note Lyotard's point that a discourse's sense and references are not the only means of meaning making:

> Signification does not exhaust meaning, but neither does signification combined with designation. We cannot be satisfied with this choice of two spaces in which discourse—the system's as well as the subject's—insinuates itself. There exists another, figural space. One must assume it buried, for it shuns sight and thought; it indicates itself laterally, fleetingly, within discourses and perceptions.[77]

Lyotard's remark about the buried figuration within discourse provides an opening to consider an important effect of the 9/11 feature films, because cinema—both documentary and feature films—can restore and make available for reflection what disappears from the daily media and what perception, whether mediated or raw, tends to evacuate.

A cinematic treatment of the dynamics of perception is especially evident in Alejandro González Iñárritu's eleven-minute version, which is effectively an appreciation of how a sublime experience requires one to confront the "unpresentable."[78] The film begins with a black screen on which flashes of bodies falling from the towers intermittently appear. They are images that the media buried after the initial coverage as well as being traumatic images that individual perception has tended to repress. Insofar as his film references a community of sense, it is one that is bound together by the temporality of trauma, which "enables people [however briefly] . . . to share a common lot."[79] At the same time, the film's flickering images reference the confusion, disorientation, and "emotional shock," which are "after effects well beyond the area directly affected by the attacks."[80] As a result, modes of comprehension after the initial shock are screened through a variety of cultural formations and genres.

Accordingly, the other ten films, emerging from different cultural perspectives, show "diverse sensory experiences," predicated on alternative phenomenologies of perception that derive from an alternative mode of imagining the in-common (i.e., an alternative community of sense).[81] As a whole, the eleven different cinematic renderings of the event, seen one after the other, make it evident that a Kantian universality does not result from such a sublime experience. Rather than affirming Kant's hoped-for global *sensus communis*, the cinematic mediations of the 9/11 event indicate that, insofar as the world displays a unity, it "is only united by fear and sadness [and that] . . . the best that movies can do is provide a continuum of feeling."[82] One can attribute a similar effect to a literary intervention, to which I now turn.

A Return to the Earthquake Sublime

My return here to the sublimity of earthquakes is to examine the aftermath of the Kobe earthquake, figured in a collection of stories by Haruki Murakami. As for the impact of the quake, "in the early morning hours of January 16, 1995, a 7.2 earthquake hit the port city of Kobe, Japan, killing over five thousand people, causing billions of dollars' worth of damage, and putting 300,000 out of their homes, including the parents of Haruki Murakami."[83] In entitling his set of stories *After the Quake* (all of which are obliquely connected to the event), Murakami creates an encounter of temporalities. The temporality of the sublime moment—as apprehension moves toward comprehension—is followed by the temporality of the quake's aftereffects, the enduring trauma, which like the quake itself is (metaphorically) subterranean, i.e., not available to explicit discursive reference. Cathy Caruth captures the (subterranean) temporality of such traumas:

> The wound of the mind—the breach in the mind's experience of time, self, and world—is not, like the wound of the body, a simple healable event but rather an event that . . . is experienced too soon, too unexpectedly, to be fully known and is therefore not available to consciousness until it imposes itself again, repeatedly, in the nightmares and repetitive actions of the survivor.[84]

As I noted it is primarily governmental authority that is the resort for those seeking reassurance in the face of events that challenge their sociopolitical presence to themselves. In the case of the Hanshin earthquake centered in Kōbe, after the government's response turned out to be inadequate, the authorities in Tokyo treated the problem as organizational, a need for a more rapid response and for structural improvements: "An emergency transportation network was also devised, and evacuation centres and shelters were set up in Kōbe by the Hyōgo prefectural government."[85] A subsequent report suggested that the trauma has been assuaged:

Once every few weeks this city is shaken by a tremor so powerful that it becomes a topic of conversation in the gleaming high-rises that tower above Tokyo and aboard the packed subways that course underground. And then, just as swiftly, conversations shift back to Japan's economic performance, the latest political scandal or, these days, Japan's baseball championship series. Such serenity is in large part attributable to government assurances that every practical earthquake safety precaution has already been taken in Tokyo, and to Japanese familiarity with geological disaster on a huge scale.[86]

Yet preparing better for the future does not provide solace for those traumatized by what has transpired. Murakami makes that case through his characters in *After the Quake,* suggesting that they experience the aftereffects of the quake not by heeding official policy responses but by reflecting on and comprehending aspects of their own lived experiences that had not hitherto found their way into consciousness.

Here two thought systems, Heidegger's phenomenological approach to thinking and Freud's version of sublimity, help elucidate what transpires for Murakami's characters.[87] In his *Was heisst Denken,* which has been translated as *What Is Called Thinking* (and could have been translated as *What Calls for Thinking*), Heidegger suggests that when certain events take place, we are enjoined to think about thinking. As he poses it in a crucial formulation, "What is it that calls on us to think?"[88] As his analysis proceeds, Heidegger displaces a cognitive approach to thinking (an emphasis on mental representations) with an emphasis on one's total presence to oneself and the world, on how things become manifest. Within such an approach, thinking is intimately tied to attention. Hence, as applied to Murakami's characters, what has happened is that at varying levels, the earthquake has gotten their attention.

To pursue Heidegger's phenomenology of attention further: recognition arises for the characters that rather than being discrete entities among other entities that are merely objects of representation, they are involved in relationships with the things in the world and with each other. In Heidegger's idiom, they become in touch with Being (as a being with). As a result, phenomenologically for Murakami's characters, sublime experiences of the quake create the conditions of possibility for senses of belonging, which are based less on conscious reasoning than on feelings or moods that had hitherto been fugitive.[89]

Murakami enacts that phenomenology as he extends the sublime moments of the quake, using his stories to defer and diversify comprehension and the modes of self-recognition it occasions, articulating it through a variety of kinds of lives. Metaphorically, he juxtaposes those different modes of comprehension in the civic sphere belonging to the communities of sense of the "little people" to the state's attempt to contain understandings, likening the state to a wall and citizen subjects to eggs:

> If there is a hard, high wall and an egg that breaks against it, no matter how right the wall or how wrong the egg, I will stand on the side of the egg. Why? Because each of us is an egg, a unique soul enclosed in a fragile egg. Each of us is confronting a high wall. The high wall is the system which forces us to do the things we would not ordinarily see fit to do as individuals. . . . We are all human beings, individuals, fragile eggs. We have no hope against the wall: it's too high, too dark, too cold. To fight the wall, we must join our souls together for warmth, strength. We must not let the system control us—create who we are.[90]

Accordingly, rather than rendering the significance of the quake through official responses, Murakami has it register on an event-provoked awareness in individual lives. For example, at the beginning of the first story, "U.F.O. in Kushiro," the quake is experienced by the nameless wife of the character, Komura, who is transfixed for "five straight days in front of the television, staring at crumbled banks and hospitals," unresponsive to her husband's voice.[91] Ultimately, when her initial shock and confusion turns to comprehension, she recognizes the emptiness of her marriage. Having often left for long intervals to visit her family, this time (five days after the earthquake) she leaves permanently, leaving behind a letter: "I am never coming back . . . the problem is that you never give me anything . . . Or, to put it more precisely, you have nothing inside you that you can give me . . . living with you is like living with a chunk of air."[92]

The life-unsettling reaction to the quake of Murakami's character, after she experiences an epiphany about her marriage, is one among a few "Flitcraft" moments in Murakami's stories. Flitcraft is the subject of a parable in Dashiell Hammett's crime novel *The Maltese Falcon*, a narrative-interrupting episode about a man, who like some of Murakami's characters is a creature of habit. In the novel, Hammett's detective, Sam Spade, tells a story to his client Bridget O'Shaughnessy (who turns out to be the murderer) about "a man named Flitcraft" who is startled when a large beam falls from a building, narrowly missing him. As it hits, a chunk of the side-walk (a small fragment of concrete) hits him in the cheek, causing a minor wound. That impact pales in comparison with Flitcraft's epiphany. "The event seemingly jars his consciousness, making him realize that he lives in an unsponsored, random world in which no normative order governs life."[93] As Hammett puts it, "he felt like somebody had taken the lid off life, and let him look at the works."[94] Flitcraft realizes that his effort of "sensibly ordering his affairs" is "not in step with life,"[95] and "after some aimless wandering in another city, he begins another life that looks quite similar to the one he left."[96] Two of Murakami's other characters also suddenly exit from their familiar lifeworlds after the quake—Junko and Miyake in "Landscape with Flatiron."

However, despite the focus on jarring effects—the "emotional after-shocks"—of the quake on those in Murakami's stories who had supposed that they had "sensibly ordered" *their* lives (like the aftershock and subsequent dramatic changes in their lives by Komura's nameless wife in "U.F.O. in Kushiro" and Junko and Miyake in "Landscape with Flatiron"), his focus is also on Japan's cultural reaction as a whole.[97] In his quake stories, as in his ethnography of the Aum Shinrikyo sarin gas attacks on Tokyo passenger trains three months later (in his *Underground*), "it is clear that one of Murakami's goals is to force the Japanese to see themselves," an attempt to present what has been for a traumatized population unpresentable, to attempt to "capture the event of trauma in language."[98] Seeing denial and avoidance as intrinsic to much of the Japanese reaction to the quake after the initial apprehension of the effects, Murakami evokes the evanescence of quake images. Recalling Iñárritu's rendering of the 9/11 images—his black screen with flashes of bodies falling from the towers at intervals—we find a similar mode of apprehension in Murakami's Komura in the "U.F.O. in Kushiro" story: "Images of it had come to him one after another, as if in a slide show, flashing on the screen and fading away."[99] Thereafter in that story as well as in the others, the quake gets scant mention or direct recognition by the characters.

To appreciate how his stories work, we have to heed both Murakami's testimony about his experience of the aftermath of the quake and his ethnography of the perpetrators and victims of the sarin gas attack. Murakami testifies that he traveled back to his former city to witness the "earthquake's shadow" to make sense of both that event and the sarin gas attack by creating "a corridor connecting the two" (seeing both events as "simultaneously" "physical" and "psychological").[100] Pointing out in his *Underground* how workings of memory displace historical events, transforming trauma into an alternative narrative, Murakami writes, "Simply put, our memories of experiences are rendered into something like a narrative form. . . . The truth of 'whatever is told' will differ, however slightly, from what actually happened. This however, does not make it a lie; it is unmistakably the truth, albeit in another form."[101] Seeing a tension between "personal memory" and "official history," Murakami has his fictional subjects reflect "the schism between the psychoanalytically determined subject and the subject of history."[102] Freudian thinking fits well here because his "therapeutic design intends the undoing of history" to liberate the subject to cope with the present.[103]

Specifically, to summon the psychoanalytic subject requires a summons to Freud's version of sublimity (his concept of the uncanny) to make further sense of the reactions of Murakami's characters (who reflect Japan's collective reaction).[104] Freud effectively reverses the direction of the Kantian version of the sublime. Instead of moving upward to a transcendent sphere of reason, the subject is sent downward, deep within its subconscious. To apply the Freudian view is thus to recognize that modes of reasoning that belong to a "mindedness" are not what shape the characters' coming to comprehension. Rather, in the Freudian frame, there is "something about mindedness itself that is 'mindless,'"[105] i.e., is awash in psychic energy whose aims are unconscious. What the traumatized Japanese subject seeks is to make sense of the experience of a traumatic event that is "uncanny," i.e., has evoked something in the unconscious that is both familiar and repressed, so that an excess psychic energy (which had been blocked) can be released.[106] If we heed the psychoanalytic aspect of what has occurred as the Japanese psyche confronts a terrifying event, we can observe that once the trauma registers itself, there can be a breakthrough to comprehension. What had been symbolically "indigestible"—mental energy that was hitherto "without an idea"—becomes effectively gregarious; it shapes a subject who is open to social recognition and intelligibility, able to negotiate the meaning of the event with others (inflected of course in this case by the Japanese cultural context).[107]

Taken as a whole Murakami's stories register relationships between individual and collective psyches. They seek to transpose individual lives into a historical treatment of how the nature of Japanese modernity (the cultural context) shapes the experience of sublime events. Accordingly, the stories in *After the Quake* simulate the ways in which the Japanese psyche creatively shapes the significance of the event for various individuals, each of whom has mostly an oblique connection with the earthquake, as they incorporate the trauma into their altered lives. Because the stories focus on individual lives, we can ask (as some of Murakami's stories imply) about the conditions of possibility for translating the effects of sublime events into collective civic moments. Inasmuch as each story presents a different kind of oblique, singular (i.e., symptomatic) reaction to the earthquake, the collection militates against a frame in which Japanese modernity as a whole can be characterized in terms of a unitary cultural *sensus communis*. Instead we can discern shared civic moments in the stories if we heed the spaces within which such moments transpire. Rancière supplies the relevant spatial framing for such moments, noting that he understands the "phrase 'community of sense' to mean a collectivity shaped by some common feeling . . . a frame of visibility and intelligibility . . . which shapes . . . a certain sense of community. A community of sense is a certain cutting out of a space and time that binds together practices of visibility . . . patterns of intelligibility . . . [derived from] cutting out a partition of the sensible. . . . Above all, it is made of some spatial setting."[108]

There are two such civic spaces in Murakami's earthquake stories, both of which are drawn from earlier periods of his personal life. One is the gathering around a bonfire at a beach: "As a child . . . I'd sneak out of the house at night, go to the sea with my friends and gather driftwood and light a bonfire."[109] In the story "Landscape with Flatiron," the two characters, Junko and Miyake, experience the bonding effect of a beach bonfire, which for both of them expresses the freedom they have experienced in their Flitcraft moments (the breaking out of their former lifeworlds). At one point Junko says, "Tell me Mr. Miyake, when you see the shapes that a bonfire makes, do you ever feel kind of strange?" (read "uncanny")—to which he responds, "It's like all of a sudden you get very clear about something that people don't usually notice in everyday life." As the conversation continues, the spatio-temporal moment of the bonfire yields a shared sensibility. After suggesting that he is not quite able to express what he is thinking, Miyake concedes that "watching the fire now, I get this deep kind of feeling" and adds, after pondering for a while:

> "You know Jun . . . a fire can be any shape it wants to be. It's free. So it can look like anything at all depending on what's inside the person

looking at it. If you get a deep, quiet kind of feeling when you look at a fire, that's because it's showing you the deep quiet kind of feeling you have inside yourself."[110]

Junko and Miyake keep meeting at the bonfire. As Junko becomes his "bonfire buddy,"[111] the bonfire becomes the space of shared moments in which they can reflect together on what they have felt inside, an earlier feeling that was never comfortably resolved and thus an emptiness that has needed to be filled. There had been a void after the sublime moment of the earthquake, as rather than moving toward comprehension, the characters had deferred their thinking. By staging an encounter within a contingent civic moment, Murakami uses the space of the bonfire to summon an unmetabolized past, overcome a "hermeneutic impasse,"[112] and end the deferral of comprehension.

The second civic space is musical, doubtless drawn from Murakami's lifelong association with jazz, which began "in 1964 when [he] was 15." He subsequently opened his own jazz bar and has since "wondered if it might be possible for me to transfer that music into writing."[113] The improvisational rhythms of jazz performances have resonances in Murakami's writing in which he has sought to represent events that defy representation within conventional discursive practices. For example, the jazz idiom surfaces in the story "Thailand," which features a relationship between a vacationing medical doctor, Satsuki, who, seeking a reprieve from her troubled marriage, decides to hang out a while in Thailand after her medical convention closes, and her guide, Nimit, who drives her around to various tourist sites. As their conversations become personal, the jazz cassette tape, playing on Nimit's car radio, becomes (like the bonfire in the "Flatiron" story) a key character with an effect on how their relationship transpires. It provokes a conversation about jazz when Satsuki asks if he minds "turning the volume up."[114] After they listen for a while, Nimit refers to having been asked once to listen carefully to an Ornette Coleman jazz improvisation, which, he was told, "is telling us the story of a free spirit." Ultimately, the music lesson turns out to be a lesson about how improvisational music can challenge reified forms of discourse in general: "Words turn into stone, Nimit had told her," in a line near the end of the story. As the story ends, an affected Satsuki is listening to the jazz pianist Erroll Garner while she falls asleep on her departing flight. She is waiting for a dream (which Nimit has promised will free her from a hard stone [something repressed] inside her, which has had to be extracted in order for her to come to effective terms with her life).[115] Again, we should note the Freudian sublime/uncanny at work in that moment: "Freud speculated that what we first forget, and only subsequently remember, is the most important element in a dream . . . 'important' . . . for an interpretation."[116]

Moving from a psychic to a political level, it is evident that Murakami draws on his understanding of jazz improvisation, both to figure his linguistic departure from the more stultifying forms of Japanese literature and to contrast the spatio-temporal moments of jazz performance with the unimaginative representations of events in official policy pronouncements. With respect to the former—his way of crafting a narrative—as a writer Murakami resists normalization. In his characterization of Jean Genet, Félix Guattari captures what it is that Murakami seeks to depart from: "Everyone who has been well brought up . . . every soul whose reflexes and mind have been duly normalized, knows how to discipline essentially heretical, dissident, and perverse voices." He adds, "Genet was not well brought up" (not effectively normalized). As a result, he writes (in a sentence that applies well to Murakami), "By way of rhythms, refrains, passwords, magical mnemotechnical formulae, he takes partial control of [a] . . . processuality of sense."[117] Like Genet, Murakami invents "a new way of language," an alternative "linguistic idiom," in his case by mixing nonhuman, psychological, and historical forms of subjectivity to challenge conventional ways of rendering what he refers to (in the "Super-Frog Saves Tokyo" story) as the "accumulated hatred" intrinsic to Japanese modernity.[118]

With his use of jazz to allegorize freedom from conventional modes of comprehension, Murakami is tapping into what has been an oppositional communitarian practice of the African American assemblage in the United States. In an episode in his novel *Atet* A.D. Nathaniel Mackey captures the *sensus communis* that a jazz ensemble achieves. The setting is Onaje's, a jazz club in Oakland, California, where a group is playing to celebrate the musical career of Thelonious Monk. In one brief passage, Mackey evokes the musical and sports heritage of African Americans, while treating how they are able to make musical sense together: "Indebted to Sonny Rollins's Blue Note recording of the piece, most notably the sense of alarm he gets from the leap to a high D in the fifth bar: We gave it the same quantum sense of duress but added a touch of our own, pulling back as if to declare the alarm false. If you can imagine the acoustical equivalent of a fade-away jumpshot you've got a good idea of the approach we took."[119]

At that moment, Onaje's as Mackey has rendered it is a civic space for the exercise of an oppositional community of sense. As the evening progresses, the group's *sensus communis* waxes—e.g., when one member of the group, Aunt Nancy, "finished her solo the two of us took up what turned out to be an extended increasingly contentious conversation," which continues as "an old-time cutting session" (i.e., as a communitarian mode of contentious acoustical thinking).[120] Mackey's episode at Onaje's is thus an instance of what Gregory Clark calls "civic jazz." One of the exemplary moments to which Clark refers involves the fashioning of an intercultural acoustical community of sense at "the Moab music festival," where the "Marcus Roberts Trio" is joined by the "banjoist Bela Fleck at the Utah stop of the tour." As Clark describes the moment:

> Here jazz would meet bluegrass, bringing together two American musics that had much to divide them. When the concert began, the four musicians—three black and one white—let their musics roll across each other, calling out in one idiom and responding in the other, exchanging idioms and gradually developing a hybrid sound in a new voice of both jazz and bluegrass.[121]

Thus what Murakami's evocation of jazz implies is that oppositional communities of sense are forged in moments that defy the longer-term torpor of the officially sanctioned national cultures through which events are comprehended. His bonfire and jazz moments, experienced by symbolic refugees from the moment of the earthquake, suggest ways of facing one's psychic and historical condition when conventional reactions bury events rather than confronting them.

Conclusion: Another Small Girl Confronts an Earthquake

In the last story that articulates his musings on post-earthquake Japan, "Honey Pie," Murakami figures the divide between denial and comprehension with yet another figuration, a contrast between confining things in small boxes and liberating things for creative thinking. The story brings my analysis full circle because one of the characters is a small girl, Sala, trying to make sense of the very large earthquake. She tells her mother, Sayoko, that she has been afflicted by a bad dream about a man who summons her, "the earthquake man. He came and woke me up. . . . He said he has a box ready for everybody. He said he's waiting with the lid open."[122] The main character, Junpei, a writer (who is likely a stand-in for Murakami), has renewed a romantic connection with Sayoko (having replaced her former husband, Takahashi, who, tellingly, works for the news media). Junpei supplies the antidote for the confining box. His remarks about his vocation ends the story (and the collection as a whole):

> I want to write stories that are different from the ones I've written so far. . . . I want to write about people who dream and wait for the night to end, who long for the light so they can hold the ones they love. But right now I have to stay here and watch over this woman and this girl. I will never let anyone—not anyone—try to put them into that crazy box—not ever, even if the sky should fall or the earth crack open with a roar.[123]

Here, Murakami's art of storytelling is his challenge to the way a politically attentive approach to a historical event can challenge Japan's cultural quiescence, its attempt to approach historical comprehension by confining the event within a small box (i.e., within conventional discursive frames). To summon Lyotard's terms, Murakami's stories bear "expressive witness to the inexpressible," while at the same time attempting, with what fiction at its best can do, the creation of an altered (often oppositional) community of sense.[124] They exemplify "the political sublime."

2. THE RACIAL SUBLIME

Two fictional episodes disclose and reflect on the reality of black family life in the southern plantation system during the slave period. One is in Edward P. Jones's novel *The Known World*, whose main protagonist, Henry Townsend, is a former slave who ultimately owns his own slaves. Henry's story begins when his freed parents have to leave him behind until they can afford to buy his freedom. The father, Augustus Townsend, has come to collect his wife, Mildred, whom he has managed to buy some years after having bought his own freedom from his earnings as a furniture maker. The plantation owner, William Robbins, whose labor force is 113 slaves, had permitted Augustus to hire himself out but had "kept part of what he earned."[1] As Augustus and Mildred are about to depart, Augustus tries to reassure the nine-year-old Henry, saying, "Before you can turn around good . . . you be coming home with us." Meanwhile, Robbins, observing the scene while mounted on his horse, "Sir Guilderham," appears from Henry's perspective as "a mountain separating the boy from the fullness of the sun." Asked by Robbins why he's crying, Henry is too fearful to say; he is to be left under the supervision of a household slave, Rita, to whom Robbins says, "You see things go right," implying that it's her job to make sure that Henry doesn't try to flee. The narration proceeds in the third person: "He would have called Rita by name but she had not distinguished herself enough in his life for him to remember the name he had given her at birth."[2]

In an earlier reading of the episode, I addressed the political pedagogy of the scene:

> Among what we learn [from the episode] are aspects of the micro-politics of plantation space missing in abstract, historical glosses—its multiple dimensions of dominance: a horse with an aristocratic name contrasted with a slave whose name is not regarded as worth recalling, a child being wrenched away from his parents without having the right to voice its misery, and a "master" who remains on horseback, well above the level of those oppressed by the exercise of his prerogatives, all framed by a historical situation in which bodies can be owned and subjected to any exercise of will but their own.[3]

While Jones's novel dramatizes aspects of the lived experience of slavery from the perspective of those who labored within the vast, imagination-challenging system of plantation gulags in the South, the other episode, recounted in Russell Banks's novel *Cloudsplitter* (a novelistic version of the life of the abolitionist John Brown), treats the veil of ignorance that shielded white Americans from the violence done to the black family structure under slavery. The scene is a conversation between John Brown's son Owen (the novel's narrator) and three African American men: one fugitive slave and two freed slaves. Addressing the free Mr. Fleete first, Owen asks, "Do you have a wife or children Mr. Fleete"? Mr. Fleete responds: "No, my wife is dead Mr. Brown. She died young . . . died without children."

> "And you never thought to marry again?"
> [Mr. Fleete] sighed and studied the pipe in his brown hand.

Owen then turns to the free Lyman Epps and says, "'I want to ask you about your wife Susan, did you come out of slavery together?'"

> "No, she came north alone."
> "You don't have any children?"
> "No, we don't. Susan has children though. Three of them. They got sold off south, sent to Georgia someplace, she don't know where."
> Lyman turned and looked at me, said nothing, and returned his gaze to the ceiling. (220–221)

Finally, Owen engages the fugitive James Cannon:

"Do you have family in Canada who will help you settle there?"

"Family? No not exactly Mr. Brown . . ."

"What is the name of the man who was your master?"

"His name? Samuel . . . Samuel Cannon."

"The same as yours?"

"Yes, Mr. Brown, same as mine. Same as his father's too. Same as my mother."

"So you were born a slave to Mister Samuel Cannon, and your mother was born his father's slave?"

"Yes, Mr. Brown. She surely wasn't Mas' Cannon's wife."

"Who was your father then? What happened to him?"

He looked away from me again. "Don't know. Long gone." (222)

After the three conversations, the veil is lifted and Owen confesses, "I'd finally lost that punishing innocence, and I felt ashamed of my inquiry" (223).

The racial sublime articulated in the inauguration of the contemporary concept of the sublime by Edmund Burke and Immanuel Kant is radically different from what one can discern from the novels of Jones and Banks. As Hermann Wittenberg points out, "The sublime, already in the classical foundations laid by Edmund Burke and Immanuel Kant, is founded on problematic assumptions of racial difference."[4] They "sought to define sublimity by using images of racial others as deficit models."[5] Without venturing from their homelands, both philosophers constructed fabulous anthropologies of the black body. Burke's version is based on a metaphorical disparagement of darkness as something terrible. For him the sublime is an "abyssal dark immensity"; it is "dark, uncertain, consumed, terrible, and sublime to the last degree."[6] Burke seals his case for the cultural deficits of the black body with a story about the "horror" evinced by a previously blind child "upon accidently seeing a negro woman."[7]

Kant's initial version of the racial sublime is more geographically situated; he imagines the black body (referencing "The Negroes of Africa") as one with "no feeling that rises above the trifling"[8] and equates the "Negro" with the "slave."[9] Challenging a long historical trajectory of a racial sublime, which has perpetuated a violence-legitimating mythology of the lessor cultural value of the black body, the Jones and Banks novels give historical and experiential specificity to the American version of that sublime. In what follows, I address the ways in which a variety of media and artistic genres extend what is accomplished in Jones's and Banks's novels by contesting the persistence of that racial sublime (a vast, difficult-to-comprehend system of oppression) with attention to what much of white America has until recently failed to witness—how it is experienced by African Americans.

Contemporary Scenes

Although its manifestations have changed, the U.S. racial sublime persists as a system of racial discrimination and officially sanctioned forms of brutality whose vastness pierces the veil of ignorance only episodically. For example, the media images of the aftermath of Hurricane Katrina in 2005 and subsequently the media dissemination of video captures of urban police officers beating, strangling, and shooting unarmed African Americans have attenuated much of the contemporary "punishing innocence" of contemporary "white" America. As I noted elsewhere (and in the introduction), quoting Michael Eric Dyson, "it has become evident in a way not previously appreciated by white America, 'the lived experience of race feels like terror for black folk.'"[10]

That terror registers itself in a wide variety of coping mechanisms, actualized (among other ways) as family strategies. In an earlier study, I addressed the issue by comparing the family problematic evinced in two exemplary films—Paul Brickman's *Risky Business* (1983) and Spike Lee's *Clockers* (1995)—emphasizing that while "many privileged white parents are worrying about making sure their children reproduce their level of privilege [Brickman's film opens with the protagonist Joel confronted by his mother who is concerned that his SAT scores are insufficient for getting him into an Ivy League school] . . . many black parents are worrying about keeping their children alive."[11] Throughout Lee's film, situated in a housing project, a middle-aged black mother watches in dismay from her apartment window while, in the project's square below, one of her sons is harassed by policing agents, and in a series of subsequent scenes in the project square, a young black mother strives (unsuccessfully) to keep her preteen son away from the young drug clockers who work for a dealer.

Popular culture is one window into the most daunting issue facing many contemporary African American families: protecting their children from violence. In other testimonies, generations of African American intellectuals (organic intellectuals in Gramsci's sense) have disseminated to both black and white publics a lesson that is crucial for black family members.[12] They must understand—as James Baldwin explains to his namesake nephew—that for the most part those "believing themselves white" belong to a world that doesn't want to know how *their* world oppresses the world in which blackness has been quarantined.[13] Baldwin goes on to refer to the knowledge culture that helps to set the black world straight: "The American negro has the great advantage of never having believed that collection of myths to which Americans cling: that their ancestors were all freedom loving heroes."[14] As a contemporary reviewer notes, "It's shocking how little has changed between the races in this country since 1963, when James Baldwin published this coolly impassioned plea to 'end the racial nightmare.'"[15] Baldwin's "impassioned plea" is indeed coolly delivered. As Edward P. Jones points out (in a new introduction to Baldwin's *Notes of a Native Son*), Baldwin, "never shouts."[16]

More than half a century later, another black organic intellectual, Ta-Nehisi Coates, has repeated and elaborated Baldwin's lesson for the current era. In Coates's case the advice is to his son and is delivered with more stridency, driven by his anguish over the murder of his loved and admired friend (and Howard University schoolmate), Prince Jones, by a Prince George County policeman, who claimed to have mistaken him for a wanted man (even though Prince Jones was ten inches taller and many pounds lighter than the fugitive). Coates had learned to live in fear, a condition of being "black in the Baltimore of [his] youth," where, among other things, "the law did not protect us," while in contrast it "protects some people through a safety net of schools, government-backed home loans, and ancestral wealth."[17]

The lack of protection to which Coates refers derives from the persistence into the twenty-first century of the "color line," which W. E. B. Du Bois had famously identified as the essence of the racial sublime. Evoking an essential aspect of sublime experience, vastness, Du Bois stated that the color line was "the problem of the twentieth century . . . our vastest social problem . . . so vast a prejudice."[18] As aspects of the color line persist, one dimension of the vastness to which Du Bois referred afflicts the contemporary African American family in the form of mass incarceration, which results from the disproportionate criminalization of young African American males. As Coates points out, the "consequences [of the rapid increase in incarceration rates] for black men have radiated out to their families. By 2000, more than 1 million black children had a father in jail or prison."[19]

Rather than recognizing in the black struggle for equality a replay of the much valorized American revolution, political leaders and law enforcement apparatuses have instead incorporated the struggle into a "war on crime," actualized as a violent (re)affirmation of the color line. As Coates puts it, "The American response to crime cannot be divorced from a history of equating the black struggle—individual and collective—with black villainy."[20] In contrast, the color line continues to favor white America, which seems to avoid the stain of criminality. When researchers "sent young whites and blacks out to interview for low wage jobs in New York City with equivalent resumes . . . whites were twice as likely to get callbacks . . . and a black applicant with a clean criminal record did no better than a white applicant who was said to have just been released from 18 months in prison."[21]

For Du Bois the entrenchment of the color line represented a tragic failure of the Reconstruction, during which for a brief historical moment there had been the possibility of a shared oppositional community of sense, yielding a black-white economic collaboration. He refers to a time in which "the ranks and file of black labor had a notable leadership of intelligence" that many white laborers had begun to appreciate.[22] There was thus the possibility that a combined labor force could "bring workers of all colors into a united opposition to the employer," a "democratic development across racial lines,"[23] which never came to fruition. What remained was the color line, a vast racial sublime painfully evident for African Americans, relatively unobserved by white America. As Du Bois lamented:

> Within and without the somber veil of color vast social forces have been at work—efforts for human betterment, movements toward disintegration and despair, tragedies and comedies in social and economic life. . . .
> The center of this spiritual turmoil has ever been the millions of black freedmen and their sons, whose destiny is so fatefully bound up with that of the nation. And yet the casual observer visiting the South sees at first little of this.[24]

Rather than an emerging structure of cooperation, the vast racial sublime that separates much of white and black America is arguably a legacy of an earlier war on ethnic Americans. As Robert Crooks suggests, the violence that took place on the western frontier (an internation frontier) of the United States during the nineteenth century shifted to urban frontiers—in his terms, a "transformation of the frontier from a moving western boundary into a relatively fixed partitioning of urban space . . . a racial frontier."[25]

It should be noted however that what Crooks designates as an internation frontier was radically reoriented by Euro-America's political agencies, which changed Native America from a collection of nations into a single race. The initial step in that transformation involved creating a dependency to displace what was initially "foreign policy." John Borneman points out that "by the mid-19th century, the European concept of a 'polity' organized by a sovereign, territorial state was juxtaposed to the Indian's lack of territorial organization, which made Indians, in the words of Chief Justice Marshall in 1831, into a 'domestic dependent nation,' as opposed to a 'foreign state.'"[26] Ultimately, an identity discourse was institutionalized, as "non-Indians employed a set of proto-race categories that defined the Indian." As a result, Native Americans were racialized and politically disempowered as both governmental and cultural discourses effected "the transformation of the aborigine from historical actor to aesthetic object; Native Americans became an artistic abstraction that served to deflect a painful history of violence and injustice."[27] Unlike the case of Afro-America, the Native American color line has become virtually invisible to white America. Nevertheless, many mixed race, Euro-Native Americans struggle with identity issues and suffer from having had their heritage turned into a series of demeaning aesthetic objects, for example, sports logos for college and professional sports teams. One has to turn to Native American literatures and films to discover the details of their identity struggles (e.g., the films of Chris Eyre and the novels of James Welch, Leslie Marmon Silko, and Sherman Alexie). Sherman Alexie's character John Smith (in his novel *Indian Killer*) is exemplary, a part Indian who was taken from his birth mother and relocated with white middle-class foster parents. As Alexie puts it, John "gently goes mad during the course of the book" and ultimately suffers from a feeling of "invisibility," an "inability to see and recognize himself as a 'real' Indian," which "propels him to search for and reenact authenticity" by killing white men.[28]

African Americans have had to deal with a different kind of invisibility (as Ralph Ellison famously suggests), a withholding of respectful recognition by white America.[29] To return to Crook's analysis of the shift from the western to the urban frontier and to the white/black color line, it's important to note his qualifier, "relatively," for contemporary racial partitioning. In some zones of mixing—especially sports and music (the latter of which I elaborate on below)—the color line has been breached. Significant sharing and mutual influence developed throughout the twentieth century and has continued in the twenty-first.

Zones of Mixing

There is an allegory that provides a way to read the vicissitudes of the color line. Years ago on a trip to the Amazon region of Brazil, I witnessed a remarkable geological phenomenon: two rivers, the Rio Negro and Rio Solimões, which ultimately become part of a single one, the Amazon, run side by side without mixing. The two rivers form a color line that does not dissipate for roughly six kilometers. One is virtually black (the Negro) and the other (the Solimões) is the color of a cappuccino. As one description summarizes it:

> The Rio Negro, as the name implies, is a river of water that looks nearly black. It is relatively clear of sediment but has obtained its tea-like color from large quantities of plant material steeping in the water as it comes down through the jungles of Colombia. . . . The Rio Solimões, on the other hand, is a creamy cafe-au-lait color due to the large amount of sediment picked up as the water flows down the Andes Mountains. . . . The difference in composition, flow rate, temperature, and density prevent the two from mixing when they initially meet. The contrast in color is so stark, this section of water can even be seen from space. Eventually, the water encounters obstacles that form heavy eddies, which churn the two rivers together.[30]

What kinds of eddies have churned the two races and have created the conditions in which the racial color line has been breached? Certainly, a major one—in some ways more effective than the civil rights cases and legislation of the 1950s and '60s—has been the expansion of commerce, especially an "emergent consumer culture" in which as Paul Gilroy puts it, "it became possible for some of North America's racial inferiors to buy and enjoy things that they were not supposed to have."[31] Notably that buying power was noticed by the formerly white-only record industry whose producers had come to understand that "fourteen million Negroes will buy records if recorded by one of their own."[32] Arguably, "black music rescued the record business in the 1920s because the Depression would kill most of it off. The race market certainly saved Columbia Records."[33]

Although African Americans were invited into the music recording business, much of the black assemblage constituted an alternative community of sense for whom musical reception differed from that of white America. For example, Mamie Smith's song "Crazy Blues" (1920), which tends to lack political meaning for white Americans, has consistently registered itself among much of the African American assemblage as "an insurrectionary social text . . . contributing to an evolving discourse on black revolutionary violence in the broadest sense . . . black violence as a way of resisting white violence and unsettling a repressive social order."[34] At the same time, as the jazz age emerged, there was considerable "ethnic dissonance"; a musical culture war developed, as "Anglos, who were committed to a model of racial hierarchy[,] . . . dismissed jazz as a remnant of an inferior culture, and others, mostly Jewish émigrés [were] incorporating jazz and aspects of its ragtime roots into a new hybrid American music in both symphonic and musical theater genres."[35]

That ethnic dissonance also registered itself *within* the jazz culture. Duke Ellington saw much of the Jewish American incorporation of African American music (in musical theater) as a reinforcement of the existing racial-spatial order. When he staged his own musical, *Jump for Joy*, his intention, he said, was "to take Uncle Tom out of the theater."[36] And after the premier of George Gershwin's *Porgy and Bess*, Ellington said, "the times are here to debunk Gershwin's lampblack Negroisms."[37] Nevertheless, there have been creative, shared moments—acoustical communities of sense—for example the one that emerged (described in chapter 1) when the bluegrass banjo player Bela Fleck played with the Marcus Roberts jazz trio. Seeing the episode as one among many instances of "civic jazz" in which, as Gregory Clark describes the moment (quoted in chapter 1), "jazz would meet bluegrass, bringing together two American musics that had much to divide them."[38] However, the encounter that Clark describes is a legacy of a series of earlier encounters. From the outset, the bluegrass genre developed within an African American musical idiom. The son of a former slave, "Arnold Schultz, an African-American fiddler [was a] childhood mentor of [Bill] Monroe," who developed bluegrass in the 1940s "as an outgrowth of old-time music."[39] Moreover, "African-American influence on bluegrass is pervasive. Slave ballads and heavy religious themes, both hallmarks of the antebellum South, have substantial place in bluegrass musicology [and] . . . the impact of the blues on the musical composition of bluegrass and the African invention of the banjo, were two other contributions to string band music."[40] And significantly, the two music genres share an experiential past involving forms of servitude; part of the legacy of bluegrass is string band music developed through the immigration of Scotch-Irish musicians to the United States: "Many were so poor that in order to afford travel expenses, they signed contracts with American plantation owners to become indentured servants."[41]

In short, the Bela Fleck–Marcus Roberts Trio encounter *restored* an acoustical community of sense rather than inventing a wholly new one. As the ensemble's different sets progress, Roberts's piano style sounds increasingly string band–like, while Fleck's banjo riffs sound increasingly less percussive and more jazz-like. Thus the musical moment that is achieved in the Roberts–Fleck encounter succeeds in (re)uniting black and white communities of sense, where the labor coalition and the possibility of "interracial sympathy"[42] that Du Bois had hoped for failed. Like many others, that moment indicates that although in some domains the "color line" is entrenched, it is attenuated elsewhere as black and white America have functioned as both divided and shared lifeworlds and communities of sense. To put it spatially, there have been zones of separation and zones of mixing. Because the way race has been lived in zones of mixing is especially evident in the experiences of "racially mixed" families, I turn here to Richard Powers's novel *The Time of Our Singing* because of the way it is attuned to the history of musical exchanges that cross racial lines as well as the way it details the fraught racial-spatial order as it afflicted mixed-race families in the mid-twentieth century, a period witnessing the tension between exclusionary Jim Crow practices and openings of social and economic opportunities formerly denied to those designated as "American Negroes."[43]

The Time of Our Singing

The family of protagonists in Powers's novel, the Daley-Stroms, parented by a African American wife, Delia Daley, and a German Jewish father, David Strom, are "essentially brought together by racism"; they meet at a 1939 Marian Anderson concert on the steps of the Lincoln memorial, after Anderson is denied the use of Washington's main concert venue.[44] Thereafter, as they raise their children in a musically rich household, managing the coherence of the family involves a struggle with the very racial order that precipitated the marriage. Throughout the novel—a family saga structured by their struggles—Powers interarticulates two kinds of mixture, musical and racial, where the former constitutes a reprieve from the enmity toward the later. The home is shaped as a musical conversation, a "singing school [in which] upstart tunes took their place on a thousand-year parade of harmony and invention"; they sang together and thereby "continued that long conversation of pitches in time. . . . In old music, they made sense. Singing, they were no one's outcasts."[45] Mixing meets mixing in the "contrapuntal interludes" the Daley-Stroms stage in ways reminiscent of America's often fraught, interracial musical self-fashioning, running from the late nineteenth century through much of the twentieth: "after dinner they came together in tunes, Rossini while washing dishes, W.C. Handy while drying" (11).[46] And in their musical game, "crazed quotations," they invented subjects and counter-subjects: "The game produced the wildest of mixed marriages, love matches that even the heaven of half-breeds looked sidelong at. Her Brahms *Alto Rhapsody* bickered with his growled Dixieland. Cherubini crashed into Cole Porter, Debussy, Tallis and Mendelssohn shacked up in unholy *ménages a trois*" (13).

Outside the family home, the Daley-Stroms struggle against the ethnic objectifications that racialize families—primarily the effects of "Jim Crow laws and practices" that created "the desperation felt by African Americans living under them" (famously exposed for a reading public in this period by Richard Wright's writings, the stories in his *Uncle Tom's Children* [1939] and his novel *Native Son* [1940]).[47] However, even sympathetic attempts to ameliorate "the problem of the black family" have reinstalled the color line: for example, the influential and (in)famous Moynihan Report in which racial inequality is attributed to the absence of father figures in black families. Hortense Spiller's response to the report effectively deconstructs that ethnicization/racialization:

> "Ethnicity" itself identifies a total objectification of human and cultural motives—the "white" family, by implication, and the "Negro family," by outright assertion, in a constant opposition of binary meanings. Apparently spontaneous, these "actants" are wholly generated, with neither past nor future, as tribal currents moving out of time. Moynihan's "families" are pure present and always tense.[48]

Powers's novel provides an elaborate politics of temporality that generates an experiential realization of what Spillers provides more tersely in her response to the Moynihan report. His character David Strom (aka "Da") puts it succinctly in his remark to his middle son (the novel's narrator), Joey: "There is no such thing as race. Race is only real if you freeze time" (94). The novel as a whole affirms and extends that remark as it interweaves diverse levels of temporality. For example, there is David Strom's biographical time, characterized as "a life of dedicated forgetting," a consequence of his steadfast commitment to avoiding ethnic identification ("he never checked 'Jewish' on any form in his life" [20]). All aspects of individual lived time are set against historically developing national time—for example, the section entitled "late 1843—early 1935" in which the narration refers to a racial intermingling that has yielded the production of varied skin tones among African Americans, the heritage of the "light skinned" Delia Daley, whose biography also includes a musical legacy, a diverse collection of musical genres: "She'd come from more places than even her hybrid children could get to, and one of those clashing places sang its signature tune" (72).

As the novel plays with the tension between scientific and artistic frames of reference, the musical trajectory is applied to Delia's biography, given her musical vocation, while in David's case, given his physics vocation, cosmological time dominates his temporal perspective (noted for example in a passage that reflects on "time's arrow," which can point in both directions, e.g., "time running backward toward some youngest day's Big Crunch" [93]). As is the case for Delia, for whom historical time is inscribed on her body (racial time implied by her skin tone), time is inscribed on David's body. His biographical time is shown on his "thickening features," which direct his gaze and on "his four gnarled fingers on his right hand, as it rises up to wipe his brow, tracing the same reflex path they've followed every day of this life" (93).

Reversing the direction that had aimed time's arrow into the past is an Augustinian moment (a riff on St. Augustine's speculation about how one can have a future that "as yet does not be") as the arrow points to the future.[49] Joey wonders, "If time, in fact, still exists, it must be a block, a resonance. . . . The lives he has yet to live through are already in him, as real as the ones he has so far led."[50] That futurity is also represented in Joey's "recurrent sightings of a beautiful elusive woman who turns out to be his own mother in her youth"—effectively a reflection on the way one imagines "an escape into the future . . . for those stuck in an unbearable present . . . The ultimate rescue vehicle (as David Strom sees it) for those who have perished in the past."[51] He is however unable to "wrap his head around" the destructiveness that time lends to the family: "He struggles . . . to do away with time. But [thinks Joey] the world will do away with all five of us before then, if it can."[52]

The temporal structure of the novel—its nonlinear rhythms as it moves back and forth across several decades and repeats events—adds to its critical rendering of the Daley-Strom family's struggle for coherence and attunement to an America that is hostile to their hybridity. Powers's use of repetition is a formal strategy that recasts the novel's substantive, experiential rendering of American's mid-twentieth-century racial sublime by demonstrating its contingencies. The novel repeatedly mimics "what *effectively occurs*" for the Daley-Stroms, freeing the event of the family's fate from inevitability.[53]

The coherence of the Daley-Strom family ultimately succumbs to the pressures of a racial order that defies their attempt to create a zone of safety within the family, free from the world's racialized ascriptions. At one point, after their oldest son, Jonah, impresses a white church audience with his singing, two of the congregation's "white women" approach him. One of them says, "I just can't tell you how much it means to me, personally, to have a little Negro boy singing like that. In our church. For us." Jonah—at this juncture innocent of the racial order that has ventriloquized itself through her words—responds, "Oh ma'am, we're not real Negroes. But our mother is!" Stunned, "the ladies fell back from this ghost. Their known world crumpled faster than they could rebuild it" (28–29). Nevertheless, that "known world" is well institutionalized; when Delia gives birth the second time, "the state puts 'Colored' on the birth certificate. 'How about "mixed" this time?' she asks . . . but mixed isn't a category" (334).

After that encounter, Jonah tries to clarify his ethnic identity. He raises *the* question that "they'd been waiting for, and every other one that would follow": "Mama," he asked. "You are a Negro, right? And Da's . . . some kind of Jewish guy. What exactly does that make me, Joey, and Root [their younger sister]?" Da responds with a double entendre: "You must run your own race," and Delia says, as she holds her two sons in her arms, "You're whatever you are, inside. Whatever you need to be" (9). However, the parents cannot protect their children from a world that insists on unambiguous racial identities. Out of the house, the boys must "take . . . a dose of torture at the hands of boys more cruelly competent in boyhood, boys who rained down on the two Stroms the full brutality of collective bafflement" (10).

Accompanying the discursive rendering of the family's struggle to manage the racial order is the novel's incorporation of the temporal aspects of visual technologies. In a very telling moment Joey describes "a photograph—one of the few from my childhood that escaped incineration." It's a Polaroid shot of Joey and his brother Jonah opening Christmas presents. Joey emphasizes his brother's eyes, taking in his present, "a three-segment expanding telescope" aimed as well at the rest of the family and their presents, looking at "mine, a metronome; at Rootie, who clutches his knee, wanting to see for herself; at our photographing father, deep in the act of stopping time; at Mama just past the picture's frame; at a future audience, looking from a century on, at this sheltered Christmas crèche, long after all of us are dead" (16). As Pierre Bourdieu has suggested, "Photographic practice only exists and subsists for most of the time by virtue of its family function. . . . The photograph itself is usually nothing but the family's image of its own integration."[54] In an age that threatened its economic viability, the family began (re)asserting itself "by accumulating the signs of its affective unity, its intimacy."[55]

However, at the beginning of the section about the photo, which is captioned "My Brother's Face," the narration hints about the relevance of another visual technology's ability to represent the family's situation, cinema. Before describing the photo, Joey describes the mobility of Jonah's face, "a school of fishes. His grin was not one thing, but a hundred darting ones" (16). As the section about Noah's face continues, Joey notes how it will record the future, as the stresses of the racial order continually afflict its owner: "The features will narrow as the months move on. The lips draw and the eyebrows batten down" (17). Thus as Joey's description of his brother's face integrates a time image, the novel moves from a photographic to a cinematic mode. The initial close-up of the face is what Deleuze famously calls an affection image, an image "abstracted from spatio-temporal coordinates," which has the effect of "undoing space."[56] But as the temporal montage of the narration continues, space reasserts itself as the children's initial innocence has to confront the humiliating vagaries of the racial-spatial order. For example, when Noah auditions for a singing school, prospects look favorable: "Twenty bars into my brother's a cappella rendition of 'Down by the Sally Gardens,'" the judges were sold. But when official word comes two weeks later, the word is, "We regret to say . . ." (19). Shortly afterward, as the family travels together for another tryout, Joey says, "My mother rode in the backseat with me and Ruth. She always rode in the back whenever we traveled together" [making it appear that their black mother is instead a servant] . . . so that the police wouldn't stop us" (21). And after the first rejection, as the family tries to catch a cab home, "On Broadway, the first three cabs we flagged wouldn't take us" (29).

Occasionally the racial tensions outside the home insinuate themselves within. "One evening toward the summer's end, just before Jonah and I returned from Boylston [where a music school had finally enrolled Jonah], he stopped Mama [playing the piano] in mid phrase, 'You could get a smoother tone and have less trouble with the *passaggio* if you kept your head still.'" A sudden silence prevails as the parents have pained looks; Delia just stared: "My father's face drained, as if his son had just spouted a slur." Jonah had not appreciated the body-music relationship belonging to African American culture: "Singing meant being free to dance" (67). And late in the novel the tensions break up the family. When the children are grown they don't all share their father's commitment to colorblindness (an inattention to demeaning forms of racial division that are in many ways officially sanctioned). Jonah wants to live in a world without "a Negro problem"; "I'm thinking maybe Denmark," he tells Joey (499). And Ruth becomes a militant rights activist, breaks with her father (her mother is deceased at this point), and points out to Joey that their parents had been "raising us like three sweet little white kids" (375). And in one of its more prescient moments the novel has Ruth talking about the need to be armed to fight police brutality: "They're shooting at us," she says (377). Ultimately the novel recognizes what Ruth has recognized. While its lyricism and virtually symphonic sentences mimic its musical narrative, which celebrates interracial contributions to a musical America, its nonlinear story of encounters for both generations articulates the relentlessness of America's punishing racial order. And hovering above both modalities is a meta narrative that suggests something about the power of historical fiction to make palpable how race is lived in an America in which aspects of the color line persist.

That persistence has asserted itself recently. Lest we assume that the hostility toward interracial marriage has abated, we should heed a series of racist rants in response to an advertisement by the Old Navy clothing chain that features an interracial couple, reported in the *New York Times*: "A simple ad for Old Navy stores has turned into a snapshot of the extremes of race relations in the United States . . . Last Friday [April 29, 2016], Old Navy posted the ad to Twitter promoting a sale with a photo of an attractive, happy interracial family in an embrace. Within hours, a backlash was apparent, with hashtags like #BoycottOldNavy and #WhiteGenocide, and messages like "Stop promoting race mixing, you degenerates," and "I don't shop at stores that are anti-White and promote race mixing."[57] Doubtless, actual mixed race families, who experience how race is lived in the United States, have had to deal with equally disturbing reactions. In recognition of such actualities, I turn from literature to ethnography.

From Aesthetic to Ethnographic Subjects

There is another option for accessing the experiential aspect of America's racial order. While, as I have suggested, historical fiction is one (what Jacques Rancière calls "avowed fiction"), another option is the ethnography, which is subject to the same epistemological protocols, because as Rancière suggests, that latter kind of text should be regarded as "unavowed fiction." Like the avowedly fictional text, "the writer and subject must orchestrate the coexistence of facts that defines the situation and mode of connection between events that defines a story."[58] The "unavowed fictions" (stories to which I turn) were assembled and published initially in June and July 2000 as a *New York Times* fifteen-part series on how race is lived in America (subsequently published as a book).

The "coexistence of facts" that emerge in the stories results from a collaboration between the *Times* reporters/ethnographers and their subjects. The primary resulting insight produced by the investigations—as the book monograph's editor, writing at the beginning of the millennium, points out—is that "two generations after the end of legal discrimination, race still ignites political debates—over Civil War flags, for example, or police profiling. But the wider public discussion of race relation seems muted by a full-employment economy and by a sense, particularly among many whites, that the time of large social remedies is past." And referring to the fifteen ethnographic investigations, he adds, "thanks to the persistence of our reporters over time, the reader of the series . . . hears what most white protagonists in the articles neither hear nor even sense: the candid reflections and voiced emotions of blacks with whom their lives are temporarily interwoven. Whites can walk away from race: it's over when they go home. With blacks, it's seldom so easy."[59] Certainly, as I have already noted, the development of video technologies and their broad distribution, along with the proliferation of social media, has made race more difficult for white Americans to walk away from, especially since the violence of local police forces against African Americans has been finding its way (televisually and through Internet media) into their homes. Moreover, they must contend with new voices from a growing protest movement (treated later in this chapter), represented by the hashtag #blacklivesmatter.

Here I want to focus on how the color line, to which recent videos of police atrocities bear witness, is represented at the turn of the millennium by the subjects of the investigations by the *Times* reporters. One of the investigations is especially revelatory because its subjects, Achmed Valdes, a white

Cuban, and Joel Ruiz, a black Cuban, who brought their close friendship with them when they emigrated from Cuba to Miami, were utterly innocent of the racial order to which they were introduced. Ruiz, for example,

> discovered a world that neither American television nor Communist propaganda had prepared him for. Dogs did not growl at him and police officers did not hose him. But he felt the stares of security guards when he entered a store in a white neighborhood and the subtle recoiling of white women when he walked by.[60]

And Valdes found the black sections of Miami to be inhospitable. However, his "transition to this world has been seamless, so much so that he does not really think of himself as an immigrant at all . . . being white and Cuban, he has not had to learn how to behave."[61] As for their friendship, although "the two men live only four miles apart, not even fifteen minutes by car . . . they are separated by a far greater distance. . . . In ways that are obvious to the black man but far less so to the white one, they have grown apart in the United States because of race. For the first time, they inhabit a place where the color of their skin defines the outline of their lives."[62]

The "epidermalization"[63] that has been applied to Ruiz places a surcharge on the orchestration of his gestures in public. He has to work hard to appear to be a customer rather than a thief in stores in white neighborhoods (he walks fast in stores to avoid security guards). As John Fiske points out, for young blacks "the store is a key site where . . . multiaxial disempowerment [of blacks] is put into practice."[64] Other venues are even more challenging; Ruiz discovers that while driving he must carefully manage his bodily comportment in the proximity of Miami's police and white drivers. He had to learn the rules that apply to how "a person with dark skin should behave in this country . . . if an officer is following our car, do not turn your head; the police don't like it. Do not stare at other drivers, especially if they are young and white and loud."[65] Before long, Ruiz finds himself retreating to his racially segregated "comfort zone . . . His entire routine, almost his entire life, is focused in a 20-block area around his home."[66]

The racial order that compromised the Valdes–Ruiz friendship is shown to have had the same separating effect on another example of cross-race friendship that began in middle school. That story, which takes place in Maplewood, New Jersey, begins with the description of a "tight threesome" who hang together at Maplewood Middle School. "Kelly, a tall, coltish Irish-Catholic girl; Aqueelah, a small, earnest African-American Muslim girl;

and Johanna, a light-coffee-colored girl who is half Jewish and half Puerto Rican"[67] are so close that, "at the end of middle school, the three were nominated as class 'best friends.'"[68] However, once they moved on to the next educational level, they found themselves in a milieu with stronger race-based judgments, especially notions about what constitutes white versus black behavior. Exacerbating the judgmental environment in the school is an institutionalized practice of "ability grouping" in which "honors classes are mostly white and lower-level ones mostly black," which has a corrosive effect on interracial friendships.[69] Although the girls strove to maintain their friendship bonds, by the time they entered the tenth grade, "the three girls moved further into separate circles of friends."[70]

Yet given the abundance of racial difference within the school, for all its "cultural jockeying," there is an "up-side—a freedom from the rigid social hierarchy that plagues many affluent suburban high schools."[71] Moreover, the school, which is very much a zone of mixing, experiences an "ebb and flow" of racial separation and mingling. For example, as high school was ending . . . the racial divide began to fade . . . Senior year was wonderful, [one student reports] when the black kids and the white kids got to be friends again."[72] And throughout the fifteen investigations, although evidence of an insistent color line kept revealing itself, there were zones of mixing in which it is breached—for example, at the Assembly of God Tabernacle in Decatur, Georgia, where black and white parishioners are drawn together through "the intensity of their Pentecostal faith," encouraged by a "mission statement, displayed prominently in the lobby, [which] challenges the congregation 'to be a multiracial, multicultural body of believers.'"[73]

Although the year 2000 investigations yielded ambiguities with respect to when and where the color line was firm versus breached, the most prescient story remains that of the Cuban friends who experience vastly difference accommodations to Miami. Especially notable is Ruiz's experience of police harassment, which led him to severely restrict his habitual geography. He learned what it means to be a black Cuban in Miami when, "in an event on Valentine's Day 1996" (briefly referred to above) he and his uncle went to "a popular restaurant in Little Havana, a bastion of white Cuban Americans" with three light-skinned girl friends." After leaving the restaurant just past midnight in a new red Nissan with one of the women driving, just twenty blocks from the restaurant "four police cars, lights flashing and sirens wailing stopped them." The cops, weapons drawn, ordered them out of the car. They frisked them and held them for some time before allowing them to leave. And most alarming for Ruiz, a "white Cuban-American" cop said in Spanish, "I've been keeping an eye on you for a while. . . . Since you were in the restaurant, I saw you leave and I saw many blacks in the car, I figured I would check you out." Ruiz's uncle was sure that the restaurant, "uncomfortable with Ruiz's mixed race group," had called the police.[74]

That episode is a relatively minor incident of police harassment, given the pervasiveness (and increasing observability) of police violence against African Americans, bidding to turn white America's episodic apprehension of such racial incidents into an increasing comprehension of something vast and disturbing. The beginning of that turn took place as a result of the television coverage of the aftermath of Hurricane Katrina, especially the police shooting of six African Americans (two of whom died) on the Danziger Bridge as they fled the rising waters. The disproportionate suffering of the black portion of the population resulting from the storm, along with that episode of brutality, awakened the nation to its racial sublime. Clyde Woods (in a remark quoted in the introduction) puts it succinctly:

> The disasters surrounding Hurricane Katrina revealed the impaired contemporary social vision of every segment of society. Despite mountains of communication and surveillance devices, America was still shocked by the revelation of impoverishment, racism, brutality, corruption, and official neglect in a place it thought it knew intimately.[75]

(De)Sublimating the Racial Sublime

The Danziger Bridge shootings became newsworthy again a decade later. The six police officers convicted on all counts for shooting six unarmed African American citizens appealed and got a new trial because a federal appeals court has found evidence of prosecutorial misconduct (anonymously posting derogatory comments about the defendants to the local news website NOLA .com).[76] One was acquitted. However, apart from the verdicts, the images of that incident, along with the many other episodes of police violence, have been broadly witnessed. What was once diffuse and speculative has gained solidity. Now pervasively witnessed, police violence has been (what I want to call) (de)sublimated. To sublimate (in the discourse of chemistry) is to change from a solid to a dissipating gas. Accordingly, (de)sublimation, as I am using the concept, is a change from what is dissipated (and thus rendered invisible) to something solid and thus apprehensible.[77] In what follows, I consider the forces and genres involved in facilitating the (de)sublimation of the racial sublime by calling attention to what has been repressed in order to venture a politically inflected reading of America's racial order.

In the immediate aftermath of Katrina, the media's angle of vision was ahistorical; much of its initial focus was on estimations of the costs of the damage. By the time it had adopted a racialized angle of vision, its focus was on looting. Nevertheless, the mainstream media's images told a story that has historical depth, which although unavailable in the popular media was supplied by black intellectuals—for example, by Emma Dixon, who referred to "the unnatural disaster of racism," which

> swept away the cars with which poor black people could have escaped Katrina. Almost a third of the residents of the flooded neighborhoods did not own the cars on which the evacuation plan relied. If the promise to the freed slaves of 40 acres and a mule has been kept, the six generations later, their descendants would own assets, and the mule would be a Buick.[78]

Certainly, the consequences of what Dixon points out were there to see. However, "for most Americans, the horrors of Katrina have devolved into nothing more than a sad, but distant memory."[79] The racial sublime, vast and seemingly unfathomable for much of white America, persists.

Popular culture texts have extended that moment nevertheless, and here I turn to the contribution of Spike Lee to revealing the racial sublime that became momentarily evident in the aftermath of Katrina. Lee, an extraordinarily productive black organic intellectual, has created a filmography that constitutes a continuing reflection on America's racial order. In particular, his documentary on Hurricane Katrina, *When the Levees Broke* (2006), provides a critical counternarrative to the official responses to the devastation, while at the same time providing a demonstration of a black politics of aesthetics that inflects the way much of the African American assemblage approaches a comprehension of the consequences of the racial order. In Lee's documentary, images and cinematic montage, along with the commentaries of locals, do the interpretive work. And as has been the case in his other films, music is also a major part of his politically oriented cinematic aesthetic—for example, his juxtapositions of the two Americas in his *He Got Game* (1998) in which throughout the film, America's color line is rendered through a contrapuntal collision between Aaron Copland's symphonic celebration of a white American West and Public Enemy's rap renditions of the exploitation and perils visited on urban black America. As the film's imagistic narrative develops, its soundscape coordinates the music with the rhythms of its image montage.[80]

The music–image coordination that operates throughout Lee's *He Got Game* is the primary formal structure of his *Levees* documentary. The documentary, whose subtitle is *A Requiem in Four Acts*, is animated by its rhythmic coordination between sound and image as it thematizes the major effect of the storm, *death*. The soundscape, created by the musician/composer Terence Blanchard, picks up the requiem figuration figured as a "tragic symphony" as Lee's image narrative discloses the primary color of the lived experience of suffering and neglect.

Along with the testimony of the talking heads are the close-ups of their faces—"affection images," which are articulated in prose in Powers's novelistic treatment of the experience of a New York, mixed-race family and are central to the effect of Lee's *Levees*, which focuses on the Katrina experience of New Orleans's predominantly black residents. As I quoted it in chapter 1, "The face is a veritable megaphone"; along with the words of the persons who experienced Hurricane Katrina and its aftermath, it constitutes much of the micropolitics of the Katrina event, which Spike Lee's *Levees* provides.[81] Whereas (as I have noted elsewhere) "the macropolitics of race in America's twentieth century . . . is articulated primarily in policy histories [in which] African Americans have been incorporated in a 'story of legal and moral ascent' and in 'simplistic accounts of moral progress' . . . the micropolitics of race is articulated through practices with which African Americans have sought to manage their day-to-day lifeworlds in the face of structures and policies of intolerance, exclusion and violence, in 'struggles against racial hierarchy,'" and in this case coping with a disaster followed by a long period of official neglect.[82] As Lee points out,

> The residents of the Gulf Coast were not a priority for this [President George W. Bush's] administration. Actions speak louder than words, and two times [in the] past . . . with earthquakes and tsunamis the United States of America have gone more than half way around the world and was there in two days. And it took the same government four days to reach New Orleans.[83]

Lee's documentary maps that neglected world, offering an "affective map" that explores New Orleans's post-Katrina lifeworld.[84] And because much of that mapping is about death (dead bodies are shown floating in the water and there are long takes of signs on abandoned houses that say "dead body inside"), Terence Blanchard's soundtrack, which is part elegiac and part redemptive/joyous (as it provides the soundscape for the "requiem" that the film's subtitle implies) captures the affective rhythms that Lee's cinematic montage effects. Ultimately, the film images capture the disproportionate suffering and death of New Orleans's black population, whose living spaces (primarily in the Ninth Ward), were most vulnerable to the flood. "Low income black neighborhoods in low-lying areas suffered a disproportionate share of the floodwater, while wealthier, whiter neighborhoods on higher land stayed dry."[85]

Doubtless, when a viewer is exposed to an actual individual death— photographically or cinemagraphically delivered—"the star [as Teju Cole suggests in an analysis of live moments of death] is likely to be death itself and not the human who dies."[86] However, when it is evident that the deaths are mostly among a vulnerable and neglected black assemblage, among the "stars" is a history of racism and government neglect, which Lee emphasizes through a variety of interviews by those who either seek self-justification or point to those responsible. The other stars are those who have suffered, not only those who mourn the dead but also those separated from family members. As the documentary makes evident, both voluntary and forcible resettlement of much of the back population harks back to the plantation period when black families were forcibly separated.

The Law Enforcement Sublime

While Spike Lee's professionally shot and edited, well-funded documentary introduced white America to black America's suffering in general and the specific hardships facing black families through governmental neglect, it has been video footage (some shot with police officer–carried or car-mounted video and some shot by bystanders with smart phones) picked up by news media that has introduced white Americans to what black Americans know well, the murderous policing that targets African Americans and operates with relative impunity. Among the stars of the show of recent police brutality was Michael Brown's body, left unattended on a Ferguson, Missouri, street for hours after he (an unarmed victim whom witnesses say had his hands raised when the bullets hit) was shot and killed by a police officer (August 9, 2014). Although "the police department had pledged to investigate Brown's death while simultaneously stating that the shooting was the result of a struggle in which Brown allegedly went for an officer's weapon . . . at that point, they had not interviewed the witnesses who claimed that Michael Brown was shot down while running away or attempting to surrender."[87] Since then video footage of other police murders in various cities have gone viral, often contradicting police department accounts of the shootings (for example, in Baltimore, Charleston, Chicago, and New York).

In the period preceding social media, the Michael Brown atrocity would have slipped from public attention rapidly, a condition that Milan Kundera, writing in the mid-1990s, captures in his novel *Slowness,* in which a character in a hotel room watching television news reflects on events of brutality that he'd seen covered in recent television news broadcasts. He surmises that such news becomes old very quickly:

> No event remains news over its whole duration, merely for a quite brief span of time, at the very beginning. The dying children of Somalia whom millions of spectators used to watch avidly, aren't they dying anymore? What has become of them? Have they grown fatter or thinner? Does Somalia still exist? And in fact did it ever exist? Could it be only the name of a mirage?[88]

Since then social media have radically altered the duration of events. The vast scope of the current police-inflicted atrocities has become evident. And as social media keep them in front of the public, the continuing attention they have generated (activating the Justice Department while becoming parts of major news outlets) is being amplified by "citizen journalism," which launched the "Black Lives Matter" movement articulated in (among other ways) "hashtag activism": for example, #blacklivesmatter, #Ferguson, #HandsUp, #MichaelBrown.[89] The veil of ignorance, which had formally shielded white America and consigned the daily effects of the racial sublime to those who experience it, is in tatters. An apologetic media, whose bias has diverted attention from police violence (for example, by focusing on the arrest records of victims of police brutality), now has competition that challenges its "truth weapons."[90] As one African American media outlet points out, in response to the police killings in Ferguson and elsewhere, "Twitter communities consisting primarily of African American citizens launched several viral hashtags that garnered substantial attention from the public and media. These hashtag campaigns effectively situate the violence in Ferguson in a context of an intensely racist culture, testifying [to] Black

experiences and rehumanizing the victim(s) amidst biased media representations and public conversations."[91]

While Twitter's durational impact is immediate (it takes place in real
time and is dialogic or conversational), there are other media with alternative durations that are supplementing the social media responses to publi-
cize the atrocities—for example, Beyoncé's music video "Formation," with
lyrics evoking Katrina and subsequent police brutality, graffiti artists in
many urban venues referencing police killings of unarmed African Americans (e.g., with "hands up" images), and an African American Quilt Guild in
Oakland, California, where quilters are "visualizing their thoughts in cloth,"
which treat "race and police brutality" among other things.[92] This latter
medium, which has a brief historical trajectory, beginning with quilting that
testified to the pervasive lynching that took place throughout the Jim Crow
period,[93] emerges from a politically engaged African American domesticity,
statements woven in the home and among African American quilting societies that testify to the dangerous world in which African American families
seek to survive official neglect and a trajectory of violence from vigilantism
to "law enforcement." The perils of this latter (in)justice agency is the main
topic of Ta-Nehisi Coates's epistolary treatise, addressed to the son he realizes he cannot protect from police violence. Having begun this chapter with
a treatment of the violence to black families under slavery, I want to end it
by engaging the continuing violence with which black families must cope
by recurring to Coates's treatise, which, inspired by the death of a friend,
describes unblinkingly the perilous world in which black families try to
raise their children.

Conclusion: The Still Imperiled Black Family

> It is necessary for communal life to maintain itself at the *height of*
> *death* . . . a community can last only at the level of the intensity of death;
> it falls apart as soon as it fails the particular greatness of danger.
> Georges Bataille, *The Unavowable Community*

> When I was eleven my highest priority was the simple security of my body. My
> life was the immediate negotiation of violence—within my house and without.
> Ta-Nehisi Coates, *Between the World and Me*

When Coates refers to the murder of his friend Prince with bitter irony, he
summons (Kantian) sublime images, overwhelming, unstoppable forces of
nature in the form of an earthquake and typhoon:

No one would be brought to account for this destruction. . . . The earthquake cannot be subpoenaed. The typhoon will not bend under indictment. They sent the killer of Prince Jones back to his work, because he was not a killer at all. He was a force of nature, the helpless agent of our world's physical laws.[94]

Given the seemingly unpunishable violence that makes the white world's law enforcement agents uninhibited in their use of weapons (adding peril to the violence within the streets of his community), Coates infers that the violence "within" the African American house (administered in his case by his father) was connected with that violence "without"; it was aimed at protecting him: "my father beat me as if someone might steal me away," for he feared losing his child "to the streets, to jail, to drugs, to guns."[95]

While it is the response to the violence within and without that shapes much of the African American community of sense, as it is articulated by African American intellectuals (exemplary is John Edgar Wideman's *Brothers and Keepers*), it is the act of writing that constitutes a major analytic response of that community. Belonging to a trajectory of critical artistic responses to their constitution as a form of "ungrievable" life and inspired by the "writers Greg Tate, Chairman Mao, Dream Hampton [who are among those] out there creating a new language," Coates writes "to communicate this evidence [of the experience of violence] to the world."[96] He thereby joins what Jean-Luc Nancy refers to as a "community of literature," a disjunctive or particular subcommunity that mounts a challenge to presumptions that a national community is consensual.[97] Nancy insists that a community's "being-in-common" involves "only a juncture"—for example, as I've put it elsewhere, "the sharing of a space of encounter."[98] Affirming that perspective, Coates insists that the African American subject has not been able to share in the primary fable of the American national community, "the American dream." Continually referring to white Americans as "Dreamers," he repeatedly states that he will not be enrolled in the fantasy that the dream applies to black America and notes that his "reclamation" was accomplished through literature—"like Malcom's [X's] through books."[99]

Here I want to refer to the writing form with which Coates joins the literary trajectory that in his terms has participated in telling "a new story, a new history told through the lens of our struggle."[100] To conceptualize the form of Coates's version of the reality of America's racial order, I enlist Houston A. Baker Jr.'s concept of literary deformation. Baker distinguishes two approaches in black literary history. The more conservative approach he allocates to what he calls the "mastery of form." Exemplary of this approach for Baker is Booker T. Washington's autobiography, *Up from Slavery*, in which Washington tells a story of American racism in a way that articulates with white American modes of reception of black America's aesthetic forms—for example, by self-consciously adopting "minstrel tones . . . reassuring sounds from black quarters," while engaging in a "rhetorical appropriation that addresses "the contours, necessities, and required programs of his own culture."[101] The more radical approach, which Baker calls the "deformation of mastery," is characterized by "distinguishing rather than concealing," achieved by enacting "a go(ue)rilla action in the face of acknowledged adversaries."[102]

Coates's *Between the World and Me* clearly belongs to Baker's "Deformation of Mastery" analytic. Selecting as his primary targets "Dreamers" and one of their supporting agencies, police departments, he accomplishes the deformation both by turning the natural sublime into a racial sublime (by describing violent policing as a "force of nature," as noted above) and by countering what he figures as the antiblack "weaponry" of the state and the education system, which assigns blackness to a lower level of worth. With an imitation of Malcolm X's "weaponized" writing, he harks back to African kingdoms and figures African Americans as "royalty," as "kings in exile," thereby exemplifying the role Baker assigns to one involved in deforming mastery:

> The Afro-American spokesperson who would perform a deformation of mastery must transform . . . an obscene situation . . . into a signal self/cultural expression [evoking a black oppositional community of sense] . . . it returns—often transmitting "standard" syllables—to the common sense of the tribe . . . not minstrelsy, but the sound and space of an African ancestral past.[103]

Finally, writing within what Foucault would call an ethics of care—in his case as a father seeking to edify a son by using his own self-fashioning as an exemplary model—Coates figures the color line as a "chasm" that separates the "plunderers" from the "plundered."[104] He hopes that as a parent, his investment in his son's well-being is not lost (as is the case for "Prince's mother").[105] Coates's *Between the World and Me* is an unabashed writing performance that seeks to desublimate the racial sublime by conveying a message from one community of sense (that which constitutes black America's self-understanding) to another, to "white" America, hoping, he writes, "to awaken the Dreamers, to rouse them to the facts of what their need to be white, to talk like they are white, which is to think that they are beyond the design flaws of humanity, has done to the world."[106] As he articulates that hope, he joins hands across the centuries with Frederick Douglass, who in 1883 also sought both to evoke black solidarity and to awaken white America to the violence of its implementation of the color line, as he "defended the propriety of 'the National Colored Conventions' against whites who objected that they reinforced the color line."[107] I give Douglas this chapter's last words:

> No reasonable man will ever object to white men holding conversations in their own interest, when they are once in our condition and we in theirs. In point of fact, however, white men are already in convention against us. . . . The practical construction of American life is a convention against us. . . . The apology for observing the color line in the composition of our State and National convention is in its necessity and in the fact that we must do this or nothing. . . . It has its foundation in the exceptional relation we sustain to the white people of the country.[108]

3. THE NUCLEAR SUBLIME

There is something shared in two of the texts analyzed in chapter 1: Haruki Murakami's version of the earthquake sublime in his *After the Quake* stories and the nuclear sublime featured in Ingmar Bergman's film *Winter Light*. In Murakami's stories, none of the characters has a firsthand experience of the Kobe quake of 1995: "The central characters in *After the Quake* live far from the physical devastation, which they witness only on television or in the newspapers, but for each of them the sublimity of the quake, the massive destruction unleashed by the earth itself becomes a turning point in their lives."[1] For them comprehension—once they recover from their initial imagination-challenged apprehension—is directed toward aspects of their lives that had operated at an unconscious level. In the case of the nuclear sublime, as it is experienced by the character Jonas Persson (Max von Sydow) in Bergman's *Winter Light*, the possibility of a nuclear engagement is something he has gleaned from the print media, which has led him to believe that because the Chinese learn to hate, they are likely to endanger the entire planet, once they have an advanced nuclear capacity. His wife, Karin, who brings him to their church's pastor, Tomas Ericsson, for solace, describes the onset of Jonas's anxiety: "It started last spring. Jonas read about China in the papers. The article said that the Chinese people were brought up to hate and that it's only a matter of time before China has atom bombs. They have nothing to lose; that's what they wrote. I don't worry about it all that much. Maybe I'm short on imagination. But Jonas can't stop thinking about it. We discuss it constantly." When the film debuted, Bergman's Jonas had a lot of company worldwide. Many had experienced a dread that had been "fostered by Hiroshima, the fear of irrational death, of mass death . . . a generalized and abstract fear [which for many was] an unaffiliated terror. It envisioned future developments, but was not directed at a specific enemy."[2] In this case the media has given Jonas specifics rather than abstractions, and he is unable to shake his fear. He commits suicide after the pastor "can offer nothing but the bleakness of his own despair."[3]

At one point in the conversation, prior to Jonas's suicide, Tomas says, "Everyone feels this dread to some extent. We must trust God." However, at the moment when he is making that suggestion, his facial expression is saying otherwise; a close up shows his face reflecting doubt and anguish. The camera then shifts to a shot of his right hand, tentatively tapping the desk as if searching for something solid. Tomas goes on to refer to the incomprehensibility of the Christian sublime: "We live our simple daily lives [i.e., in the small local world] and atrocities [in the vast distant world] shatter the security of our world. And God seems so very remote . . . I feel helpless." As I noted in chapter 1, the Pastor's conversation with his parishioner is an encounter of sublimes. As it unfolds, the Christian sublime, conveyed by a pastor who has lost his faith and is thus unable plausibly to summon God's comfort for a suicidal parishioner, is no match for the nuclear sublime, mediated for a traumatized Jonas by the print media, which brings a remote, menacing geopolitical entity to his home doorstep.

Tomas's anxiety associated with the Christian sublime bears comparison with fears of a nuclear apocalypse because the Christian deity, like an allegedly dangerous geopolitical entity, has always been available only through hard-to-decipher media: scriptures, the words of prophets, "saints," mystics, architectural edifices, and so on. Moreover, anxiety associated with the remoteness of the Christian sublime and reliance on media has a long history. For example, during the rise of the Christian church in late antiquity (between the third and fifth centuries) a shift occurred in the way Mediterranean people experienced the Christian sublime. As Peter Brown explains, "'Divine power' did not only manifest itself directly to the average individual or through perennially established institutions: rather 'divine power' was represented on earth by a limited number of exceptional human agents [Brown refers to saints and sorcerers], who had been empowered to bring it to bear among their fellows by reason of a relationship with the supernatural that was personal to them, stable, and clearly perceptible to fellow believers."[4] What resulted was an intensification of interpersonal scrutiny by those anxious for news of the divine: "Men watched each other closely for those signs of intimacy with the supernatural that would validate their claim [of 'divine power']."[5] Bergman's Tomas Ericsson has thus found himself in a venerable situation; he has sought validation, but no amount of scrutiny has convinced him of the existence of the divine. He has found the signs of God's sponsorship and concern for humanity to be scarce to nonexistent, and the available media—scriptures, institutionalized liturgical practices, and Christian discourses (alleged sources of the "good news")—are inadequate for him to maintain his faith. The "will to believe" and idea that the divine is a "hypothesis" (the way William James acknowledged the presence of a creator) are clearly insufficient for Bergman's Tomas.[6] By the end of his conversation with Jonas Persson, he says, "Jonas, there is no creator."

In the case of contemporary sublime events—difficult-to-comprehend natural and human-created dangers—people have to rely primarily on the corporate broadcast media through which the dangers and consequences are conveyed and interpreted. As a character in Don DeLillo's novel *White Noise* exclaims, "Terrifying data is now an industry in itself. Different firms compete to see how badly they can scare us."[7] Although the spread of social media now provides a measure of competition for attention, major television networks continue to dominate the (bad) news. DeLillo's novel (written in the mid-1980s, before the proliferation of social media) is arguably the best critical analysis of broadcast-mediated sublimes. Its narrative is about characters whose lives are disrupted by what the broadcast media euphemistically refer to as an "airborne toxic event." Apprehension grows rapidly as the population of a small university town seeks reassurance from the media about the level of danger from a moving toxic cloud. While in a mass exodus, a "traffic flow," they are accompanied by a radio voice (one among many voices that function as characters throughout the novel) that says, "Abandon all domiciles. Now, now. Toxic event, chemical cloud."[8]

At a crucial juncture during the town's mass exodus, the novel's featured family, the Gladneys, is listening to their car radio, seeking more information about the toxicity. They hear "a woman identified as a consumer affairs editor began a discussion of the medical problems that could result from personal contact with the airborne toxic event . . . 'Convulsions, coma, miscarriage,' said the well-informed sprightly voice."[9] Panic sets in as the novel effectively evokes Edmund Burke's primary focus on the sublime, its fear-inducing effect ("the strongest emotion which the mind is capable of feeling") up-to-date for the corporate and media age. However, while the novel's characters manifest fear, panic, and disorientation, the novel thinks about (fearful) thinking. As I have noted (in a passage that helps me transition to the problem of the nuclear sublime), DeLillo's *White Noise*

> is not a traditional consciousness raising novel aimed at alerting people either to imminent dangers or their dire consequences, as in . . . Nevil Shute's *On the Beach* [1957], a best-selling depiction of the death of the human race as a result of nuclear war. . . . DeLillo's novel does its work not by raising consciousness but by revealing the dilemmas and aporias of consciousness, by showing . . . the extent to which consciousness is owned and operated by modern media scripts.[10]

Heeding DeLillo's thinking about thinking—his approach to a fear-inducing sublime event, which foregrounds the way media dominate the discourse on danger—I turn to the question about thinking that Martin Heidegger famously poses, because his analysis of thinking about thinking provides an appropriate grammar for the two glosses on apocalyptic thinking related to the nuclear sublime that I want to explore, one by the think-tank futurologist Herman Kahn and the other by the philosopher Jacques Derrida.

"What Is Called Thinking?"

As I note in chapter 1, Heidegger's title contains a productive ambiguity.[11] It can be translated as either "what is called thinking" or "what calls for thinking." The latter option opens his treatise to a focus on events that are, in his words, "thought-provoking." The primary such event for Heidegger had an extended duration; it was the historical emergence of technological thinking, which for Heidegger rendered humanity's relationship with things "unthought."[12] The antidote according to Heidegger is "to learn thinking," to recover that which the "dominion of technology" and its associated model of thinking as *ratio* (i.e., as technologically oriented rationality rather than as a phenomenological relationship with things) causes to "remain hidden."[13] I invoke Heidegger on thinking about thinking not only because of the critically important grammatical insights he offers but also because the two prominent thinkers between whom I stage an encounter share Heidegger's focus on the importance of thinking about thinking, albeit in vastly different ways. The two thinkers, Kahn and Derrida, are from quite different "textual communities."[14] Kahn belongs to the very large one of techno-scientific security analysts, while Derrida participates in a relatively small one, a coterie involved in "nuclear criticism." Both reacted to the nuclear sublime with a focus on thinking but divided themselves dramatically with respect to the modality of thinking. While Kahn, "the heavyweight of Megadeath Intellectuals"[15] and the epitome of a techno-scientific thinker, argued that we should regard nuclear war as "thinkable," the philosopher Derrida, a nuclear critic, argued that thinking requires a resistance to techno-scientific discourse.

Turning first to Kahn: despite being an exemplar of the technological thinking that Heidegger condemned, Kahn nevertheless shared with Heidegger an advocacy of learning to think about thinking—in his case not to accept a thought model in which nuclear war is "unthinkable" but instead to think about the possibility of preparing to either win or survive it. Kahn's advocacy during the cold war of "thinking about the unthinkable" and his analysis of thermonuclear war, which preceded it, calls for strategic rather than apocalyptic thinking. Like late antiquity's saints and sorcerers, Kahn attracted considerable scrutiny; he was regarded by both policy officials and much of the mass public as "an exceptional human agent," one who conveyed the news that the nuclear age is an occasion for thinking rather than avoidance.

As a member of two think tanks, initially the Rand Corporation and subsequently the Hudson Institute, Kahn dedicated himself to the advocacy of planning for the possibility of nuclear war. Responding to negative reactions to his musings on thermonuclear war, he begins his *Thinking about the Unthinkable* with a chapter, "In Defense of Thinking," where he notes how common it is historically for "social inhibitions" to "reinforce natural tendencies to avoid thinking about unpleasant subjects."[16] Thereafter, "obsessed with the riddles of deterrence," he elaborates a theory of how to deter the Soviet Union by creating a credible threat, specifically by implementing an effective second strike capability, under the assumption that the United States could survive a nuclear attack.[17] And in his prior analysis in *On Thermonuclear War* he advocated accepting the possibility of such a war and argued that it is winnable, reckoning it as a catastrophe without precedent but one that would be nevertheless limited.[18] In an (in)famous, controversial passage, he wrote, "I will tend to ignore, or at least underemphasize, what many people might consider the most important result of war—the overall suffering induced by ten thousand years of postwar environment."[19]

While the willful amorality of what Kahn ignored may seem peripheral to what was his more empirical focus, much else that was more central to his contribution was also ignored. As Louis Menand points out, "What is missing from his analysis is not morality; it's reality. The reason his scenarios are fantastic to the point, almost, of risibility is that they deliberately ignore all the elements—beliefs, customs, ideas, politics—that actual wars are fought about, and that operate as a drag on decision-making at every point."[20] Apparently "reality" was not part of Kahn's concern. As one of his Hudson Institute associates reported to a Kahn biographer, when asked what working with him was like, "Nothing was ever finished. It was terribly sloppy. It was an enormous myth that anything was studied. Not really. He didn't study anything. . . ."[21] Kahn's polemics were based primarily on excogitation rather than research. He was a fabulist, masquerading as a scientific rationalist.

Lest there be any doubt, Kahn is the prototype for the eponymous Dr. Strangelove in Stanley Kubrick's satirical comedy, *Dr. Strangelove* (1964), about the consequences of the United States' Kahn-influenced weapons development, brinksmanship, cold war profiteering, and "opportunities for partisan gain"—all achieved by exaggerating the Soviet threat.[22] Near the end of the film, "Strangelove's rhapsodic monologue about preserving specimens of the race in deep mineshafts is an only slightly parodic version of Kahn" (although the wheelchair-bound, somewhat spastic body, played by the actor Peter Sellers, bears more of a resemblance to Joseph Goebbels).[23] While Kubrick's film exposes much of the absurdity of the cold war deterrence *dispositif*, Derrida's response to Kahn (and other nuclear weapon enthusiasts) is a critique rather than a parody of techno-scientific discourse. His essay on the nuclear sublime, which mimics much of Heidegger's critique of technological thinking, provides an extended critique of what he calls the "techno-scientific," "closed circuit" discourse of defense intellectuals.[24]

Interrogating the "event" of the "nuclear age" with a Heideggerian mode of questioning, Derrida identifies the kind of thinking called for. Rather than, like Kahn, forecasting a potentially violent future that would require the use of nuclear weapons, he ponders the conditions of a dangerous present that the existence of the nuclear weapons *dispositif*—weapons manufacturers, laboratories with influential nuclear scientists, "armed forces," missile silos, decision makers, strategic analysts (Kahn among others)—has wrought.[25] At the outset he advocates thinking rather than planning: "We have to recognize gratefully that the nuclear age allows us to think through

[the] *aporia* of speed," i.e., to confront the space-time compression within which overwhelmingly destructive force can be unleashed: "A gap of a few seconds may decide, irreversibly, the fate of what is still now and then called humanity."[26]

Derrida goes on to detail the locus of enunciation for the "we" to whom he has referred, which as he lists other aspects of thinking called for, turns out to be practitioners of the humanities. Obliquely referencing the human suffering that Kahn intentionally ignores, he writes, "So we are not experts in strategy, in diplomacy, or in techno-science known as nuclear science, we are oriented rather toward what is called not humanity but the humanities . . . this specialty entitles us, and doubly so, to concern ourselves seriously with the nuclear issue."[27] He suggests that the very lack of expertise is a competent incompetence: "given our techno-scientifico-militaro-diplomatic incompetence, we may consider ourselves, however, as competent as others to deal with a phenomenon whose essential feature is that of being *fabulously textual* through and through."[28] Seeing the preparation for destruction as a "war over speed" to create a will-have-been—a future anterior that has been available from the outset of the nuclear age ("*At the beginning there will have been speed*")—he suggests that with respect to the possibility of nuclear war, we are in the realm of fiction. We face "the necessity and the impossibility of thinking the event, the coming or venue of its first time which would also be a last time."[29]

Two things become evident as Derrida proceeds to distinguish his nuclear criticism from Kahn's techno-science: one is the role of carefully crafted grammatical expressions that capture an imagination of an event that could come about when its very possibility is in part a function of making it thinkable; the other is the blurring of lines between the fictional and the real. Jacques Rancière's distinction (noted in chapter 2) between "avowed fiction" and "unavowed fiction" (e.g., Kahn's) is what Derrida is instructing us about.[30] For Derrida, nuclear criticism must tell a different story from the one privileged in the unavowed fiction in techno-scientific discourses, which counsel speed, a rush toward nuclear confrontation. He suggests that instead of being in such a hurry, we are obliged to "decelerate," to be dissuaded from "rushing to a conclusion on the subject of speed itself," i.e. (to repeat the quotation), we need time to "think through the aporia of speed."[31]

Urging a "critical slowdown," Derrida points out that "the very process of calculation" has destructive consequences. Evoking the fabulations of techno-scientific thinking, as they are articulated in the form of the gaming practices of Kahn and other deterrence thinkers, he refers to "the games that simulate the process [which], escape all control."[32] Most significantly (a crucial move in Derrida's critique) he raises the question of "life" against those who would calculate how many lives are expendable for a state to survive a nuclear confrontation: "Today, in the perspective of a remainder-less destruction, without mourning and without symbolicity, those who contemplate launching such a catastrophe do so no doubt in the name of what is worth more in their eyes than life ('better dead than red') . . . nuclear war—as a hypothesis, a phantasm, of total destruction—can only come about in the name of that which is worth more than life, that which giving its value to life, has greater value than life."[33]

No Value without "Life"

His wry remark notwithstanding, Derrida recognized that if a nuclear war was to extinguish life, questions of value would be moot. Writing about "the ultimate peril posed by nuclear weapons . . . extinction" of the life-world, Jonathan Schell points out that such an event begs all questions about what is at stake. While "every catastrophe short of extinction leaves behind witnesses who can record what has happened, . . . when the last act is played there will be no one left to see it."[34] Although posing that reality— an "absolutization of humanity"—begs some issues (it "proposes to lead us away from the twists, perversities, and gaps that continually preside over the nuclear age"), it is nevertheless a reality that is either wholly evaded or impoverished within the thinking of strategic analysts.[35] For example, decades ago the syllabus for one of my war strategy–enthused colleague's course on nuclear war included on a list of questions the course would address, "What values are at stake during a nuclear war?" Obtuse-to-reality though that question may be, pondering its illogic shifts one's focus to the lifeworld, which contains *everything* of value, ranging from the trivial to the profound (e.g., from the trivial—enjoyment of a tasty sandwich that hits the spot—to the profound—the satisfaction one may gain from a life full of interpersonal moments of mutual support and intimacy, which generate the feeling that one has contributed to the satisfactions of others). A *Wibakusha* (Japanese A-bomb survivor) effectively answers my colleague's question: "Such a weapon has the power to make everything into nothing."[36] And the poet Aaron Kramer, pondering years of silence about Hiroshima, captures a small part of the "everything" in a poetic gesture toward some of what he values in the nuclear-threatened lifeworld with these simple lines:

> I love the silver bellies of minnows,
> The golden crusts of pies;
> I love the twilight's lavender banner,
> My sister's hazel eyes.[37]

Such an aesthetic appreciation of the nuclear-threatened lifeworld is even more intense for those who have witnessed the devastation of a nuclear attack—for example, Masuji Ibuse, who interviewed many in Hiroshima who had watched their lifeworld get partially extinguished by the atomic bomb. In his novel *Black Rain*, based on his experience of the bombing's aftermath (he collected diaries and interviews with victims of the bombing), he has his narrator/protagonist Shigematsu Shizuma lament the annihilation of the condition that had sustained his daily aesthetic appreciation of life: "Emerging from the main gate of the Clothing Depot, I'm struck by the desolation of the lotus pond." He reminisces about his former daily enjoyment of the surroundings: "the glossy black sheen of the crows' plumage in the morning blends well with the green of the rice plants, and equally well with the rice fields after they have started to turn yellow."[38]

The insensitivity of strategic thinking to intense and vivid aspects of one's experience—an aesthetics of the lifeworld—is simulated in one of Don De-Lillo's stories, which features two futuristic World War III warriors, circling the earth in a laser firing satellite. The narrator (a veteran on his "third orbital mission") describes what has happened to his young assistant (who is on his first mission). "Vollmer's perceptions have changed during their mission":

> A note about Vollmer. He no longer describes the earth as a library globe or a map that has come alive, as a cosmic eye staring into deep space. This last was his most ambitious fling at imagery. The war has changed the way he sees he earth. . . . He doesn't see it any more (storm spiralled, sea-bright, breathing heat and haze and colour) as an occasion for picturesque language, for easeful play or speculation.[39]

In contrast with the narrator, who makes it "a point to talk about small things, routine things . . . the commonplace," Vollmer has moved on to mimic strategic thinking; he has concerned himself with "enormous subjects. He wants to talk about the war and the weapons of war. He wants to discuss global strategies, global aggressions . . . he has stopped describing the earth as a cosmic eye; he wants to see it as a game board or computer model"; he wants, the narrator says, "to get me into a theoretical argument: selective space-based attacks versus long, drawn out, well-modulated land-sea-air engagements."[40]

However, by the end of the story, Vollmer recovers an ability to appreciate other parts of his existence, among which is his childlike wonder of the aesthetics of the lifeworld:

> He spends all his time at the window, looking down at the earth.
>
> The view is endlessly fulfilling. It is like the answer to a lifetime of questions and vague cravings. It satisfies every childlike curiosity, every muted desire, whatever there is in him of the scientist, the poet, the primitive seer, the watcher of fire and shooting stars . . . all at once and little by little [he has recovered] . . . his boyish longing to fly, his dreams of strange spaces and eerie heights, his fantasies of happy death . . . all these are satisfied. All collected and massed in that living body; the sight he sees from the window. "It is so interesting," he says at last. "The colours and all." The colours and all.[41]

As DeLillo's story attests, the aesthetic value of being intimately attuned to the lifeworld, which is effaced in the thought world of strategic analysis, can be effectively restored in literary texts.

From Nuclear Criticism to Artistic Challenge

Whereas Derrida challenges "techo-scientifico-militaro" thinking in a genre known as "nuclear criticism," in which he renders the target, techno-scientific discourse, as fabulous (as "unavowed" fiction), DeLillo's challenge is artistic; it is "avowed" fiction, which exposes the discontinuities of the way the lifeworld is epistemologically and ethically inhabited. Gayatri Spivak puts it well: "The protocols of fiction give us a practical simulacrum of the graver discontinuities inhabiting (and operating?) the ethico-epistemic and ethico-political . . . an experience of the discontinuities that remain in place in 'real life.'"[42] Spivak's remark speaks to Derrida's suggestion that "we" in the humanities have the competence to respond to the issue of nuclear annihilation because (to repeat his quotation), "given our techo-scientifico-militaro-diplomatic incompetence, we may consider ourselves, however, as competent as others to deal with a phenomenon whose essential feature is that of being *fabulously textual* through and through."

If we accept Derrida's suggestion and seek specification for how that "competence" should be focused, we are enjoined to explore the way humanities genres—literary fiction, the arts more broadly, and philosophical texts—have responded to "the bomb" (where the bomb should be understood in terms of its extended existence as a network of installations and the material, discursive, imagistic, political agencies, and scientific laboratories from which the fabulous prognostications justifying its potential use draw their support). In contrast with the abstractions of technoscientific security analysts who, like Herman Kahn, ignore or diminish the significance of the lifeworld (especially the bios) that the bomb has victimized and continues to threaten, are works in the humanities that traffic in reality.

The "First American Sublime"

Evoking with lyricism and grammatical efficiency Kant's rendering of the negative pleasure of the sublime in his *Critique of Judgment*, Gene Ray offers a gloss on the difference between two kinds of sublime encounter—the aesthetic experiences of the power of nature and that associated with "genocidal catastrophes":

> In bourgeois aesthetics, exemplified by Kant's 1790 *Critique of Judgment*, the pain of imagination's failure before the power of raw nature was compensated by reason's reflection on its own supersensible dignity and destination. Nature's threat to dominate the human was contained by human capacities for self-admiration. In the wake of Auschwitz and Hiroshima, however, the ruined dignity and destiny of human reason and its moral law can offer no compensatory pleasure.[43]

Here, I want to note that while I am in accord with Ray's observation, nevertheless when we contemplate the "first American sublime"—the European settlers' experience of the "power of raw nature"—we find an endorsement of another "genocidal catastrophe," once those involved in the "American Revolution" began to implement their version of a (collective) "self-admiration." It took the Euro-Americans a while to turn their initial awestruck apprehension of sublime landscapes into a self-confident American version of comprehension. As Chandos Michael Brown points out, the "first American sublime" was initially mediated by elements of the European thought world: "Intellectuals on the far side of the world [Thomas

Jefferson and others involved in creating the "American Revolution"] looked eagerly to English and continental savants to help them make sense of their place, even as they inhabited a landscape that few across the Atlantic could imagine."[44] However, once the Euro-American "ethnogenesis"[45] (the whitening of the continent) was under way, that "first American sublime" was constituted as an "ideological sublime"; "Nature" was cast as a warrant for "imperial expansion."[46] For example, as I have noted elsewhere, "in a telling moment . . . while [Thomas] Jefferson is enjoying the long view afforded by [his estate] Monticello's hilltop purchase and the outward orientation of its structure, he 'constructs a visible scene as an icon of historical change'. . . . After he remarks on the 'disruption' that nature creates, he has nature promise a pacified locus of possession."[47] It was presumed by Jefferson (and other American "founders") that the "summons of nature" was meant for Euro-Americans: "America's indigenous nations were [regarded as] ineligible to stand against a Euro-American future."[48]

Among the genres that both reflected and sponsored such a viewpoint was landscape painting. Emphasizing

> vastness and virtual emptiness (of a significant indigenous habitus) . . . the tendency in the painting initially narrating the Euro American territorial and cultural expansion [articulated] what Albert Boime calls a "magisterial gaze," which foregrounds a prospect from which Euro Americans can look from within their cultivated and organized spaces of domesticity toward a future in which they will organize and domesticate the vastness of the untamed West.[49]

By the nineteenth century, among those involved in inventing the American natural sublime was Thomas Cole, whose immense canvases (imitating the sublime of nature as vast) ascribed to (one of his main subjects) the Hudson Valley "natural majesty"; he saw it as possessing "an unbounded capacity for improvement by art," and went on to celebrate a future of an imposition of a Euro-American built habitus: "Without any great stretch of the imagination we may anticipate the time when ample waters shall reflect temple and tower, dome in every variety of picturesqueness and magnificence."[50] Where are the Native Americans in Cole's landscape imaginary? In his *Landscape with Tree Trunks*, he reproduces a "romantic mythology, the cult of the 'noble savage' . . . Barely visible in reproduction, but clearly evident on the canvass, is the tiny figure of an American Indian by the bottom of the waterfall." By then (1828) the scene was an anachronism inasmuch as "European

Figure 3.1 Fanny Frances Palmer's *Across the Continent*

colonization for generations had made traditional native American form of life impossible in this area [the Catskills]."[51]

As the Euro-American imperial expansion progressed westward, violently effacing the Native American lifeworld, the celebration of white dominance is exemplified in Emanuel Leutze's huge canvas (which was hung in the U.S. Capitol): *Westward the Course of Empire Takes Its Way* (1862). The canvas is an early confirmation of W. J. T. Mitchell's observation that landscape is the "dreamwork of imperialism."[52] Mimicking the imperial erasure of indigenous America (and Leutze's title) is yet another large canvas that celebrates the white continental ethnogenesis (while being explicit about the erasure of native America), Fanny Frances Palmer's *Across the Continent: Westward the Course of Empire Takes Its Way* (1868, "published and widely distributed by Currier and Ives"; figure 3.1).

The painting's westward moving train is exiting the white population of a town on one side of the tracks and is partially obscuring, with the smoke from its stack, two Native Americans on horseback on the other side.[53] It is one of many nineteenth-century landscape paintings that pictured the "first American sublime," making evident that the Euro-Americans' fascination with the natural sublime (which eventuated in possession and settlement) did not extend to a sympathetic view of the ethnoscape that had preceded them.

There were other genres contributing to the "first American sublime" and to the effacement of Native American possession as well. As Larzer Ziff points out, referring to texts by Thomas Jefferson, Timothy Dwight, and Nicholas Biddle, Euro-Americans conducted a "literary annihilation" of Indianness.[54] He notes, for example, that Nicholas Biddle's rendering of the Mandan Buffalo Dance (using many Latin expressions), resulted in a perspective so distant from a "corporeal presence" that his text effectively buried what it represented.[55] A variety of other genres were also complicit in the erasure of Native American continental presence. One such genre is cartography. Starting from the east: among the most notable initial instances of the cartographic erasure of Indianness was Cotton Mather's exact map of New England in his *Magnalia Christi Americana* (1702), in which all that showed was "two tribal choronyms in the heart of New England's dominions—Nipnack Country and the Country of Narragansett—there are no further signs of actual Indian presence."[56] The map is dotted with crosses, reflecting its preoccupation with church history. A century and a half after Mather's symbolic conversion of New England into a Christian imaginary, James Fenimore Cooper, in yet another genre, contributed an essay to an illustrated book on the picturesque in which he evacuates history from the landscape as he contrasts the landscapes of Europe, on which are "impressed the teeming history of the past," with the American landscape, which has "an air of freshness, youthfulness, and in many instances . . . rawness."[57]

Contrary to Cooper's dehistoricizing of the American landscape, what he perceived as "the seemingly youthful and raw vistas of the West contained a rich history which he was unable to discern because he wholly neglected a Native American perspective."[58] As Matthew Dennis points out in his analysis of Iroquois landscape practices, what was seen by Euro-Americans as "wilderness" was "the product of centuries of cultural modification . . . a landscape shaped by the desires of its denizens to provide themselves with a prosperous, secure, and fulfilling existence," for example, through clearing, burning, modifying water flows, and so on.[59] Similarly, as the ethnologist Keith Basso learned while traveling with western Apaches, for them "the past lies in features embedded in the earth—in canyons and lakes, mountains and arroyos, rocks and vacant fields which together endow their lands with multiple forms of significance that reach into their lives and shape the ways they think."[60]

Cooper's erasure of an "American history" in his musings about the sublimity of American landscape is in accord with a legal erasure to which he contributed in his novels, the evacuation of "Indian" claims to the land. For example, in his *The Pioneers* (1832), seeking to deal with "the difficulties of establishing a sense of national identity in the face of the nation's complex and conflicted relationship with the past," Cooper shaped his narrative to dispossess the "Indian's" right to the land by inventing a past that rendered North America as a white inheritance through a right of conquest.[61] At one point his protagonist, Natty Bumpo, says, "Might often makes right here as well as in the old country. From what I can see."[62] As Susan Scheckel puts it, "Cooper rewrites the American Revolution by editing out the violence of conflict . . . [to] dispel the Indian problem."[63] In effect, Cooper's writing was complicit with the way chief justice John Marshall wrote his briefs. Together, they "relegated (Native Americans) to a place in the history of a nation not their own."[64]

Writing (in the genre of legal discourse) was one among many of the technologies that articulated Euro-America's space-possessing/indigenous-effacing comprehension in response to the first American sublime. Among the most significant accompanying the Euro-American ethnogenesis was photography, which was employed in the process of mapping and surveying western landscapes. Accompanying General George Wheeler's cartographic survey of the West (authorized by the U.S. Congress in 1872, during the years of the extermination and territorial containment of Native American nations in the West) were his photographers William Bell and Timothy O'Sullivan, whose photographic views and the names attached to them participated in the recoding of the western landscape. As I have noted elsewhere, "owing especially to the work and writings of Charles Mason and Jeremiah Dixon (creators of the famous Mason and Dixon line) in the eighteenth century, the use of the 'survey' as a device that aided and abetted Euro-America's imperial expansion had already become 'assimilated into the discourse of landscape description.'"[65]

While within the Euro-dominant mode of writing the history of the western landscape the cartographic survey is merely a scientific technology, Albert Boime points to its imperial effects: "The charting of uncharted areas, the systematic mapping of the continent, is first and foremost the surveyor's actualization of the magisterial gaze. All the conflicts over boundaries—regional, national and international—masked by the rhetoric and bombast of Manifest Destiny are expressed in the surveyor's language of lines of longitude and latitude."[66] And in his novelistic version of the surveying adventures of Mason and Dixon, Thomas Pynchon affirms Boime's view of the politics of violence implemented by the cartographic survey. As Pynchon's Mason and Dixon continue to chart territories westward,

> they discover that "Previous lines run through the supposedly boundless forest," and after being joined by a delegation of Indians and reach what is called "a certain warrior's path," they are given to understand that they have gone as far west as they should proceed [for they are encroaching on another] . . . civic Entity . . . they are involved, as Mason puts it, in "trespass, each day ever more deeply."[67]

At a minimum, technologies of perception, mainly the cartographic and photographic interventions into the American West, disseminated images that legitimated the acts of possession that followed the process of surveying. They helped to shape what I have called elsewhere a "violent cartography."[68]

Although in a territorial sense, Native America succumbed to the violence of possession, Native American writers and artists have responded to the violence of Euro-America's sublime imaginaries by focusing their attention on what I deem the "second American sublime," the toxicity visited on much of what remains of Native American living space by uranium mining, nuclear waste dumps, and nuclear test explosions.

The "Second American Sublime"

What can we surmise about the second American sublime, the vastness of nuclear tests in western landscapes along with the uranium mining and nuclear storage dumps that have added to the radiation perils, which like the ultimate effects of the natural sublime, have disproportionately victimized the remnants of indigenous America residing in the West? The initial Euro-American reactions to the experience of that second American sublime is well expressed in the oft-cited remarks of Brigadier General Thomas Farrell, who was awestruck and linguistically challenged as he tried to find words for his witnessing "of the first atomic explosion at Alamogordo, New Mexico" on July 16, 1945:

> No man-made phenomenon of such tremendous power had ever occurred before. The lighting effects beggared description. The whole

country was lighted by a searing light with the intensity many times that of the midday sun. . . . Thirty seconds after the explosion came, first the air blast pressing hard against people and things, to be followed almost immediately by the strong, sustained awesome roar which warned of doomsday and made us feel that we puny things were blasphemous to tamper with the forces heretofore reserved to The Almighty. Words are inadequate tools for the job of acquainting those not present with the physical, mental, and psychological effects. It had to be witnessed be realized.[69]

Locating the general's reaction within the "nuclear sublime," Rob Wilson writes, "Farrell's confrontation with figurative inadequacy and inexpressibility comes about because a terrifying *abyss* has suddenly—objectively—opened between cognition (the language of the self) and its corresponding object (nature dematerialized and sublimated into atomic energy)." Going on to connect that experience with the historical trajectory of the sublime, as it has been thought with respect to "nature," Wilson adds, "In more *aesthetic* terms, this widening gap between man's strongest language and the death-inducing forces of nature was what Longinus and myriad neo-romantic critics after him had privileged as the rapture (*hypsos*) of the sublime," which "awed" General Farrell as he contemplated with "*uncertainty*" over the "moral/political consequences of such force in American hands."[70] Although Farrell and others involved in the "bomb project" were initially overawed, they soon turned to a celebration of their control over technological power as an instrument of mastery. Carol Cohn charts the shift from apprehension to masterful comprehension:

> The entire history of the bomb project . . . seems permeated with imagery that confounds man's overwhelming technological power to destroy nature with the power to create—imagery that invests men's destruction and asserts in its place the power to create new life and a new world. It converts men's destruction into their rebirth.[71]

Once the awe-provoking, language-vexing apprehension of an atomic explosion migrated toward a celebratory comprehension, the possibilities of mediation and contestation of how nuclear technology was to be understood were controlled by the American military and the Atomic Energy Commission. Collaborating, they "limited access to the test sites," to "information about the explosions," and "regulated the production of visual

artefacts." As a result, the "process of absorption and adaptation into existing culture"—i.e., into the collective national comprehension—"was heavily controlled," and "the process of negotiation that usually characterizes
such adaptation was severely limited."[72] What was ultimately available to
public comprehension was an "abstract visuality," for example, "ill-defined
records of a rising column of smoke—images similar to traditional news
photographs depicting catastrophic fires, industrial accidents and torna-
does."[73] And the reports of the effects of atomic bombs on Japanese cities
were also focused on abstract aesthetics rather than the catastrophic human
costs; e.g., *Life* magazine on the "atomic explosions at Hiroshima and Nagasaki: 'white smoke leaped on a mushroom cloud'; it was a 'huge ball of fiery
yellow,' and 'a big mushroom of smoke and dust,' and later 'a tremendous,
ugly waterspout,' and a 'pillar of swirling particles.'"[74]

While the U.S. military subsequently censored reports on the victims of
the bombing (the immediate deaths and those that followed from radiation
sickness) as well as censoring artistic versions (e.g., preventing the release
of Ito Sueo's 1946 documentary *The Effects of the Atomic Bomb on Hiroshima
and Nagasaki*), a more thorough official censorship has been in place with
respect to the "slow violence" (the subsequent sickening of populations)
that has resulted from atomic testing and uranium mining).[75] At the beginning of the nuclear age in the United States, the mediation of public
comprehension of the direct effects of the vastness of nuclear explosions
belonged to both controlled and independent media. The public was not
apprised by the press or syndicated broadcast news of the subsequent slow
violence resulting from nuclear tests and uranium mining.

It has been that slower violence that has constituted the aftereffects of
the "second American Sublime" on America's Native American nations.
For example, the effects of toxicity from uranium mining on the Navajos
living in Monument Valley (the region in the Utah–Arizona borderlands
where John Ford filmed eight of his westerns) became known only after
Elsie Begay, a Navajo living in the valley, submitted a formal request for the
results of the Environmental Protection Agency's (EPA) testing of the radiation level in her valley. What she obtained revealed a level of toxicity that
had exposed the Native American population of the valley to "100 times the
level considered safe" by EPA standards.[76]

Rebecca Solnit understands what the Euro-American spatio-temporal
gaze misses, as it sees the desert space of the nuclear test site ("a blank on
many maps") as empty. As she puts it:

Space itself isn't an absolute, or at least the spaciousness of landscapes isn't. Up close, aridity means that even plants are grown far apart from each other. . . . It is rock—geology—that dominates the landscape . . . here the earth is naked, and geological processes are clearly visible. It is geological time and geological scale that dominate the landscape, dwarfing all the biological processes within. . . . The very rocks on the ground have lain in place so long around the test site that their tops and bottoms are different colors. And any disturbance leaves a lasting scar.[77]

Here I turn to fictional Native American texts that reflect on such lasting scars (found among other things on the stones of the testing site). While the media owned and operated by the "boat people" (Native American writer Sherman Alexie's term for Euro-American settlers) have expressed little or no concern over the radiation poisoning of the landscapes of America's indigenous peoples, Native American writers and artists have reflected on and publicized the effects.[78] I refer briefly to works that I have analyzed elsewhere, the Laguna Pueblo writer Leslie Marmon Silko's novel *Ceremony* and the landscape paintings of the Kiowa-Caddo artist T. C. Cannon.[79]

As I have noted, "Silko's *Ceremony* provides . . . a counter text to Euro-America's version of western landscapes and ethnoscapes."[80] The novel's protagonist, Tayo—half Laguna and half "white" and a veteran of World War II—"returns to a territory undergoing a drought, which imperils the cattle-raising Native Americans in his old community." The novel focuses both on the significance of the landscape for Native Americans and on their victimization from nuclear mining and testing. It distinguishes a landscape that for Native Americans is regarded as a "living companion" from one that for Euro-Americans is "merely a series of exploitable objects." Rendering effects of the "atomic age," the novel states: "Trinity site, where they exploded the first atomic bomb, was only three hundred miles to the southeast at White Sands. And the top secret laboratories where the bomb had been created were deep in the Jemez mountains, on the land the Government took from Cochiti Pueblo."[81] As Silko's story nears completion, the dramatic narrative has Tayo undergoing a cure through a purifying ceremony with a shaman. However, the way the novel locates him spatio-temporally constitutes its challenge to Euro-America's second (nuclear) sublime: "Tayo's cure involves a recognition of the consequences of the nuclearization of tribal lands. Significantly it is at an abandoned uranium mineshaft where he completes his personal ceremony and at the same time sees the destructive effects of the mining and testing of nuclear weapons on Indian lands." Ultimately, the novel "brings the poisoned landscape to life, giving it a Native American significance by having Tayo perceive the way that life and death are intertwined in a piece of uranium ore": "a grey stone streaked with powdery yellow uranium, bright and alive as pollen."[82]

The effects of the invisibility of nuclear peril in Native American landscapes, represented in Silko's fiction, has been thoroughly addressed ethnographically in an investigation by Valerie Kuletz, who distinguishes the very visible testing of nuclear bombs in the West with the invisible perils of radiation nuclear fallout, uranium mining and nuclear waste dumps. Focusing part of her study on the Indian Nation featured in Silko's novel—the Laguna Pueblo—Kuletz provides a brief ethnography of one nuclear poisoned village, Paguate in New Mexico, where the Laguna Pueblo Dorothy Purley, who had contracted thyroid cancer from the radiation, describes the fate of others in her family: "My mother died of it . . . my brother died of it! My aunt! How many aunts and how many uncles have died! And you know it's just a shame that DOE [the Department of Energy] doesn't believe what's going on."[83] Kuletz's investigation reveals a violent cartography, as it treats two overlapping landscapes, the nuclear and the "Indian" (where the former has been devastating to the latter). We can therefore revise the question in my colleague's course syllabus, "What values are at stake during a nuclear war?" to the question of the values that were acknowledged to be at stake during the Euro-American cold war. As Kuletz makes clear, the "Indian" landscape was a "sacrifice zone," incorporated into a discourse on wastelands, thereby "justifying the relentless plunder of the region through highly environmentally destructive extractive technologies." It was a designation that justified "the region's use as a large scale waste dump and weapons testing range in the minds of policy makers."[84]

Kuletz challenges the erasure of Native American presence in the contemporary period of the "second American sublime" with elaborate maps (a counter-cartography) that correlate their presence with the areas of nuclearization: testing, mining, and waste dump creation. However, as she suggests, Native Americans have actively fought the "erasure," part of a strategy of domination that has led to the nuclear devastation of their landscapes by military and commerce-related nuclear projects to which most of the rest of the U.S. white population has been indifferent, manifesting a "tendency to dismiss inconvenient facts."[85] In the process of resisting erasure, the Native

American Nations residing in the region have generated rejoinders to the wasteland discourse, which has designated their lands for degradation and to the techno-scientific and legal discourses aiding and abetting their disenfranchisement. As Kuletz puts it, "Scientific discourse may serve as a mechanism of exclusion in public hearings and in government documents at every stage of the nuclear cycle, but it hasn't entirely silenced the traditional Indian voice with its [cosmo-ontological] appeal to the heavens, the stars and the earth [for example, Indian voices have noted the spiritual significance of places where nuclear waste has been dumped]." She adds, "Sometimes the voice of the people is the only record we have of what is going on within the dark zones of the nuclear landscape."[86]

Discourses of rebuttal and resistance have not been the only challenges by Native American activists. Using images rather than voice, the Kiowa-Caddo artist T. C. Cannon created a silent rejoinder to the nuclearization of the "Indian" landscape with images. Like Silko's fictional Tayo, Cannon was a Vietnam veteran who returned home with a renewed sense of the violence visited on his people and their landscapes. His images are both ironic commentaries on the stereotypic stoic, nonspeaking "Indians" and political statements about the nuclear poisoning of the landscapes within which they reside—for example, with the portrait images *Double Self-Portrait with Atom Bomb* and a variety of versions of *Village with Bomb*.

The Pacific Nuclear Sublime

As is well known, the geography of nuclear poisoning resulting from the U.S. government's nuclear policy extended well outside its borders. The within-border willingness to cast Native Americans outside of the spaces of "moral solicitude" is a posture I've noted elsewhere (in an analysis of the neglect of indigenous peoples in Immanuel Kant's moral geography): "For indigenous people to achieve moral solicitude, in a Kantian world, they would have to have a coherent political culture that functions, interpretively, within a European state-oriented political imaginary."[87] The peoples of the Pacific Islands have also suffered from a geographic myopia. They too have been outside the geography of moral solicitude. As Epeli Hau'ofa points out, "As far as concerns Oceania, derogatory and belittling views of indigenous cultures are traceable to the early years of interactions with Europeans. . . . In a number of Pacific societies people [e.g., Europeans and Euro-Americans] still divide their histories into two parts: the era of darkness associated with savagery and barbarism; and the era of light and civilization, ushered in by Christianity."[88] The continuation of a moral geography that diminishes the moral status of Oceania—"small island states" regarded as "much too small, too poorly endowed with resources, and too isolated from centers of economic growth" to be visibly equal global partners—contributed to the egregious disregard that allowed them to be marked as a space for nuclear testing.[89]

The accompanying text to Peter Goin's photographic exhibition, *Nuclear Landscapes*, reviews the rationale for the atrocities visited on Oceania:

> Although American scientists developed the atom bomb, they could not predict its force and effects. The military was determined to continue the testing program in order to learn more about the bomb's potential. . . . President Truman authorized a nuclear testing zone in the Marshall Islands, located 2400 miles southwest of Hawaii. The United States assumed responsibility of the Marshall Islands under the United Nations trustee system. On any specific atoll, there were few inhabitants, and they had little political power or representation to contest the American government's determination to conduct nuclear tests in the islands.[90]

What followed was the forcible removal of Marshallese Islanders, e.g., from Bikini Atoll (and some of the peoples of the Aleutian Islands) where much of the testing, both aerial and in the ocean, took place, and as a result of the fallout carried by wind and ocean currents, the poisoning of much of the population of the Pacific Islands. As in the rest of Oceania, the population of the Marshall Islands was scattered, in their case over thirty-one atolls. For the United States, a powerful nation-state with a consolidated population, contained by fixed geopolitical boundaries, the Pacific sublime was experienced as a vast but empty area (much like the Euro-American experience of western sublime a century earlier, effectively rendered in the history of Euro-American landscape painting). Although as Hau'ofa points out, as an area of habitation, Oceania is very large—a "sea of islands . . . a large world in which peoples and cultures moved and mingled unhindered by boundaries of the kind erected much later by imperial powers," it did not appear significantly large within the United States' nation-state–oriented cartographic imaginary.[91] And, as Hau'ofa also points out, it was diminished within the Euro-American cultural imaginary.

The diminution of the value of Pacific populations was owed to the same technologies that had symbolically evacuated the indigenous presence as they shaped the America's western imaginary—technologies of perception that rendered their spaces as relatively empty and sparsely populated. While the Pacific imaginary was like much of the U.S. western desert, regarded as a "waste space," the U.S. government was preoccupied with a space of antagonism elsewhere, the very large Soviet Union against whom the nuclear arsenal, whose testing took place in the Pacific, was aimed. For U.S. policy-makers, the USSR was a sublime object in a Burkean sense during the cold war, a vast and threatening geopolitical entity, a source of terror that precipitated the nuclear standoff that characterized a major aspect of U.S. "defense" policy (which was encouraged by the futurology of the above noted Herman Kahn and other "defense intellectuals").[92]

How was the Pacific invented as an appropriate site for nuclear testing? Bracketing for a moment the ethnographic imaginaries within which Pacific Islanders are accorded diminished status (a sparseness of population and low level of civilizational development), cartographic protocols were involved in suggesting that the islands where the tests were to take place were "remote"—for example, the Aleutians, where Amchitka was chosen in 1971 for a test deemed too large for the Nevada test site.[93] As Eichenberger et al. point out, entrenched versions of geologic and cartographic thinking led to the choice of Amchitka, which was "perceived as remote." Of course, as they note, "What is remote to some people is home to other, though fewer people." Moreover, Amchitka's "remoteness" was perceived "in part [as] a consequence of conventions in map projections: The familiar Mercator Projection places it well out of the way for those traveling between North American and Asia . . . [a projection based on the] . . . propensity for Americans and Europeans to tear the world down the International Date Line in order to flatten it [which] further isolates Amchitka in a corner."[94] And of course prior to the mid-twentieth-century development of the Pacific as an area for militarization—a militarized Pacific imaginary was initiated in the writings of Alfred Thayer Mahan on the strategic importance of sea power— the nineteenth-century Pacific was the "last uncharted space" a *terra incognita*, "knowable by way of archeology, travelogues, Pre-Raphaelite paintings, ethnographic photography, and Crystal Palace exhibitions," and it was also alternatively made "illegible" (e.g., by Herman Melville's *Moby-Dick*) and legible (e.g., in Walt Whitman's "Passage to India") but nevertheless for them a product of literary fantasy rather than on-the-scene ethnography.[95]

Ironically, it was the presence of American and Japanese soldiers in the Pacific during World War II that led to a more nuanced de-exoticized version of the island ethnoscapes, even though the islanders were given image roles they "did not always choose for themselves," and were frequently "pictured . . . savages, servants, victims (especially of progress), or childlike students whose wartime experiences . . . were ultimately educational and uplifting."[96] Nevertheless, both the Allied and Japanese militaries recycled and regenerated multiple and conflicting images of Pacific Islanders, and thus served to "enlarge and complicate the colonialist photographic archive," even though the islanders were put in poses that were chosen by military photographers.[97] However, ultimately, the dissemination of that enlarged photo archive produced a reassurance that the western self could justifiably impose its will and power on the Pacific. In the last analysis, "the military gaze was a variety of the colonial."[98] And as was the case in the survey of the western desert of the United States, "Photography itself 'represented technological superiority harnessed to the delineation and control of the physical world, whether it be in boundary surveys, engineering schemes to exploit natural resources, or the description and classification of the population."[99] As Lamont Lindstrom points out, during World War II, as the Allies and Japanese constructed each other with racist stereotypes, "Standing back in the referential shadows are Pacific Islanders whose homelands were invaded by Japanese and Allied forces alike."[100] As the structure of geopolitical antagonism shifted during the cold war, the military gaze remained averted, with the United States and Soviet Union as the primary players in the exchange of perceptions, while the Pacific Islanders remained "in the referential shadows," still burdened with an imagistic legacy from the earlier antagonism.

Narrativizing What Photography Has Fixed

While Herman Kahn has had decades of nuclear weapons–enthused fellow travelers in his area of the academy—a "security theory" textual community of sense that has shaped much of the discipline of "international relations"—rather than reprise the traditional discourses of securitization (developed within an axis of government, mainstream academic security studies, and weapons manufacturers) that legitimate the nuclear *dispositif* (the aggregation of "discourses, institutions . . . administrative measures, scientific statements," etc., which constitutes the apparatuses associated with nuclear weapons), I want to focus instead on the question of the value attributed to lives and the technology-assisted moral geographies within which lives are valued versus devalued.[101] When Herman Kahn admitted, "I will tend to ignore, or at least underemphasize, what many people might consider the most important result of war—the overall suffering induced by ten thousand years of postwar environment" (cited above), his focus was on the aftermath of a nuclear war. His "thinking about thinking" ignored (willfully) the "overall suffering" resulting from the preparation for such a war. That willfulness has been situated within the nuclear *dispositif* responsible for that preparation. As a congressional report stated, after the Atomic Energy Commission's operational records were made public, "The saddest irony of our atmospheric testing program is that the only victims of United States nuclear arms since World War II has been its own people."[102] However, which "people" needs specification. Carole Gallagher discovered in her investigation of the health consequences of nuclear testing in the Nevada desert that the AEC had made life-threatening bio-political distinctions when they designated that site as a nuclear testing ground: "In one 'top secret' AEC memo, the people living downwind of the Nevada Test Site during the atmospheric testing era were described as "*a low-use segment of the population*" (emphasis in original).[103] And as regards the Pacific Islanders, photographic, cartographic, and ethnographic technologies located them in a space and biopolitical frame that deprived them of the moral solicitude provided to continental peoples, encouraging the United States and France to militarize the Pacific, heedless of the violence imposed on its peoples.

In order to restore the moral solitude effaced by technologically mediated perception (primarily photography-assisted cartographic surveys in the U.S. desert and the Pacific), I turn to cinematic rejoinders that effectively displace fixed images with moving images. Cinema provides counter-visions, revealing aspects of lifeworlds that the violent acts of possession—involved especially the nuclearization of western and Pacific land- and peoplescapes— have overcoded. As Gilles Deleuze has insisted, the mobility of the cinematic camera destabilizes spectatorial positioning, thereby discrediting fixed, institutionalized perceptual practices.[104] To Deleuze's insight on the importance of perceptual mobility I want to add the tensions in cinema elaborated by Martin Lefebvre between landscape as narrative and landscape as setting.[105] He points out that "the gaze by which landscape emerges in painting [is also] manifest in the work of filmmakers." However, crucially for purposes of critical distance from institutionalized landscape imaginaries, some filmmakers "have freed the film's setting from its service to the story."[106] In such cases, "landscape . . . is *space freed from eventhood* (e.g., war, expeditions, legends)."[107] So while setting, as Lefebvre notes, is the space where the story or event takes place, landscape can have different connections with setting—at times in a supporting role as background or setting to events and characters, and at times as "a completely distinct aesthetic object."[108]

In films in which landscape is a "distinct aesthetic object," the film tends to offer a "counter-historical" perspective in which (for example) it "destabilizes revered styles of militarism and patriotism derived from official and popular history."[109] Heeding that insight, the films I analyze here treat both landscapes and ethnoscapes as distinct aesthetic objects in ways that challenge the predatory economic and militarized gazes that constituted the modes of comprehension emerging from the landscape and nuclear sublimes that eventuated in the evacuation of some and the poisoning of other Native Americans in the West and the displacement and poisoning of many islanders in the Pacific.

Sean Penn's *The Pledge*

Were we attentive only to the plot of Sean Penn's *The Pledge*, we would be following a story based on a Durrenmatt novel whose protagonist, a police detective, Jerry Black (Jack Nicholson), defers his retirement to try and solve a series of murders of young girls after having promised the mother of one of the victims to find the perpetrator. The film narrative focuses on an ambiguity. It is never clear whether the clues Black is following point to a serial killer or are a manifestation of his pledge-driven obsession with solving the case. However, if we heed the film's aesthetic objects (the film's non-narrative treatment of a land- and ethnoscape), which are disconnected from the film narrative, we can observe a challenge to the sublime that I want to emphasize in my reading of the film, one that has played into a "peculiarly American status quo of domination and blindness . . . an unconscious enterprise that asserts the present as the only temporal dimension: a depthless phenomenological now where awe and entertainment encircle one another."[110]

The spatial setting of the film is the Reno area of the state of Nevada, which from the point of view of the film narrative is irrelevant. It is merely the space in which the action takes place—the discovery of a murdered seven-year-old girl, the interruption of Jerry Black's retirement party with the report of the crime, the decision of the police to blame the killing on a Native American, and Jerry Black's subsequent search for the actual perpetrator after he watches the "Indian's" confession being coerced and promising the girl's mother that he'll solve the crime. However, *The Pledge* is a film in which aspects of the land- and ethnoscapes are "freed from the eventhood"—in this case from events of the crime and those associated with Jerry Black's search for clues. The camera's exploration of aspects of the land- and ethnoscape recover a history of encounter and atrocity that the phenomenology of everyday life in the West, a "status quo of domination and blindness" and a "depthless phenomenological now," has evacuated.

As I have noted (in an earlier analysis of the film), "surrounding one man's drama is an institutionalized space, a western venue with a significant temporal trajectory. Reno and its surrounds [a consolidated and recently white-dominated region of the West] exist in both ethnic and geopolitical time."[111] That surrounding milieu—both the land- and ethnoscape—explored by the camera with zooms, pans, depth of focus and close-up shots—stands apart from the film's narrative that follows Jerry Black's investigation. To manage the dramatic narrative, much of the camera's attention is on Black's face. Those shots, constituting what Deleuze calls affection images, carry the burden of the film's treatment of the psychic intensity of Black's quest to fulfill his pledge. As Deleuze points out, affection images, which are "abstracted from spatio-temporal coordinates," have the effect of "undoing space."[112] However, there is a disjunctive story that is revealed as the film narrative proceeds, and what is evacuated with face shots returns as landscape shots. To put it simply, that story is about the historical whitening of the West as the space is incorporated into Euro-American nation building, the virtual effacement of the Native American population, and the discrediting of those who remain.

Here I want to point to several scenes that tell that parallel story. Whereas the close-up and the tracking shots articulate Jerry Black's investigatory story, his psychic and clue-gathering experiences, respectively, it is the close-up, the long take, and the depth of focus shots that tell the spatio-temporal story (of the Euro-American ethnogenesis). In the context of the two sublimes I have elaborated, that story implies that the result of the mediated comprehension through which Euro-America, in both its westward movement in the nineteenth century and its uranium mining, nuclear testing, and waste dumping in the twentieth, was heedless of the value of Native American lifeworlds.

As is well known, before nuclear radiation poisoning afflicted the health and longevity of Native Americans in the West, alcohol did part of that job.

Two close-up long takes early in the film refer obliquely to that aspect of the destructive result of the Euro–Native American encounter. In an early scene in which Black is ice fishing on a frozen lake, the camera enters his small hut and lingers with a long take of a bottle of Glenfiddich whisky on a shelf. In a later scene at Black's retirement party, the camera does long takes of alcoholic drinks being carried on a tray and of a drink in the hand of one of the police officers dancing.

The alcohol shots would have been inconsequential were it not for later scenes that refer subtly both to the degradation of the Native American population of the area and to white hegemony. As the retirement party proceeds, there is a cut to a snowfield where a plump white teenager is snowmobiling (there are long takes of his face that is so white that pink blush patches show). When his snowmobile breaks down and he climbs off, he is shown virtually unable to manage on foot in the deep snow. The camera then cuts to a Native American who is more physically attuned to the snowscape; he is shown running gracefully through deep snow to his truck with his animal traps in hand. After a snowboarder discovers the body of the murdered seven-year-old and later ID's the Native American's departure from the murder scene, the "Indian," Toby Jay Wadenah (Benicio del Toro) is being interrogated and coaxed into admitting the crime. The camera cuts to a police detective who has drawn a degrading caricature of an Indian while watching the interrogation on closed circuit.

If those scenes seem inadequate to support an interpretation of the film's parallel story of the Euro-American violent ethnogenesis, a scene later in the film, after Black has bought a gas station/convenience store near the scene of several murders in order to locate himself near clues, makes the case unambiguously. A Native American stops for gas at Jerry's store, and a

> (doubtless allegorical) Indian-white interaction takes place. . . . After Jerry fills the tank of the Indian customer's car, he has difficulty getting the credit card machine to record the Indian's American Express card. As he botches the transaction several times, having difficulty making the slide mechanism on the recording machine work, the two men stare awkwardly at each other. An ex-policeman on unfamiliar commercial ground is failing to process smoothly the credit card of a person whose people have been historically discredited (on their former ground) . . . calling to mind a history of fraught Anglo-Indian transactions and negotiations.[113]

Adding to the "image facts" that point to the Euro-American takeover of the territory, late in the film, as Jerry, his girlfriend, and her daughter (whom Jerry ultimately uses as a decoy to lure the murderer), are watching a Fourth of July parade, the plump pink and white boy from the earlier snowmobile scene goes by with his vehicle atop a float.[114]

Accompanying shots of the sparse Native American portion of Nevada's ethnoscape (in which the "Indian" population had dropped from roughly 50 percent in the early 1860s to slightly more than 1 percent by 2004), are landscape shots that often juxtapose Euro-American settlement with a nature that looks unsettled—for example, early in the film with a tracking shot of Jerry's car traveling from the lake, through a tunnel, and into the city of Reno, and, thereafter, cuts to unsettled landscape that interrupt the crime narrative, all suggesting that the context of the drama has a violent historical trajectory that precedes it.[115] In *The Pledge*, the landscape shots make oblique reference to the slow violence through which Native America was violently evacuated as the landscape became a product of a white territorial imaginary.

Cinematic landscape shots perform many functions. In *The Pledge*, the "extreme long shots and deep focus shots using a bird's eye view of high angle camera set up" serve as a way of "looking back."[116] In contrast, in the text to which I now turn, the Pacific is filmed as a different kind of imaginary, enacted in Terrence Malick's film *The Thin Red Line* (1998). Malick's interpretation of nature is more active than Penn's rendering of the Nevada scene. His landscape shots are ontological rather than historical. They are telling us in effect "who the landscape thinks it is"—something alive—at a historical moment in which the Pacific Islanders' lifeworld exists as a "shadow reference" in the midst of a U.S.–Japan battle during World War II.[117] Recalling Derrida's juxtaposition of a valorization of the lifeworld against a techno-scientific preoccupation with weapons and antagonisms, Malick's cinematic focus aligns itself with the life-affirming, humanities-oriented community of sense that Derrida evokes. Leo Bersani and Ulysse Dutoit's summary statement of what his film does captures that focus. They see the film as "a kind of kinetic argument against the invasive movements of war."[118] What I want to show is *how* the film makes that argument, as it performs as a counter-history event that challenges conventional security-oriented forms of war comprehension.

As is well known, Malick's signature images are sublime landscapes. He enacts a "visual language . . . focused on the rhythm of the world: the visual rhythms of light and dark, of architectural forms, of people positioned as figures in a landscape that always seem[s] terrifying and vast."[119] However, as is the case in Penn's *The Pledge*, his landscape, long takes, and sequences are disjunctive with the narrative occasions of his films—for example, the drama of the killing spree of Kit (Martin Sheen) and Holly (Sissy Spacek) in his *Badlands* (1973) and the battle for Guadalcanal in *The Thin Red Line*. Given Malick's preoccupation with the problem of evil, his sublime land-scapes are Hitchcockian; they host both beauty and terror, invoking a "dual perception of nature as beauty and threat."[120] Similarly, in Malick's *Thin Red Line* what appears beautiful and serene—for example, the brief idyll of Witt and friend (detailed below) among the islanders of Guadalcanal in their peaceful habitus is suddenly disrupted when a military patrol boat shows up outside the lagoon, heralding the violence that is to be visited "in the heart of nature" and causing Witt (Jim Caviezel) and friend to scramble for cover before they are apprehended and returned to the war machine.

Malick's film thinks through what his characters say and see, with the latter tending to outweigh the former. Early in the film, in a voice-over, the main protagonist, Witt, wonders what it means to have "war in the heart of nature." Rather than having another character respond, Malick's answers are nondiscursive. While the war narrative is about the battle for Guadalcanal, which involves as the major episode a tension between soldier-imperiling commands of the insensitive Colonel Tall (Nick Nolte) and the resistance to the commands of the more ethically sensitive Captain Staros (Elias Koteas), another narrative is under way. The image sequence suggests, in answer to Witt, that war is an invasive disturbance to the vitality of the lifeworld's land- and peoplescape. In accord with Derrida's above-noted resistance to apocalypse, the film states, primarily with images, that life is what calls for thinking.

Life is on the agenda in the film's above-noted opening sequence, where Witt and another soldier are AWOL from their army unit, living in a com-munity of islanders whose lifeworld is peacefully attuned to the land- and seascape. Witt and his fellow soldier's absorption into the everyday rhythms of the islanders, swimming, dancing, playing, singing, as they ritually as-semble and disperse throughout the day, contrasts with the war machine's regimentation from which they have temporarily escaped. Antonio Benitez-Rojo's view of archipelagoes in his analysis of the Caribbean as a counter-rhythmic culture machine that resists the war machine fits well with the way Malick has filmed the people of Guadalcanal. In conceptual accord with Malick's brief cinematic ethnography of Guadalcanal, Benitez-Rojo thematizes the "culture of the Peoples of the Sea" as a practice of a some-times fraught attunement with nature, a culture that is a "flux interrupted by rhythms which attempt to silence the noises with which their own social formation interrupts the discourse of Nature," a culture expressing a "desire to sublimate social violence through referring itself to a space that can only be intuited through the poetic."[121] Animating that perspective with moving images, Malick, an "esoteric visual poet," combines his cinematic ethnography of the islanders with a poesis of nature.[122] Like the fluidly choreographed movements of the islanders, his nature is filmed as a series of movements and flows; it becomes a "silent actor with a complicated semiotic burden"[123] as its motions become oppositional to the violent, forward movement of the military intervention in the island. As I put it in an earlier reading:

> the landscape shots in TRL present a nature that is alive and resonat-ing. . . . The trees and grasses are shown swaying in gentle breezes, while refracting light and shadow, much like the effect of a rotating kaleidoscope. The camera's framing of the landscape catches those moments in which nature is deployed as exuberant life, while men-at-war are actively engaged in extinction.[124]

While the U.S. officers in charge of the invasion are effectively relays of the military gaze, Witt's way of seeing (conveyed through Malick's camera work) articulates the invasiveness of war "in the heart of nature." Bersani and Dutoit capture that character–camera work homology. Referring to "Malick's nearly obsessive filming of Witt's face" (figure 3.2), they suggest that it "could be thought of as the camera's envy of the human eye" and go on to note the way that film form conveys the (ambiguous) ethico-political import of the film:

> The voice-overs question the moral being of the world; Witt's look indiscriminately registers the world's appearances. The circular mo-bility of Malick's camera, as well as the visual discontinuities that break up the narrative line of battle (for example, with "unrelated" images of nature), could be thought of as Malick's imitation of Witt's mode of filming, his attempt to avoid projecting a moral or aesthetic identity on the world he films, to allow his camera to be mildly but thoroughly invaded by objects as Witt's eyes are.[125]

Witt is not the only "camera" in the film. Accompanying the landscape-as-actor are soldier-actors with alternative ways of seeing, especially the binary constituted by Witt and First Sergeant Welsh, aka Top (Sean Penn). While the

Figure 3.2 Witt in Malick's *The Thin Red Line*

latter, admonishing Witt for being AWOL, claims that there is only one world, Witt insists that he has seen another (and the viewer has seen it with him). The Top–Witt encounter is thus similar to the Kit–Holly encounter in Malick's *Badlands*. In both, a predatory orientation (Kit and Top) encounters an aesthetic one (Holly and Witt). And in both cases, the viewer, once instructed by Holly and Witt, are able to see what some of the characters (involved in practices of violence) cannot. Thus what Malick's *Thin Red Line* offers is not primarily a war film but rather an invitation to a life-affirming community of sense. The film's proliferation of ways of seeing, which begins with Witt and his companion's idyll, is not a simplistic celebration of the need to be attuned to nature. For example, when Witt asks an islander woman why the children don't fight, he is told that they do. The antagonisms are simply not evident to his untrained eye. Malick allows islander culture its esoterica rather than suggesting that it's wholly transparent. Rather than merely valorizing a particular way of life, Malick exploits cinema's ability to restore what the militarized gaze has evacuated. The film is among other things a counter-anthropology that revalues (without unambiguously celebrating) a part of the lifeworld that has been historically devalued within the frames of twentieth-century geopolitical antagonisms.

Conclusion: The Encounter of Technologies

Having begun by staging an encounter between techno-scientific and humanistic ways of thinking (Herman Kahn's versus Jacques Derrida's)—alternative responses to the nuclear sublime—much of my focus has been on the way technologies of perception—landscape painting, literature, photography, cartographic projections, and surveying—contributed to the selection of the living spaces of peoples residing in the United States' western deserts and in Oceania for nuclear poisoning. After being initially awed by the challenges to comprehension of the enormous, life-threatening effects of nuclear explosions (a nuclear sublime), U.S. political and military agencies absorbed nuclearism into security-oriented forms of comprehension. After World War II, as the cold war progressed, destructive forces have been unleashed on land- and peoplescapes—the Native American peoples in the Far West (who survived the first American sublime and were subsequently victimized by the second) and many peoples in the Pacific Islands (regarded as "remote" from important population centers)—both of whom have no relationship with the geopolitical antagonisms that have been the excuse for adapting nuclear radiation to the weapons of war.

To the technologies of perception that failed to discern significant life in the spaces selected for nuclear poisoning, I have juxtaposed the technology of cinema, which can provide a counter-comprehension by restoring what other forms of perception tend to evacuate. Sean Penn's *The Pledge*, located in the American West, and Terrence Malick's *The Thin Red Line*, located in the Pacific, have as their narrative occasions a crime story and war story, respectively. However, viewed with the appropriate discernment—with attention to their non-narrative moments, focusing on the shots and sequences that disrupt the narrative line—both films make present lifeworlds that have resided in the shadows of the dramas of the planet's most powerful players. Allowing formerly devalued worlds to emerge from the shadows that other technologies of perception have made, the films are occasions for an alternative moral cartography, i.e., for peoples and places to emerge from the shadows, become objects of an "empathic (mode of) vision," and achieve the "ethical weight" to which they are entitled.[126]

4. THE INDUSTRIAL SUBLIME

By the beginning of the twentieth century, artists in the New York region, impressed by a techno-industrial sublime associated with large architectural projects, had begun to depict bridges, especially the enormous ones connecting New York to New Jersey and interconnecting New York's five boroughs. On their canvases, the landscapes of the famous Hudson School (treated in chapter 3) were displaced by urban scenes. Although many of the paintings were celebratory in mood, some expressed a degree of ambivalence—for example, Colin Campbell Cooper's *Manhattan Bridge from Henry Street* (figure 4.1), which "suggests a visually disruptive presence of the bridge's eastern pier as it terminates the view down Henry Street; the out-of-scale bridge looms over shabby picturesque tenements, an ethereal token of technological solutions to urban decay."[1] And rather than merely displacing the "natural sublime," some canvases registered the transformation—for example, Martin Lewis, *Railroad Yards, Winter, Weehawken* (c. 1917) (figure 4.2), which "stands as a lonely sentinel, measuring time's passage and the eclipse of the natural sublime."[2]

Other artistic genres also expressed ambivalence, for example, Fritz Lang's film *Metropolis* (1927). Visually beautiful and thematically dystopic, it renders the machine age as both "awful and immensely stimulating."[3] However, in general the new artistic genres of the early twentieth century welcomed a machine age that was heralded by "President [Calvin] Coolidge

Figure 4.1 Campbell Cooper's *Manhattan Bridge from Henry Street*

Figure 4.2 Martin Lewis's *Railroad Yards, Winter, Weehawken*

[who] famously declared, 'The Man who builds a factory builds a temple.'"[4] While the machine age was generally celebrated for its advantages by artists operating in the eastern United States, where the Native American presence had become largely nonexistent, its spread westward was decisively destructive for what remained of that other America.

To pick up that theme I refer back to my remarks in chapter 3, where I wrote,

> As the Euro-American imperial expansion progressed westward, violently effacing the Native American lifeworld, the celebration of white dominance is exemplified in Emanuel Leutze's huge canvas . . . *Westward the Course of Empire Takes Its Way* (1862). . . . Mimicking the imperial erasure of indigenous America (and Leutze's title) is yet another large canvass that celebrates the white continental ethnogenesis (while being explicit about the erasure of native America), Fanny

Frances Palmer's *Across the Continent: Westward the Course of Empire Takes Its Way* (1868).

Drawing special attention to how the smoke from the train's stack in Palmer's canvas participates symbolically in effacing Native America by obscuring "two Native Americans on horseback," I suggested that both canvases have undeniable narrative intent; they invent landscape as a summons to conquest; they participate (in W. J. T. Mitchell's terms) in the "dreamwork of imperialism."[5] However, as they articulate landscape and technological sublimes (combining awestruck fascination with immense landscapes and also with technology), the paintings perform as media that is inhibited by their static framing. Lacking historical extension and depth, their ability to convey the temporality of the necropolitical Euro-American imperial project on the continent (the conquest and destruction of Native America) is limited by their form.

Machines in the Gardens

Because the moving images of cinema provide more adequate testimony to that necropolitics, I turn here to a film that focuses on the same U.S. landscape, beginning with a long sequence of a solitary passenger heading westward on a train. The film, Jim Jarmusch's *Dead Man* (1995), supplies abundant time images. It historicizes the regional populations as it brings the viewer inside the train to witness a changing white ethnoscape, as a variety of new passengers enter (people differentiated historically and regionally) during the journey of the protagonist, William Blake, from Cleveland, Ohio, to the Far West. With cuts to Blake's gaze through the train's windows, the film also surveys the changing landscape, portrayed as a historical deathscape. The intent with my reading of the film is to suggest that before (the remnants of) Native America were victimized by nuclearization (the uranium mining, radioactive waste dumps, and nuclear testing, described in chapter 3), the demise of the more robust and thriving version was hastened by Euro-American industrialization. While landscape painting was involved in the symbolic turning of an awe-inspiring sublime landscape's vastness into purposeful land management and dispossession (by picturing Native America as unfit for coeval participation in modernity), it was industry, especially steel manufacturing, that was the primary material enabling factor in their rapid demise. Steel railway tracks and locomotives opened their lands to settlement and markets, and that same metal, used in the production of weapons and ammunition, enabled a force of arms with which they could not compete. This latter manufacture was celebrated in Euro-American popular culture genres—for example, dime-novel western adventure stories, which represented the gun as "a magical machine, endowing its owner with ultimate powers of 'civilization' against 'savagery.'"[6]

The film makes that case more with images than with its dramatic narrative, an observation enabled if we heed the distinction between setting and landscape (treated in chapter 3). To repeat: setting, as Martin Lefebvre suggests, is the space where the story or event takes place. However, landscape can have different relationships with setting—at times in a supporting role as background to events and characters and at times emancipated from that role, functioning as "a completely distinct aesthetic object."[7] As I added, "in films in which landscape is a 'distinct aesthetic object,'" what is offered is "a 'counter-historical' perspective."[8] In the case of Jarmusch's *Dead Man*, the setting is the space of William Blake's journey from Cleveland toward his death in the Far West. However, what the landscape scenes articulate is a more collective story, which challenges pious histories of Euro-America's "winning of the West." It's a story well summarized in Kent Jones's film review: in *Dead Man*, "there is no American West. There is only a landscape that America the conqueror has emptied of its natives and turned into a capitalist charnel house."[9] Jarmusch emphasizes his version of the landscape-as-distinct-aesthetic-object with his cinematic punctuation, which separates shots of the landscape from the shots containing characters.

Rather than a general synopsis, I provide story background as I treat the scenes and shots most relevant for my analysis. The film begins with a long monotonous journey undertaken by its main character, William Blake (Johnny Depp), who leaves the city of Cleveland bereft of attachments (deceased parents and a failed engagement) to take a position he has been promised as an accountant in the Dickinson steel mill in the town of Machine in the Far West. Blake serves as what I have elsewhere called an "aesthetic subject," a character in an artistic text whose psychological state is less important than what one learns about "the forces at work in the spaces within which they move and [as their journey makes available to the reader or viewer] the multiplicity of subject positions historically created in those spaces."[10] Before we see Blake, the film's first shot conveys the historical role of steel. Taken from outside the moving train, the camera focuses on the train's wheels running along the tracks, accompanied by the sound of

Figure 4.3 Johnny Depp as William Blake

steel on steel. There is then a cut to our first view of William Blake, which gives us a glimpse of another kind of manufacture. He's wearing a plaid suit and bowler hat and is seated across from another suit-wearing passenger (figure 4.3).

As the train begins to fill with passengers, shown wearing self-made clothing—attire representing the regions through which the train passes, first homespun-wearing passengers and then animal hide- and fur-wearing types—Blake's outfit contrasts as it testifies to the existence of clothes manufacturing, which has not yet pervaded the entire country. The homespun clothing wearers enter the train as it passes through the middle landscapes, made famous in nineteenth-century landscape painting, while those wearing buckskin, buffalo hide, and animal fur enter when the train begins to reach the Far West. As the journey progresses, the film cuts between shots of Blake's bored face, the new passengers who enter, and the outside of the train, with a focus on the steel driving mechanisms that turn the wheels. At this stage (confined to the train trip), the film rehearses two different temporalities. One is biographical, focused on the character, William Blake. During the train trip we learn of his prior life (disclosed in responses to an interrogation by the train's stoker, Crispin Glover), his current situation as he becomes an increasingly exotic object, drawing stares from the train's new passengers, and his future prospects (also disclosed in the conversation with the stoker, to whom he displays his letter promising the accountant's position

Figure 4.4 Dickinson Metal Works

in the Dickinson Metal Works in Machine). The other temporality is a collective or national history involving the forces that have led to the displacement and/or extermination of much of Native America. In addition to the shots outside the train, which emphasize the role of steel manufacture, which has contributed to the opening of the West to white settlement, are shots of abandoned Native American teepees, seen through the train's windows. And in an especially telling scene, the last passengers to enter the train—hunters in buckskin and buffalo hide—are carrying another steel manufacture, loaded rifles. At one point they leap to their feet and fire at a buffalo herd, while the stoker refers to the millions of bison that white America had already killed, destroying much of Native America's food source.

When Blake finally alights from the train in the town of Machine, he walks slowly up a main street, filled with derelicts and signs of death (wall-mounted and piles on the ground of animal and human bones) toward an icon of the industrial age, the enormous steel manufacturing factory, Dickinson Metal Works (figure 4.4), which dwarfs the rest of the small town of Machine. When he finally enters the factory and shows his letter to the office manager, John Scolfield (John Hurt), he learns that the job has been given to another person long ago. Insisting on seeing the owner, John Dickinson (Robert Mitchum), Blake enters his office, only to be threatened by Dickinson, who points a rifle at him, forcing him to make a hasty exit.

As is the case with the train, the factory contains two disjunctive tempo-ralities; the outer office is filled with accountants working at desks (cleaving to the rule of the number), while the inner office contains an anachronism, a man dedicated to an earlier instrument of power, the rule of the gun.[11]

While the violent factory owner, Dickinson, represents the old West, the accountants represent the invasion of a technology that helped to rational-ize the industrialization phase of capitalism, double-entry bookkeeping. As Werner Sombart puts it, "Capitalism and double entry bookkeeping are absolutely indissociable."[12]

The scene therefore defies the famous slogan that emerges from the clas-sic western films of John Ford, "Words won the West." Displacing words with numerical protocols, *Dead Man* shifts the emphasis from Ford's theme of the triumph of Euro-American discursive culture to Euro-American polit-ical economy. Nevertheless, while challenging Ford's version of the winning of the West, *Dead Man* contains subtle references to Ford's films, one of which is Ford's persistent theme of white settlers turning a wilderness into a garden (thematized in *Stagecoach* [1940], *My Darling Clementine* [1946], and *The Man Who Shot Liberty Valance* [1962]). *Dead Man* seems to have the last of those films, *Valance*, in mind when we see the paper flowers made by the young woman, Thel (Mili Avital) with whom Blake has an intimate liaison while briefly in Machine. The cinematic reference is arguably the cactus rose that Tom Doniphon (John Wayne)—the man who lives by the gun—brings Hallie Stoddard (Vera Miles), the wife of Ransom Stoddard (James Stewart), the man who lives by the book. Stoddard, unable to attune himself to the old West, cannot appreciate those roses because his reference is the "real roses" he has seen in the East. And it is likely that the long train ride at the outset of *Dead Man* references Ford's first feature film, *The Iron Horse* (1924), which is about the building of the transcontinental railroad, the route taken by Jarmusch's William Blake.

However, the most significant intertextual reference of *Dead Man* (which builds itself off Ford's garden metaphor, assisted by the image of the flowers) is literary. Doubtless the town of Machine, dominated by Dickinson Metal Works, references Leo Marx's classic study, *The Machine in the Garden*, which thematizes the disruption that the industrialization of the machine age does to the Jeffersonian "pastoral ideal." Looking at the intrusion of the machine on the pastoral landscape, as it is represented in nineteenth-century Amer-ican literature, Marx refers to "the ominous sounds of machines, like the sound of the steamboat bearing down on the raft or the train breaking in upon the idyll at Walden [which] reverberate endlessly in our literature."[13] He also surveys the main proponents of manufacturing, among whom is Tench Coxe (an economist and ally of Alexander Hamilton) who strenuously promoted manufacturing. Jarmusch uses Coxe's first name as the last name of one of his characters, a trapper, Benmont Tench (Jared Harris) whom Blake meets in the "wilderness." As Marx notes, "For Coxe the machine is the instrument . . . of America's future power," and like most Euro-American sponsors of western settlement, Coxe symbolically erased Native America. According to Coxe "Unimproved land . . . is 'vacant'—a 'waste.'"[14]

Nevertheless, the critical edge of Jarmusch's *Dead Man* is aimed less at the machine's disruption of the pastoral ideal than on the assault on Native America. Once Blake becomes a fugitive, pursued by John Dickinson's three bounty hunters hired to avenge the death of his son Charlie (having returned fire and killed Thel's intended, Charlie Dickinson, who interrupts them in bed, Blake is wanted as a murderer), he is led through a "wilderness" landscape by the film's other aesthetic subject, the Native American, Nobody (Gary Farmer). That odyssey reveals an enormous gulf between Euro- and Native American practices of comprehension. When Nobody first comes upon the wounded Blake (Charlie's bullet, which killed Thel, had passed through her and was embedded in Blake's chest), he refers to the bullet in Blake's chest as "the white man's metal," a commentary on the destructive effect of the steel manufacturing that "won the West."

Thereafter, Blake and Nobody continually misunderstand each other. Every time Nobody asks if he has tobacco, by which he means he wants to trade in order to create an interpersonal bond, Blake replies that he doesn't smoke. And at one point Blake tells Nobody that he hasn't understood a word Nobody has spoken. However, despite the misunderstandings, the relationship between the two is meant to testify to the significance of poetry in an age that is increasingly dominated by commercially oriented technology. For Nobody, this Blake is an avatar of the late poet, William Blake. As a result of Nobody's constant insistence that this Blake is a "dead man" in this sense as well as a result of his mortal wound, their journey is focused on a subjective duration, a process of Blake-from-Cleveland's journey toward his death and his becoming as a poet. Blake's journey to the West therefore turns out to be an identitarian journey as well as a spatial odyssey. Migrating from the persona of an accountant to that of a poet, his identity journey restores an aspect of humanity's aesthetic existence that the rationality-serving technology of calculation has effaced. That process of becoming is

Figure 4.5 Haida House

affirmed by Blake himself, when he encounters two freelance bounty hunters, Lee and Marvin, whom he manages to kill, thereby continuing to live
up to Nobody's ascription that he is a "killer of white men." When they ask
him before he fires his gun if he's the William Blake on the wanted poster,
he replies, "Yes I am, do you know my poetry?"

Ultimately, it is poetry and spirituality that the film juxtaposes to the destructive effects of industrialization. At the end of the film, there is a telling
referential montage. A nearly dead Blake is led along the street of a Makah
Native American village, a walk that repeats his earlier walk up the street
in the town of Machine. This street is dominated not by a steel mill that
stands for the industrial sublime but by a large Native American ceremonial
structure, a "cosmos house" that resembles the large wooden plank houses
typical of the Native American nations of the Northwest Coast, which were
constructed to be located symbolically at the center of the universe.[15] Specifically, it's a Haida House–type building (figure 4.5), which represents a
spiritual sublime. It's an actual rather than the metaphorical temple President Coolidge ascribed to factories. Unlike Blake's reception at the Dickinson Metal Works, he is neither welcomed nor abjected. Before he enters
the building, the village street along which he walks is strewn with death
symbols. However, unlike the street in Machine, the street in the Makah
village testifies to a surviving material culture; it has useful implements,

e.g., antlers that are tools in contrast with the bones of animals in heaps in the town of Machine. However, utility is marginal to the scene. Rather, emphasizing the spiritual coding of the village, the camera explores the various ways in which life and death are symbolized—totems and a ceremonial sea canoe made to carry the dead to the spirit world. It is a culture that seems to embrace death as part of life, in comparison with death as part of the desecration of a lifeworld represented in the town of Machine.

Although Jarmusch's film endeavors to show the remnants of the Native American lifeworld in the Far West that remain (even using the Makah language without translation), the more critical aspect of the film is an engagement between the violence of steel manufacture, which has enabled the rule of the gun (at the end of the film there's a shootout between Nobody and the remaining bounty hunter that Dickinson has hired, Cole [Lance Henriksen]) and the sublimity of poetry's reflections on life and death, for example, the line from William Blake's "Auguries of Innocence," uttered by Nobody:

Every Night & every Morn
Some to Misery are Born
Every Morn and every Night
Some are Born to sweet delight
Some are Born to sweet delight
Some are Born to Endless Night.

What is the critical effect of such an engagement? Treating a later stage of capitalism, financialization, Franco Berardi provides an appropriate frame. Like Jarmusch, Berardi is concerned with conformist thinking and the liberating force of poetry. In terms of the former, in Jarmusch's film his characters, Lee and Marvin (an obvious reference to the actor Lee Marvin, who performed in traditional westerns), are shown looking identical, each incapable of any singularity. And in terms of the latter, Berardi, seeking a "line of escape" from "the list of priorities that capitalist conformism has imposed on society," turns to poetry, which he describes as "insolvency in the field of enunciation," a genre that "is going to play a new game: the game of reactivating the social body."[16] Poetry, he suggests, provides a counter-rhythm to the "rhythmic disturbance" occasioned by capitalism's "desolidarization"; it mounts a challenge to the destruction of the conditions of possibility for shared and creative communities of sense.[17]

As for the form of the challenge mounted by Jarmusch's film: its vehicle is an aesthetic subject, a naive character who ultimately becomes a poetic

Figure 4.6 Hybrid William Blake

and ethnically hybrid subject who deviates from the typical heroic characters in classic westerns (figure 4.6). We witness the destructive effects of the industrialization visited on Native America through his eyes and experiences. As one commentator puts it, "Blake is a complex stratification of marks: not just the white record of Western violence, he is marked by Nobody as a native warrior, and, by his own hand, with the blood of a slain fawn, the Becoming Native American of Blake."

"Coding [Blake] as variously Indian and white, human and animal, animate and inanimate, Jarmusch transforms his protagonist into a transcendent site of becoming" and, I would add, into a vehicle for transforming the Euro-American narrative of an expanding nationhood from a triumphal destiny (turning wild nature into a space of cultivation, settlement, and commercial progress) into a destructive force, enabled by an industrial technology that destroyed a lifeworld.[18] As the stoker says to Blake during his train journey, "Machine, that's the end of the line," a remark with many levels of meaning—the end of the line geographically, the end of the line for Blake (soon to be deceased), and the end of the line for Native America, unable to compete during a steel- and machine-enabled invasion of their landscape.

As a political reflection that enfranchises an expanded array of subjects, Jarmusch's film suggests that there are multiple loci of perception and enunciation through which the industrial sublime is experienced and brought into political discourse. Significantly, the encounter between his two aesthetic subjects, Blake and Nobody, is an encounter between two liminal subjects, a displaced middle westerner who, like Ford's Ransom Stoddard in *Valance,* is not attuned to the violence in the Far West and a displaced Native American who returned from a foreign venue, where he absorbed experiences and exotic cultural texts that robbed him of a local identity. By rendering the West through their experiences and the gazes through which they as liminal subjects register the desolation of a formerly thriving Native America, the film challenges those texts that have consolidated the collective identity "American" in their versions of how industrial technology has been experienced. The well-known texts on Euro-America's industrial sublime legitimate a singular national narrative, seen through the perspectives of Euro-American citizen/subjects, who view the white possession of the continent as an unambiguously liberating political process. They neglect the narratives of those at whose expense that possession occurred. In the next section I reflect on the blindness within the insights of one of those texts.

From the Pastoral Ideal to the Industrial Sublime

Among the most cited analyses of the Euro-American cultural response to industrialization is David E. Nye's *The American Technological Sublime,* which constructs the "American" technological sublime primarily through the celebratory moments and general enthusiasm with which it is welcomed by those who functioned comfortably within a whitened continent. Consolidating Americans and their "social context" into unitary identities, his comprehensive treatment of the sublime—articulated in a wide variety of genres (treatises, paintings, tourist brochures, etc.)—privileges a historical genealogy of changing sublimes. He begins with the change from awe-inspiring natural phenomena, especially the large landscapes, moves on to immense technological innovations, represented by factories, locomotives, electrical systems, and huge architectural and cultural pieces, and turns ultimately to the most destructive form, the atomic bomb.[19] Treating the temporality of the sublime experience, he emphasizes the dynamic through which what was initially sublime becomes familiar enough to be banal rather than awe inspiring, echoing a late nineteenth-century remark by the son of John Quincy Adams (the historical editor–diplomat Charles Francis Adams): "Whatever constantly enters into the daily life soon becomes am unnoticed part of it."[20] In contrast with Kant's temporality and

Figure 4.7 J. M. W. Turner's *Rain, Steam and Speed*

mood articulated in his Analytic of the Sublime (which as I note in chapter 1, posits a negative pleasure as the subject's consciousness closes the gap between apprehension and comprehension), Nye's focus is on the positive pleasure of witnessing something awe inspiring, and his temporal model is absorbed in the ephemerality of novelty, the dynamic of banalization.

Pursuing his narrative, Nye provides abundant testimony of Euro-Americans about the pleasure they derive from the sublimity of technology, while at the same time noting the negative reactions and warnings of those who resist that enthusiasm and enjoyment. Attempting to avoid what he refers to as the "imperial we," he describes the different ways in which (Euro-American) commentators and travelers reacted to what he calls the "technological sublime."[21] Rather than a comprehensive critique of all of the dimensions of the sublime that Nye covers, I focus here on his treatment of one of the phenomena that has been central to my analysis, the railroad. Inattentive to the perspectives of those who experienced the nation-destroying effect of the development of a transcontinental railroad (Native Americans, as I have suggested), Nye views rail technology through the commentaries of Euro-Americans—for example, "The railroad seemed the most obvious example of a liberating machine."[22]

Doubtless it has been for some. For instance, examining "Victorian and early modernist representations of women's experiences of locomotion and the liminal spaces of the railway," Anna Despotopoulou notes the complex dialectic of liberation and inhibition that surrounded the democratization

Figure 4.8 William Blake's train from the front

of travel for women as she addresses the sublimity of the railway experience, its challenges to the traditional comprehension of gender roles.[23] Connecting the spaces of train travel with the subjects liberated from domestic space, Despotopoulou treats the newly mobile women as liminal subjects whose experiences (articulated in Victorian literary texts) provide a micropolitics of the railway sublime, in contrast with macropolitical treatments that focus on collective national consequences of rail technology.

That macropolitical perspective is arguably articulated in J. M. W. Turner's famous painting from that same (Victorian) period, *Rain, Steam and Speed: The Great Western Railway* (1844), in which he creates a bridge from the landscape to the industrial sublime (figure 4.7). By including "elements like rain and speed," Turner "redefined the sublime to encompass not only nature, but in the image of the train, the mechanical wonders of nineteenth-century civilization."[24] Significantly, Turner's train is rushing toward the spectator, who is thereby located in the train's changing present. The image conveys to the viewer a technologically enabled collective future for the nation (in contrast with a similar shot in *Dead Man*). Jarmusch's shot of the train rushing toward the spectator (figure 4.8) is speeding toward a future of death and desolation for liminal subjects.

Despotopoulou's focus on other liminal subjects, women who experience the railway sublime in a different way, mounts a similar resistance to a collective national narrative. Her text, like Jarmusch's film, articulates the ambiguities and ambivalences associated with the industrial sublime, contradictory experiences that have also surrounded what is undoubtedly the major icon of industrialization, the factory. To treat those contradictions, I turn to a complex and markedly ambivalent rendering of the industrial sublime in a film that thematizes a factory experience, Michelangelo Antonioni's film *Red Desert* (1964).

Industrializing Postwar Italy: The Factory

Just as artists had participated in the natural sublime with their large canvases celebrating the imagination-challenging immensity of American landscapes, artists subsequently treated the factory similarly. Exemplary is Charles Demuth's *My Egypt*, which likens a huge grain-processing factory to something as sublime as an Egyptian pyramid (figure 4.9). Demuth's factory achieves sublimity by looming temple-like over the viewing subject.

However, apart from the aesthetic appreciation that enormous factories inspired, it is well known (as I have suggested) that the role of the factory in industrialization (like that of the train) has been liberating for some and destructive to others. To reflect on that ambivalence and at the same time pass through the façade of the factory to engage the movement and energies of the bodies within, I engage Antonioni's *Red Desert*, which explores an industrial sublime with a focus on a petrochemical factory complex situated in the city of Ravenna in Italy, roughly a century after the historical setting of Jarmusch's rendering of the consequences of the machine age in the American West. It's a cinematic text, which like Despotopoulou's exploration of the sublime in literary texts, constructs its historical scene through female liminal subjectivity. And like Jarmusch's William Blake, Antonioni's protagonist is badly adjusted to the scene in which she finds herself. However, in contrast with the narrative intent in Jarmusch's *Dead Man*, Antonioni evinces ambivalence in his rendering of the industrial sublime. The industrial prosperity (part of Italy's "economic miracle," which changed Ravenna after World War II) is a source of both appreciation and dismay for Antonioni. As a result, "the feelings in the film evinced in its dramatization are . . . fundamentally contradictory and intractable, [for] . . . on the one hand, Antonioni would say, the world created by the advance of technology is undoubtedly *beautiful* [an aesthetic he achieves with color, the first time he ventured away from black and white films]. . . . On the other

Figure 4.9 Charles Demuth's *My Egypt*

hand . . . this new world is very close to hell. A wasteland is a wasteland after all . . . and if a 'new beauty' has been born, . . . the phenomenon is shot with poison."[25]

Antonioni's industrial sublime is therefore partly Kantian and partly Burkean, evoking awe and anxiety, respectively. The latter, Burkean mood is conveyed by Antonioni's protagonist, Giuliana (Monica Viti), a deeply neurotic subject through which the wasteland of the new Ravenna and the petrochemical factory are experienced. Where poetry is the possession of Jarmusch's character, Blake, in Antonioni's case poetry is a function of film form. Stylistically rather than linguistically differentiating his protagonist from himself, Antonioni's point of view in the film (as Pier Paolo Pasolini explains) is expressed through the "'free indirect point-of-view' shot."[26] As "the characters enter and leave the frame . . . editing comes to consist of a series of 'pictures' . . . So that the world is presented as if regulated by a myth of pure pictorial beauty that the personages invade."[27] The film's painterly heritage goes beyond its punctuation with pictorial tableaux. The hues and architectural foci of many framing shots evoke particular art historical styles—for example, the monochrome, color-muted style of Giorgio Morandi, the "deserted agora of Giorgio de Chirico,"[28] and the color patches of Mark Rothko. With its interplay between shots of the vastness of the industrial landscape and its pictorial moments, often suffused with added color, the film plays with the contradiction between beauty and sublimity. While for Kant, the difference between the experience of a beautiful and sublime object is a difference between apprehending the form of an object and apprehending its size, both of which experiences must eventuate in subjective finality (a universalizing *sensus communis*), Burke emphasizes the contradiction between the two experiences. Like Kant, he sees the sublime object as "vast" while the beautiful object is small and of a pleasing (e.g., "delicate") form.[29] However, while Kant ultimately sees both objects as pleasing (immediately in the case of the beautiful and momentarily deferred in the case of the sublime), Burke holds onto a contradiction between the two. Although they are "sometimes found united," he writes, they can be nevertheless contradictory— e.g., "Black and white may soften, may blend, but they are not therefore the same."[30]

Burke's color example provides a propitious opening for an examination of the way Antonioni's film manages a dissonance between the beauty he observed in industrial landscapes and buildings and the negative effects of industrialization on natural beauty. While the film narrative about inter-personal relationships involves a complex emotional triangle, the extra-narrative effects supplied by the camera are articulated through "chromatic dissonance," which expresses Antonioni's above-noted ambivalence about Ravenna's industrial development.[31] He refers, for example, to the "beauty" of the factory scene dominating the horizon, with its "smokestacks and refineries," but also to the way industrial development "denudes [life] of surprise and disembodies it . . . making trees into obsolete objects."[32] This latter worry is expressed at the end of the film, when Giuliana's son Vale-rio asks about the yellow smoke issuing from the petrochemical factory's smokestacks. Giuliana responds, "Because it's poisonous."

Ultimately, as Pasolini points out, *Red Desert* has two protagonists. One is a character; Antonioni looks at the world "by immersing himself in his neurotic protagonist [Giuliana], reanimating the facts through her eyes."[33] The other is Antonioni's cinematic poesis in which he "allow[s] the cam-era to be felt." The second or "real protagonist is style."[34] As a result, like Jarmusch's *Dead Man*, the comprehension of the technological sublime is mediated by film form. In the case of *Red Desert* it's an emotion-resonating soundtrack along with a series of color-resonating tableaux (generated with "obsessive framing"), which gives us an industrial sublime viewed through and experienced by a maladjusted subject whose attempt to cope with the invasion of technology on the landscape reveals its imagination-challenging destructive effects.[35]

As is also the case with Jarmusch's approach to the industrial sublime, the image narrative in *Red Desert* does most of the work. Crucially, like Jar-musch's cinematic punctuation, Antonioni makes the industrial landscape an aesthetic object: "One of his radical innovations was to detach shots of places and things from shots of characters."[36] However, while Jarmusch's film is in black-and-white, a visual trope that conveys the presence of a historical past, Antonioni uses color to provide the intensities for his em-phasis on a subject's embodied sense experience of the industrial sublime. That emphasis is verbalized in the film when in a conversation with her husband Ugo, Giuliana describes a dream in which she connects her bodily sensations with the industrial landscape; she says that she imagines herself sinking into quicksand.

Throughout the film, the viewer is affected by the two protagonists, Giuli-ana and the camera. However, rather than being wholly separate dimen-sions of the film narrative, those two protagonists recognize each other.

Figure 4.10 Giuliana with wall color patches in Antonioni's *Red Desert*

The camera recognizes Giuliana through the way scenes are orchestrated through her gaze. And Giuliana recognizes what the camera is saying by occasionally testifying to its cinematic statements. For example, in the only direct discursive reference to the film's chromatic narrative, she says that she intends to paint the inside of her shop with light blue and green colors, for the walls and ceiling, respectively—said as the camera lingers over the test patches of paint on the walls (figure 4.10). And in another moment she reinforces the vagaries of perception that Antonioni's camera explores, when she refers to the difficulty of looking.

To summarize the interpersonal narrative briefly, the film begins with a traumatized Giuliana walking to the petrochemical plant complex where, once inside, she is introduced to her husband Ugo's old friend Corrado (Richard Harris), who has come to try and recruit workers for an overseas commercial venture. Ugo (Carlo Chionetti) explains to Corrado that Giuliana's nervous behavior is owed to the trauma of an auto accident, which has affected her more psychologically than physically. He adds that now she plans to start a retail business in a small shop she has acquired. Intrigued by her, Corrado goes to find her in her shop, and they ultimately have a brief love affair (it becomes evident in a scene in which Giuliana awakes from a nightmare that she has become unable to respond to her husband's amorous advances).

Figure 4.11 Giuliana and Valerio

However, the romantic narrative pales in comparison with the sublime industrial or technological landscape that the camera-as-protagonist maps. As the credits are run, Ravenna's industrial sublime comes into view as a blur—the way it is experienced by Giuliana, who with her son Valerio makes her way through a monochrome, deliquescent landscape, filled with polluted groundwater and piles of industrial waste surrounding a petrochemical factory complex that is belching steam and flames. As factory noises are heard, steam from its stacks makes vision even more difficult. At this point, the monochrome scene is subtlety interrupted with a dash of red, and as the camera (and Giuliana) approach the factory, we see yellow-colored pipes and hear a high-pitched sound resembling the wailing of a soprano voice.

Once the credits are finished, we see orange flames jump from the factory's stacks and there is more yellow coloring standing out on tractors and cranes. Giuliana and her son also stand out in the otherwise monochrome industrial landscape. She has on a green coat and he a brown one (figure 4.11). After a strange episode, testifying to her psychic imbalance (she buys a half-eaten sandwich from a workman), we follow her approach to the factory as the camera pans a line of striking workers and focuses briefly on one strike breaker being led away to safety by two policemen. Antonioni's beginning factory scene thus takes us back to the very beginning of cinema and the first film by the inventors of the movie camera, the Lumière brothers Louis and Auguste, who did a forty-five-second-long film of workers leaving a factory. As Harun Farocki points out, "The first camera in the history of cinema was pointed at a factory . . . [although since] it can be said that film is hardly drawn to the factory."[37] However, Antonioni's focus is more on the factory than its labor force. Once his camera enters it, we see many dials that attest to modern technologies of calculation, and we see Giuliana's husband Ugo in conversation with Corrado, whose blond hair stands out in comparison with the rest of the chromatics of the scene. As they negotiate about the laborers Corrado wants to recruit, we see bright-colored patterns on one wall. Then a blue tank appears as they walk further. Shortly thereafter Giuliana appears, coming down stairs with bright red pipes in the foreground. She then passes by a large overhead orange-colored venting pipe.

At this point it is evident that Antonioni, using color as an essential part of the identity/difference aspect of his narrative, is painting like Cézanne, whose "colors and forms alone sufficed to do [his subjects] honor" (as Peter Handke, who learned to see landscape by following Cézanne's artistic path through L'Estaque, puts it).[38] However, unlike Antonioni, Cézanne was loath to bring his color-oriented aesthetic to industrial landscapes. "When refineries sprang up around L'Estaque, he stopped painting there."[39] In contrast, Antonioni "painted" in his industrial landscape; he added color not only to the factory's structures but also to the trees and grounds nearby. As he says, "I want to paint the film as one paints a canvas; I want to invent colour relationships, and not limit myself to photographing only natural colours."[40] Rather than (like Cézanne) leaving the industrial landscape to practice his aesthetic elsewhere, Antonioni stayed with the industrial landscape and worked at overcoming his initial aesthetic estrangement, while at the same time dramatizing the experiences of a new industrial class, not the striking workers shown at the outset when Giuliana approaches the factory (a class featured in many Italian films of the period, e.g., Mario Monicelli's *The Organizer* [1963]), but an "emerging technocracy of middle-ranking managers and skilled workers . . . a new class . . . coming into existence in this extraordinary landscape."[41] It's a landscape that he saw as "beautiful" (in this mastery of man over matter) but that it was "horrifying to think that birds which fly though these fumes are going to fall dead."[42] Ultimately, Antonioni's *Red Desert* summons a "cinematic sublime" to make comprehensible his conflicted view of Italian modernity's industrial sublime. He "plays with the idea of the sublime by disrupting the possibilities for any straightforward interpretation of what we see," both with the forms imposed by his camera and his painting and by screening much of the landscape through the liminar, Giuliana's fraught modes of perception.[43]

Coloring the Industrial Sublime

By way of transition, I want to emphasize one of Antonioni's painterly inspirations, the canvases of Mark Rothko. There is an unmistakable Rothko moment in the scene in Giuliana's shop, the moment the camera focuses on a wall with three color patches associated with Giuliana's experimentation with the colors to be applied to her shop's walls and ceiling (noted above, figure 4.10). David Forgacs points out that Antonioni was "stimulated" by Rothko and other "color field" painters (of the New York school) and quotes a letter Antonioni wrote to Rothko, saying "that he found one of his paintings . . . to be of 'a phenomenal purity and force.' The way the steel coloured rectangle in the upper part of the canvas was isolated from the dark background [which] created . . . a feeling of 'cosmic panic': 'it is painted anxiety.'"[44] The colors therefore often resonate with Giuliana's moods throughout the film, giving industry's intervention into Ravenna's landscape a double emotional resonance.

Antonioni's is not the only approach to the industrial sublime that found Rothko's canvases especially adequate to the combination of awe and anxiety associated with the industrial age. They also inspired some of the works of the photographer David Maisel, whose work came after the more destructive effects of the various "economic miracles," spurred by the rise of industry, had run their course. Attracted to postindustrial sites, "to open-pit mines and power plants . . . military installations, hazardous waste sites, and the post apocalyptic megalopolis which is Los Angeles," he photographed from the air to capture "a medley of terrains, transformed by humankind."[45] Like Antonioni, Maisel engages in radical experimentation with visual materials. Focused on the contradiction between the beauty and toxicity of postindustrial landscapes, he is inspired by a history of landscape photography (e.g., the work of Timothy O'Sullivan, who surveyed the West) and the color canvases of Mark Rothko.[46] It was when he switched to using color that abstract painting exercised an influence on his work, in which "colors [came to be] active protagonists in his compositions" (see for example the Rothko-like image *Terminal Mirage #1*, figure 4.12), which bears comparison with the colored wall patches in Giuliana's shop in *Red Desert*.[47]

Figure 4.12 David Maisel, *Terminal Mirage #1*

Significantly, Maisel sees his images as political. Quoting Wim Wenders, he states, "The most political decision you make is where you direct people's eyes."[48] Following up on that politically attuned direction, I turn to more renderings of postindustrial sites, with an emphasis on ruins, which represent a later stage in history's industrial narrative.

Postindustrialism: The Ruins Sublime

Matt Bell's novel *Scrapper* (2015), whose protagonist, Kelly, makes a living off the leftover hardware in Detroit's abandoned industrial buildings, invokes the postindustrial ruins sublime. His opening paragraph is a lyrical homage to the industrial history sedimented in a vast ruin of a plant:

See the body of the plant, one hundred years of patriots' history, fifty years an American wreck. The remainder of a city within the city, a fortress of squared buildings a mile long and five blocks wide. Three million square feet of interior. A century of reinforced concrete and red brick and steel crossbeams still standing despite injury, of parking lots stretched around miles of emptiness, their lights long ago darkened, their torn and opened fences made an invitation to the gutting.[49]

Bell's text suggests that the sublime of the ruined plant, like much of the rest of the city, challenges one's historical imagination: "Everywhere you look, everywhere see the barely imaginable past" ("urban stones of memory").[50] Because the contemporary city of Detroit featured in Bell's novel, like many cities that contain industrial ruins, has lost much of its manufacturing, its abandoned industrial plants constitute "a charged scenario where imaginations of modernity and historical temporality surface in the very vocabulary of its architectural construction/destruction."[51]

Crucial to an understanding of that scenario's political implications are the practices through which the ruins are imagined and perceived. For example, throughout Bell's novel there's a disjunction between the author and his protagonist, a difference between an aesthetic of the postindustrial sublime (the author's descriptions of the industrial landscape) and an asset stripper (his protagonist), whose drama involves not only his stripping vocation but also the rescue of an abused boy. However, that storyline is less politically compelling than what can be gleaned from the economic history of the decaying urban landscape within which it unfolds.

Industrial ruins are loquacious, but they speak quite differently from what is stated by "monuments": ancient castles, temples, cathedrals, and public buildings. In this latter case, ruins articulate a romantic sublime. Monuments from various historical periods, e.g., "dilapidated columns, ingeniously wrecked temples and . . . the charming gothic tower," tend to be treated as historical relics that confer value on the classes and sects for whom they are a heritage; they are "welcome decorations that instilled a sense of enchanting historicity."[52] In contrast with such "romantically apprehended ruins . . . contemporary industrial ruins are more likely to epitomize a sort of modern gothic . . . which focuses on 'dark urban nightscapes, abandoned parking lots, factories, warehouses and other remnants of post industrial culture.'"[53] Apart from the gothic mood that such ruins can evoke is the kind of historical narrative they deliver. Rather than reinforcing a hierarchical order by bestowing "sign function value" on the particular social groupings that can claim them as their historical legacy, they speak of the demise of a different kind of hierarchy, a defunct repressive industrial order:[54]

> Ruined factories are replete with the traces of . . . redundant power, poignant reminders of the ordering functions necessary for the maintenance of industrial networks . . . remaining signatures of hierarchy and authority [for which now] . . . no one is there to listen or obey. . . . The signs of production with its sequential order become elliptical as walls erode and the rooms appear to be at the center of formless labyrinths.[55]

Figure 4.13, a shot of a ruined part of Ford Motor Company's famous, Albert Kahn–designed Rouge River plant (spread over two hundred acres and containing up to ninety-three buildings), speaks to the above passage. Once part of Kahn's elaborate design of the Rouge River complex, which provided for sequential operations in which workers became cogs in a system rather than craftspersons (the essence of the Fordist factory), the building no longer reveals its work-structuring effects. "Nature" is in the act of reclaiming space. The pictured ruin also speaks against one of the dominant myths of capitalism. As Tim Edensor notes, "In one sense, modern capitalism proceeds by forgetting the scale of devastation wreaked upon the physical and social world, for obliterating traces of this carnage [by] foster[ing] the myth of endless and seamless progress." In countering that myth, the ruin instead connotes the historical fragility of industrial capitalism with one example among many that depict the "debris of successive industrial cultures."[56] Ultimately the sense that Edensor conveys about how "the objects, spaces and traces found in industrial ruins" speak is about the "radical undecidability of the past."[57] But I want to add that they also summon a future anterior, a will-have-been that encourages a focus on the future bequeathed by industrial capitalism's fragility. They point to "a world in which the fragility of things [affects] the quality of life available to the human estate in its entanglements with other force fields . . . [challenging comprehension because] the categories and sensibilities with which we habitually come to grips to the world make it difficult to fold that sense deeply into theory and practice."[58]

Figure 4.13 Andrew Moore, photo of Rouge River ruin

The "Sweatshop Sublime"

As is well known, the (now attenuating) power of labor unions has managed only to slow the process through which manufacturing production has exited from U.S. cities like Detroit (a *Time* magazine survey of the ruins of Detroit industry identified five former factories) and moved to areas where the labor pool is much less expensive and more easily exploited.[59] Commenting on the Fordist factory located in the "third world," Stefano Harney distinguishes the coercively imposed working rhythms in the Taylorist/Fordist factory during the industrial age's profitable years in cities like Detroit with the political reality of those impositions in third world extractive factories: "The Fordist and Taylorist factory had an outside, however unstable and unjust. Control of cooperation at work was given up, but was supposed to return individually, at least for white men and settlers, in politics and rights, and votes. In the European model imposed on the colonies, there was no return."[60] The present, neocolonial sweatshop, full of exploited laborers facing accelerated morbidity, reproduces the political reality to which Harney refers.

Yet it is notoriously difficult to get the attention of consumers of the products of exploited and abused workers in third world factories. Referring to the contemporary "sweatshop sublime," Bruce Robbins reflects on the "rare moments," while getting dressed in first world dominant countries, when one can imagine what occurs in those factories—moments when "you are launched . . . to the outer reaches of a world system of notoriously inconceivable magnitude and interdependence, a system that brings goods from the ends of the earth" (e.g., moments when you happen to read the label on the shirt you are putting on).[61] He goes on to enlist the Kantian sublime, which (as I have noted) involves an experience of something so vast that it challenges the imagination. In this case, that vastness belongs to the complex supply chain that creates the conditions of possibility for making that shirt available. The ethico-political issue that concerns Robbins is how fleeting the recognition is that what we casually enjoy in our immediate local world often has debilitating effects at a great distance. His problem is about how "we" (we who have pretentions to political influence) can focus enough to connect our small world with the larger world of labor exploitation.[62]

Among the venues of labor exploitation to which Robbins refers is Haiti, where there is a Disney factory in which women sew Pocahontas shirts (among others) sold in Walmart stores for $10.77 each. Following up on Robbins's example, I turn to a brief ethnography carried out in Port au Prince of "a Disney worker at the N.S. Mart (Plant Number 32)" in the Sonapi Industrial Park, where she sewed Pocahontas and Mickey Mouse shirts.[63] A single mother with four children living in "a one-room windowless shack," the worker could afford to leave her children only a total of thirty cents to feed themselves each day. Before leaving, the researcher "asked the family what they would eat that night. 'Nothing' they responded." While the shirts she sews sell for $10.77, her earnings amount to twenty-eight cents for sewing 375 Pocahontas shirts in an hour, in a "hot, dusty, and poorly lit" plant, i.e., considerably less than 1 percent of the price of each shirt.[64]

We don't have to look outside the United States to find sweatshops. Much of the "third world" exists within the first. "Waves of immigrants [many illegal and thus especially vulnerable] . . . shored up old sweatshops and created new ones [in the United States]. By the 1980s California was fast becoming the largest garment manufacturing and sweated labor hub in the United States."[65] However, my focus is on the genres through which our attention is summoned to witness the precarious lives of sweatshop workers rather than the cartography of the oppression. If we turn the clock back to the late nineteenth and early twentieth centuries, it was literature and photography that played major roles in creating public (and official) awareness of the exploitation of workers in the garment industry. With respect to literature, one early example is a novel by Cornelius Mathews, *The Career of Puffer Hopkins* (1842), which "features a scene between a master tailor and his wretched skilled employee, Fob, exiled to outwork in his garret"[66] (the earlier history of sweated labor in the garment industry is a history of the movement from domestic space to the factory floor). With respect to photography, "the cumbersome cameras that penetrated the dark corners of late-nineteenth-century cellars and attics were beginning to document a special kind of visual field," slums and sweatshop venues. Jacob Riis's photographic study (in the 1880s), which eventuated in his *How the Other Half Lives* (1890), is exemplary for providing photographic evidence, where the prior visual field was assembled through a less evidentiary genre, the illustration.[67]

More recently, another genre, the lithograph, has been applied to the problem of sweated labor, Sue Coe's "sweatshop series" published in the *New Yorker* in 1994. Focusing on "globally exploited labor," Coe's lithographs turn factories with supposed "industrial efficiency, U.S.-style . . . into charnel houses."[68] Her focus is on such garment industries as the Fruit of the Loom textile company. This image is of an elderly Chinese floor worker, who at age seventy-two was still working in a sweatshop for $4.25 an hour (figure 4.14).[69]

What Coe is able to convey with a single image of a Chinese woman sweatshop worker is suggestive but minimally informative compared with what has been done with documentary cinema subsequently. Here I want to review briefly a documentary to which I refer in an earlier investigation, Lotta Ekelund and Kristina Bjurling's *Santa's Workshop: Inside China's Slave Labour Toy Factories* (2004).[70] The documentary, based on interviews with factory managers, workers, and local critics, revealed that in the spray-paint division of the Huangwu No. 2 Toy Factory (which supplies Walmart and Dollar General, among others) the production goal for the more experienced workers requires them to "paint 8,920 small toy pieces a day, or 1,115 per hour . . . one every 3.23 seconds in order to earn $3.45 for eight hours" (the quota is somewhat smaller for newer workers, whose pay is accordingly less).[71] The work, often fifteen to nineteen hours per day, seven days per week, is debilitating: it "wears off their skin, leaving them with sore, blistered and bleeding hands and fingers," and when they're not behind their

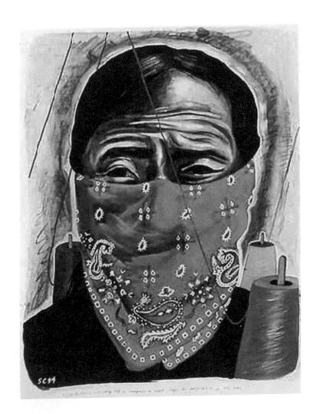

Figure 4.14 Sue Coe,
Chinese Floor Worker

machines, they "live within the confines of the factory walls in virtual prison cell accommodation or even sleep on the factory floor" (the factory hires 90 percent women because, as a manager says, "they're easier to manage").[72]

The Chinese factories are relatively stable institutions with years of longevity. In contrast, the sweatshops in Mexico, near the U.S. border (over four thousand, which sprang up after the NAFTA agreement) are more subject to the vicissitudes of labor markets. They often pick up and move to such venues as Indonesia, where, as one former worker, Carmen Duran, who had been employed in a now-defunct Sanyo television plant puts it, "they can pay less and make more." The form of the documentary *Maquilapolis* (made by Vicky Funari and Sergio De La Torre), in which Carmen's story unfolds, is unusual. Carmen, whose health was compromised by the toxic environment in and outside the Sanyo factory, and another worker, Lourdes Lujan, who had worked in another nearby factory, are not mere informants. They became activists (*promotores*), who achieved severance pay (in Carmen's case) from Sanyo and (in Lourdes's case) from the cleanup of her former factory's toxic, abandoned site. During the documentary, they serve as commentators on the realities of sweatshop practices. However, doubtless the most revealing documentary is about the sweatshops of the shoe company Nike, which at one point had moved to the place to which Sanyo had fled in order to find cheap labor, Indonesia (where by 2000 "more than one third of [their] products were produced"). However, "after almost four years of labor struggles, which had moved the minimum wage up to $2.20 a day . . . Nike moved [some of its operations] into Vietnam, where the daily wage is a meager $1.50."[73]

Certainly, reports on Nike's sweatshop practices and the intervention of activist, anti-sweatshop campaigns have roiled the firm and have resulted in slight changes in their production practices and massive changes in their publicity (aimed at "crisis management" to counter a "potential moral panic").[74] However, no investigation is more telling than the one reported in the documentary *Behind the Swoosh* (2011), a film that follows the visit of Jim Keady and the friend he recruited to join him, Leslie Kretzu, to Indonesia, where for a month they tried to live on $1.25 a day, the typical wage that Nike's subcontractor pays their workers. Keady (a well-conditioned athlete, shown energetically defending a goal in a soccer game at the outset of the documentary) undertook the experiment after resisting the demand of his university (St. John) that as a coach he cooperate with the new Nike contract with the Athletic Department (a $3.5 million endorsement contract) and wear Nike products. The results are well known; they both lost considerable weight (twenty-five pounds, in Keady's case) and had to deal with illness and melancholy while living in a nine-by-nine cement box with no windows or furniture in stifling heat. Their one-month experience only begins to approach the level of deprivation of the Nike wage-earners who live that life month after month—for example, four women neighbors living in an eight-by-eight box with their children, while sharing a bathroom with five other families. Many worked overtime just to get by—up to sixteen-hour days, seven days a week.

Rather than detail the rest of the documentary and the minor effects its publicity had on Nike's policies (it seems that have curtailed some of the violence against those trying to organize unions, and now menstrual leaves for women are permitted),[75] I want to comment on the unusual ethnographic strategy that Keady and Kretzu undertook. Clifford Geertz famously attributed *his* ethnographic strategy to reading culture behind the backs of his subjects (after which he wrote scholarly monographs "interpreting" exotic cultures).[76] By contrast, Keady and Kretzu engaged in an auto-ethnography in which their bodies rather than an interpretive discourse displayed the results. Rather than reading culture, they embodied it, providing irrefutable evidence about the lives they simulated. And crucially, rather than seeking merely to overcome the challenge of the sweatshop sublime (connecting their local world to the larger world of the exploitation involved in producing commodities) in going from apprehension to comprehension about the sweatshop sublime, their strategy was excursive rather than discursive. They moved to the venue of production and registered it on their bodies, surfaces on which were inscribed the violence of global sweatshop practices.

Conclusion: Overcoming Inattention to Violence

In an earlier investigation, I refer to the way "the arts, especially literature and film (both fictional and documentary) 'bear,' what Marco Abel calls, 'the *pedagogical* potential for activating an *ethical* mode of encounter with violence.'"[77] As I have suggested (with the assistance of Bruce Robbins), our attention to forms of oppression that silently speak in the products we use is brief and difficult to sustain, given the distance of that oppression and of course the interpretive chaos mediating what is the case at that distance. The documentaries to which I refer in the section on the sweatshop sublime provide an antidote in that they substitute documentary time, which is among other things, "a technology of memory," for the temporalities of everyday life.[78] There for all to see is an archive that the tricks of consciousness cannot easily erase.

In chapter 5 I turn to another sublime—the 9/11 or "terror" sublime—which has a much stronger purchase on everyday individual and collective consciousness, as officials, citizens (and noncitizen immigrants) around the globe and a wide variety of media struggle to come to terms with events that (in Don DeLillo's terms, applied to the 9/11 destruction of the World Trade Center towers) have "no purchase on the mercies of analogy or simile."[79] That line alone earns DeLillo considerable space in chapter 5, where my focus is on the difficulty of discerning the complex post-9/11 world of terroristic violence and the reactive practices/policies of violent securitization and militarization that DeLillo and many others oppose with the weapons of the arts, weapons that create (in Walter Benjamin's terms) a "moral shock effect."[80]

5. THE 9/11 TERROR SUBLIME

Shortly after the 9/11 attack on the World Trade Center towers, I wrote,

> A body falling through the air from over 90 stories up; a doomed
> worker, hopelessly waving a white flag from a window near the top;
> the two towers imploding with thousands still trapped inside! It was
> like a disaster movie without a touch of redemption. I wanted to see
> it as the worst film I have ever seen. But it happened, and, to borrow
> one of Don DeLillo's expressions, it was like "an aberration in the
> heartland of the real."[1]

While suggesting that the event was an imagination-challenging sublime
experience, my remark evokes the genre of the disaster movie, acknowl-
edging that such experiences engage a consciousness that is always already
attuned to the interpretation of disasters by a history of one's media ex-
posure. Kartik Nair, reflecting on one of the 9/11 event's most stunning
images, the photograph by Richard Drew "of a man falling down the side of
the North Tower," referred the image to cinema as well, in his case to the
three *Spider-Man* films (2002, 2004, and 2007) that *followed* the event. He
refers for example to the moment in *Spider-Man 2* when Spider-Man (Tobey
Maguire), hit by the hands of a clock flung at him by Doc Ock (his neme-
sis), "loses his grip and takes a dive down the north face of the building."[2]
Mine and Nair's reactions indicate that such events are both "premediated"

and "remediated,"[3] as prior and subsequent media attachments and experiences (in national narratives, canonical texts, popular culture materials, and so on) deliver the ideational and figurative frames that shape the way an event will be anticipated as well as contributing to the contentious process through which it will be (and will have been) subsequently comprehended.

Judith Shulevitz offers another example, pointing out that, "In the aftermath of the attacks on Sept. 11, Joseph Conrad's *Secret Agent* (1907) became one of the three works of literature most frequently cited in the American media."[4] Although like the 9/11 attack on the World Trade Center, the object of the attack in that novel is architectural (London's Greenwich Observatory), Conrad's plot does not present a similar terrorist narrative. In *Secret Agent* the attackers are *agents provocateurs* who have infiltrated the anarchist cell rather than the anarchists/terrorists, who are also featured in the novel. Nevertheless, I turn to Conrad's novel as a prelude to my analysis of the 9/11 terror sublime, not to locate the novel as the first instance of a genealogy of terror attacks treated in the arts but to invoke a critical remediation of the novel in a Stan Douglas video installation. In *The Secret Agent*, Douglas's 2015 video installation version of the novel, the action is relocated to Portugal. Its historical moment is the "Carnation Revolution" of 1974. Revisiting "a pivotal moment of modernity and progressive thrust towards a more egalitarian society," *his* plot bears comparison with the way the aftermath of the 9/11 event unfolded: "The plot centers upon an ambiguity; the violent, clandestine illegal action [an overthrow of a totalitarian regime] provokes rigidification of harsh control and repressive measures and also public acceptance of the actions."[5] However, apart from the relevance of the plot, Douglas's video installation, with a screenplay based on Conrad's novel, remediates Conrad's focus on anarchism in a film about the events of modernity, which achieves a critical reactualization of the story by mobilizing several alternative perspectives. The installation deploys the action on six different screens, a composition in which any attempt at narrative closure of the event is foreclosed. Like his other "audio-visual and photographic works," the installation destabilizes both the conceptual and perceptual conditions of the event with a disarticulated "flow of montage [that is] . . . derived from stress on the simulatedness of all representation."[6]

Douglas's installation treats a relatively brief, idea-saturated historical moment, which transpires within more long-term temporalities. It contends for attention with traditional organic attachments based on broadly distributed, society-wide systems of thought, articulated in such texts as bibles, sagas, tragedies, and canonical histories, as well as with broadly distributed political ideologies (variations of socialist, communist, democratic idea systems), all of which contend to shape the anticipatory frames within which events become intelligible. Doubtless the influence of those longer term idea systems has attenuated, as former allegiances to particular historical narratives have faced increasing competition in the modern media environment. Although it is difficult to isolate the precise historical moments when those attenuations have occurred, Deleuze's suggestion about the break between pre– and post–World War II societies is exemplary. D. N. Rodowick offers a convenient summary, as he addresses the distinction between the movement and time images in Deleuze's two volumes on cinema. The two treatments articulate two alternative image regimes, which Deleuze correlates with historical changes in commitments to historical narratives. Whereas "prewar societies were sustained by organic ideologies (democracy or socialism) that functioned as universals defined by a notion of history as progress," postwar societies became less attached to such a linear narrative, reflected in the Italian Neorealism–influenced cinematic styles in which chronologies are no longer teleological but are, through direct time images (based on editing), discontinuous and frequently "unpredictable" and "elliptical."[7]

I want to note that although this historical picture is conceptually fruitful, it is nevertheless oversimplified because all histories are—as Fernand Braudel has famously pointed out—"conjunctural" rather than linear.[8] Broad-based political ideologies have often been in contention with persisting traditional organic attachments (religious, for example), which they never wholly displace. As a result, attempts by governing authorities and mainstream media to hijack events by evoking systems of legitimation that remediate events, locating them within reassuring authority-sustaining frames, are often contested. At a minimum, layers of ideational temporality afflict all attempts at moving from the initial apprehension of sublime experiences toward reassuring and consensual modes of comprehension. It becomes contentious as to whose accounts and actions will dominate in a situation in which there will be no universal *sensus communis*. Having already abandoned Kant's temporal models of the move from apprehension to comprehension (as a purely cognitive, universalizing dynamic), in this chapter I pursue interpretive contention over the 9/11 terror sublime experience with special attention to a politics of aesthetics—specifically to the temporalities articulated in some of the artistic texts that have weighed in to respond to the 9/11 events (as well as one that has in effect anticipated it). I start with a prelude, another pass on Bergman's film *Winter Light*, to begin a reflection on the issue of anticipatory versus consequential mediations.

Jonas Persson Redux

In chapter 3, in my second iteration of the character Jonas Persson in Bergman's film *Winter Light*, I refer to his experience of the nuclear sublime, pointing out that Jonas was terrorized because he located himself as a likely victim of a threatening force that is both ideational/affective (Chinese alleged hatred of others) and technological (their coming possession of a nuclear device and an ability to send it to distant locations). Dwelling on a form of agency existing in a distant world that could at any moment violently impact his local world, he imagines that the people in that remote world have both the will and the technology to wreak havoc in his. For Jonas, the fabled "nuclear proliferation" problem, which has been an object of analysis and policy prescriptions for government leaders and agencies and academic security–preoccupied scholars since the 1940s, is something he takes personally. The film's dialogues and face shots of a troubled Jonas reveal someone in the grips of personal trauma (figure 5.1).

As regards the temporal connection between events and trauma, Jonas is precocious. He is traumatized because he *anticipates* a catastrophic event. The usual event–trauma sequence is quite the reverse. Ordinarily, catastrophe *precedes* trauma, for trauma usually manifests (in Gene Ray's words) a "structural belatedness": "whether catastrophic or messianic, 'events' are necessarily traumatic. If 'events' could be merely assimilated to the given order of things, they would not be 'events.' But the structural belatedness of trauma is such that we will not be able to know, before choosing and acting, which kind of 'event' has arrived (or is in the process of arriving)."[9] Nevertheless, there are sense-making collectives, both small and large, that mediate anticipation, traumatic and otherwise. What I want to dwell on at this point is the failure of Jonas's available communities of sense to provide solace—the small one constituted by his marriage and the very large one constituted as (what I called in chapter 3) "the Christian sublime." Jonas's wife Karin tells Pastor Tomas that she and Jonas discuss the problem constantly but she is unable to provide credible reassurance because (as she avers) she knows relatively little about the world outside her domestic situation. Tomas (as I note in earlier chapters) also has a credibility problem.

Figure 5.1 Jonas in Bergman's *Winter Light*

He has lost his faith in the divine solace that is allegedly delivered by the Bible's textual protagonist. Afflicted by God's silence, he can no longer trust in the existence of the character whose story and promise the Christian Bible describes. As his conversation with Jonas shows, unable convincingly to summon reassuring words from Christianity's canonical text, Tomas can speak only of his personal affliction rather than of the solace that trust in God is alleged to promise.

Organic Textual Communities

Whether through faith or through other interpretive motivations that determine the lessons of cultural texts with considerable historical duration (sacred or otherwise), attempts at stabilizing the communities of sense allegiant to such texts will inevitably involve contention. Here I want to explore briefly some organic communities of sense with long historical trajectories in order to recover that contentiousness and provide a threshold for approaching the contemporary textual struggles for comprehension in the post-9/11 world, the world subsequent to the destruction of the twin towers of the World Trade Center. The concept of a textual community with which I am concerned is introduced by Brian Stock in an analysis of the spread of literacy in twelfth-century Christian Europe. His focus is on the new "textual communities" formed as "narrative arts aimed at delineating proper versus heretical modes of religious practice developed."[10] Notably, in opposition to mainstream religious authority, dissenting textual communities emerged simultaneously. Moreover, "the textual community" was not only textual; it also involved "new uses for orality," for once a group had developed a shared understanding of (for example, a liturgical text or the Bible) and "had passed the threshold of literacy," there was no "necessity for the organizing text to be spelt out, interpreted, or reiterated. The members all knew what it was. As a consequence, interaction by word of mouth could take place as a superstructure of an agreed meaning, the textual foundation of behavior having been entirely internalized."[11]

Stock's example treats an organic textual community involved in a centuries-long struggle over how to interpret sacred texts and how to police the heresies that are an inevitable outcome of religious orthodoxies.[12] There have been other historical textual communities shaped by culturally pervasive genres. For example, the coherence (or lack thereof) of ancient Greek societies is played out in the Greek tragedies. The playwright Arthur Miller provides an account of the sublimity of the original experience of the tragedies. While on a trip to Sicily, he was dropped off by his driver at the ruins of an ancient Greek theater. On seeing the remains of the theater, he remarks that he had "felt something close to shame at how suffocatingly private our theatre had become" and proceeds to imagine the community of sense that must have emerged from each performance of a Greek tragedy in that theater: "Surely," he writes, "one sound was never heard in this place—applause; they must have left in amazement, renewed as brothers and sisters of the moon and sun."[13] However, Miller's assumption notwithstanding, rather than simply representing cultural cohesion, the Greek tragedies, notably those written by Aeschylus and Sophocles (before they lost their critical edge with Euripides), dramatized the dilemma of justice in a society radically split between competing cosmologies.[14]

A later community-sustaining textual genre, the Icelandic saga, also reflected divisiveness as well as cohesion. The sagas, which reached their influential peak in the twelfth century, were often read aloud in public gatherings. They were, as one scribe puts it, "about worthy men meant to both entertain and point to the distinction between good and evil."[15] Those storytelling events indicate that the sagas were written to be spoken, which made them suitable both for entertainment and for moral lessons at any hour, "night or day, by light or in darkness."[16] The most famous of the sagas, *Njal's Saga*, is one whose narrative spans the period in which Christianity displaced an earlier religious cosmology; it comes across stylistically as a "homily" focusing on virtuous men trying to ward off evil designs and ending, it seems, in an "indictment of violence."[17] That saga, like many of the famous family sagas, was designed to help the Icelandic community negotiate ways of keeping the peace in a community that values "fame" and "honor," which were often achieved through violent conflict in a dangerously riven social formation in which lawfulness often conflicted with the valuing of manly virtue.[18]

Rather than being merely *subject* to interpretive conflict, the Icelandic sagas were *about* interpretive conflict, for example, that between the old Norse religion brought to Iceland from Norway when the island was settled, and Christianity, which was spread in Iceland by proselytizing missionaries centuries later and ultimately imposed by chieftains who had converted. Thus at one point in *Njal's Saga* it is noted that for the first time someone is outlawed for blasphemy, indicating that those with Christian allegiance had begun to colonize the law. Whereas the sagas remain unchanged, even though their cultural authority has lapsed, there is another textual community whose text is meant to change continually. It is the Jewish scholarly community, devoted to an ongoing interpretation of the Talmud. Never fixed, the Talmud is a growing text whose continuing expansion is driven by scholarly commentaries. Although in contrast with the written Torah, the Talmud was initially a compilation of the oral law, written down by rabbinical leaders in response to the chaos attending a diasporic people trying to maintain its spiritual coherence. Without going into the nuances of the Talmud's components (a "Mishnah" written in Hebrew and "Tannaitic" writings in both Hebrew and Aramaic), I want to note one radical way in which the textual community surrounding it has evolved over many centuries.

In a radical philosophical approach to the text, the French philosopher-rabbi, Marc-Alain Ouaknin, identifies the essence of the Talmud as its resistance to closure. He points out that from the point of view of one of its more radical commentators, Rabbi Nahman of Breslav (b. 1772), the purpose of adding commentary to the Talmud is the undermining of authority. The growing Talmud should maintain an enigmatic relationship to divine will in a way that will summon continual interpretation.[19] As an "open work" that seeks renewal rather than "reconciliation," for Nahman "the Talmud seeks to undo any mastery," and (crucially, in a passage that aligns Nahman's Talmudic perspective with aspects of contemporary critical thinking), rather than the text being the expression of subjects, it makes them in opposition to the "prefabricated subjectivity" that traditional institutions sponsor.[20] When properly understood, the Talmud, according to Ouaknin, "restores life, movement, and time to the very heart of words."[21]

Historically, the Talmudic textual community is relatively insulated. Although it is without doubt that Talmudic scholars writing in a wide variety of geographic locations—ancient Babylonia, medieval Spain, and so on—have absorbed local writing styles and literatures from writers outside their community, any hybridity that entered the text was unintentional. Talmudic writing has maintained an esoteric inclusiveness in contrast with the history of Christian writing, which has been aggressively exoteric over the centuries. Because Christianity is a proselytizing religion, Christian discursive practices have required contentious encounter; they have included not only "dogmatics" (rules for guiding practices within the faith), but also "apologetics" (discourses aimed at challenging the faiths of "nonbelievers," or believers in something else). In contrast, the Talmud is designed for instruction *within* Jewish communities.

However, whatever may have been the intentions of those involved in constructing and disseminating religious canons (whether esoteric or exoteric), historical encounters with alternative religious cultures and their texts have influenced the evolution of the texts that have shaped both their modes of worship and their practices of an everyday ethos. For example, as I have put it elsewhere, "The Hebrew bible has evolved on the basis of what Hebrew shares with other Semitic languages . . . [in] philological work in which the meanings of Hebrew words have changed. Philologists have had to examine the terms and expressions in Aramaic, Classical Syriac, Acadian, Ugaric, and Classical Arabic."[22] Similarly, as Peter Brown has shown, what emerged as the Christian "thought world" was influenced by paganism: "Throughout the fifth century, Christianity and paganism worked together in such public representations as architectural detail and decoration; in the ancients' 'thought-worlds,' potentially exclusive explanatory systems coexisted." To the extent that Christianity ultimately separated itself from paganism, the change was "glacial."[23] Rather than being representatives of a triumphant and intransigent faith, Christian holy men were negotiators who worked continually at creating a compromise between their spiritual understandings and paganism's way of constructing the supernatural world.

The Jewish canon as interpreted in the contemporary period has resulted from centuries of the erasure of non-Jewish influences, and the Christian canon, which has also incorporated oppositional thought worlds, does not explicitly register its debts to alterity.[24] Teaching and liturgical practices have proceeded as if the text has been historically inviolate, attributable to divinely chosen or self-elected individual authorities or to revelation. We have to turn to key historical moments to recover the extent to which that canon has been susceptible to the contingencies of encounter. One such moment involves a dialogue that occurred in 1524—in the "recently conquered Tenochtitlan, now known as Mexico City"—between twelve Spanish friars seeking to convert indigenous Mexicans and the Mexican scholar-priests. That encounter between "radically dissimilar worlds" created a "shared world—violently transformed [so that] epistemological, geopolitical and cosmological maps would be changed forever," doubtless with subtle effects on the way the Christian textual community subsequently evolved.[25] Although "such textual and literary exchanges constitute a neglected and important part of American literary history," its effects have been difficult to explore because of "the destruction of much of the archive following conquest—and its non-alphabetic nature."[26] Following the changes that have created the Talmud as a living text avoids those difficulties because that book constitutes its own archive; over the centuries, layers of commentary have been added to the margins of the pages rather than replacing the texts on which they comment.

Contemporary Disciplinary Canons

A reflection on the particular oppositional strand of Talmudic practice that Rabbi Nahman enjoins and Ouaknin celebrates enables my analysis of the contemporary textual communities that have responded to the 9/11 event, because what has characterized interpretive struggle (inscribed *within* the Talmud) is often witnessed in contemporary struggles over canons (inscribed in clashes *among* more exoteric publications). For example, borrowing the concept of textual community from Brian Stock's reading of the Christian contention over heresy, the anthropologist George Marcus analyzes contemporary academic "textual communities" involved in struggles over academic canons, literary and social science in particular. At the outset he indicates how the idea of a canon, which begins in practices of religious orthodoxy, has migrated into academia:

> *Canon* itself connotes sanctity, orthodoxy, and discipline in a church context, and this lends ideological intensity to critique, but the broader referent is that of authority embodied in the selection and reading of *literal* texts. Thus, the rhetoric of critique has been formed and its terms defined specifically within literary theory, and has spread from there as "the issue of the canon" to other related fields.[27]

Although clearly the readers/interpreters of the canonical text, the Talmud, have been both a textual and an interpretive community, Marcus finds himself exiting from Stanley Fish's well-known concept of interpretive communities to employ the concept of textual communities, which he finds more adaptive to issues of canons in the disciplines he examines—literary studies, anthropology, history, and art history (and a null case, science)—disciplines in which (with the exception of science) struggles over the canon have been "text-centered."[28] Rather than approaching academic textual communities from within a particular textual allegiance, Marcus approaches them as an ethnographer, interrogating them as literatures and inquiring into the dynamic through which they have attained degrees of disciplinary authority. He ends with an appreciative commentary on Salman Rushdie's novel *Satanic Verses*, which "engages with canonic authority in the most canonic, fundamental(ist) sense" with a text that "is precisely not canonical, but rather challenges the very notion of such authority."[29] What Marcus surmises about Rushdie's challenge to textual authority is central to the writer Maurice Blanchot's commitment to the challenge that the literary vocation must undertake. For Blanchot, the purpose of literature, its "mission," is "to interrupt the purposeful steps we are always taking toward a deeper understanding and a surer grasp upon things."[30] Embracing the contingency of the past and future, Blanchot saw literature's purpose as "interrupting the time of the assured orders of retrospective presentation, narrative, and history."[31]

Blanchot's perspective goes to the heart of the critical thinking by stressing the importance of interrupting entrenched narratives. One of those narratives is the one that the 9/11 event has discredited. Don DeLillo describes that effect succinctly (in a passage I quote part of in chapter 1): "In the past decade the surge of capital markers has dominated discourse and shaped global consciousness. All this changed on September 11th. Today, the world narrative belongs to terrorists [and as a result] . . . this catastrophic event changes the way we think and act, moment to moment, week to week, for unknown weeks and months to come, and steely years."[32] I want to add that the event has an even more pervasive impact on chronology. It has changed the way we archive the past, recognize our present, and anticipate the future. Moreover, the event transpires in an age in which traditional textual allegiances have attenuated. As Victor Burgin suggests, "In the storm of representations that rages in contemporary life, the forms of continuity that were inhabited from the inside . . . are dissolved in a mediatic solution of perpetual contemporaneity, as if the only modes of inhabiting the world were live transmissions and instant replay."[33] Nevertheless, as the array of canonical texts through which temporality has been heretofore inscribed has lost their ideational traction, the void created by the diminution of their influence has been filled by critically reflective artistic genres, both literary and visually oriented artistic texts. I turn first to one of the most compelling literary accomplishments.

DeLillo and Post-9/11 Trauma

Decades ago C. Wright Mills addressed himself to the problem of adjusting discourse to catastrophe, specifically the way to shape a critical discourse at the historical moment to which he was responding, the rise of National Socialism in the first half of the twentieth century: "When events move very fast and possible worlds swing around them, something happens to the quality of thinking. Some . . . repeat formulae; some . . . become reporters. To time observations with thought so as to mate a decent level of abstraction with crucial happenings is a difficult problem. Its solution lies in the *using* of intellectual residues of social-history, not jettisoning them except in precise confrontation with events."[34] As is well known, the U.S. government's response to the 9/11 event was formulaic. The United States was attacked by a globally dispersed cell, but rather than adjusting to that new reality, "the Bush administration . . . feeling nostalgia for the Cold War," treated the event within a tired geopolitical narrative and attacked states. And much of academic discourse articulated an anachronistic state-centric narrative of the security crisis, reinforcing the Bush administration's approach to their "war on terror."[35] As DeLillo puts it, "That narrative ends in the rubble and it is left to us to create the counter-narrative."[36] Picking up that challenge from the point of view of the vocation of the writer, DeLillo dedicates himself to addressing the challenge of the 9/11 sublime—an event he describes as "so vast and terrible that it was outside imagining even as it happened."[37] It is truly a "paradigmatic" event, he suggests, because (as a line in the novel states) "everything now is measured by after."[38] Treating the aftereffects of the event as a problem of aesthetic comprehension, DeLillo's aim is both to understand the perceptual world of the perpetrators (who "share the codes and protocols of their mission" and fail to see the vulnerability of everyday humanity in their midst) and to make sense of our collective trauma: "The event itself has no purchase on the mercies of analogy or simile. We have to take the shock and horror as it is. But living language is not diminished. The writer wants to understand what this day has done to us."[39] DeLillo therefore saw his task as fulfilling what Mills suggests in response to an earlier catastrophe, achieving an event-adequate language to cope with the sublimity of one of history's traumatic moments. Because, as he writes in his *Harper's* essay, "plots reduce the world," he wants to enlarge and complicate the world.[40] It's not the first time he has contended with terrorism. In his novel *Players* (1977) in which the terrorist subjects attack the New York stock exchange, he has a passage on the terrorists' rationale that anticipates one in his 9/11 *Harper's* essay: "They have money. We have destruction."[41] His later remark, after the attack on the World Trade Center, is "We are rich, privileged and strong, but they are willing to die."[42]

DeLillo's novel *Mao II* (1991, fourteen years after his *Players*) is a more thoroughgoing treatment of terrorism; it anticipates the confrontation he emphasizes in his post-9/11 writings between terrorists and the novelist. In *Mao II* his protagonist, the writer Bill Gray, refers to the writer-terrorist encounter DeLillo was to revisit years later: "There's a curious knot that binds novelists and terrorists." As the passage proceeds, the writer concedes cultural dominance to the terrorists: "Years ago I used to think it was possible for a novelist to alter the inner life of the culture. Now bomb-makers and gunmen have taken that territory. They make raids on human consciousness. What writers used to do before we were all incorporated."[43] The other "raid on human consciousness" after 9/11 came out of Washington, DC. DeLillo's textual confrontation is therefore also with U.S. policy-makers who brought to the event an anachronistic view of the geopolitical world. Given the inadequacy of old narratives, derived from a moribund, macropolitical community of sense (a geostrategic legacy of the cold war), DeLillo wants to contribute to an altered community of sense, one that will ultimately substitute a micropolitical sensibility that substitutes comprehension for disabling collective trauma and misguided interpretation. And crucially, unlike the situation of the traumatized Jonas Persson in Bergman's *Winter Light*, it's a *post*-event trauma, the temporality of which Cathy Caruth (whose perspective I summon in chapter 1 as well) characterizes:

> The wound of the mind—the breach in the mind's experience of time, self, and world—is not, like the wound of the body, a simple healable event but rather an event that . . . is experienced too soon, too unexpectedly, to be fully known and is therefore not available to consciousness until it imposes itself again, repeatedly, in the nightmares and repetitive actions of the survivor.[44]

DeLillo's *Falling Man*

DeLillo's novel animates Caruth's version of trauma through its characters' post-9/11 dispositions and interactions. Although one critic complains that DeLillo's novel (like other examples of post-9/11 literature) measures a "cataclysmic public event . . . purely and simply in terms of the emotional entanglements of [its] protagonists . . . [a] retreat into domestic detail," the novel, which certainly uses the family drama (a defining feature of novels), thinks well beyond those "entanglements."[45] To appreciate the power of the aesthetic comprehension of the event that DeLillo's novel supplies through its aesthetic subjects, I want to re-evoke the Kantian and Freudian aspects of the sublime I introduce in chapter 1. As I point out there, for Kant the task of moving from apprehension to comprehension in the face of the sublime is momentarily blocked because the object is too great and its appearance too sudden for our faculty of imagination, so that (to repeat Kant's remark) "our faculty of imagination breaks down in presenting the concept of a magnitude and proves unequal to the task."[46] Strangely (I want to add), for one who has founded philosophical romanticism, displacing the locus of knowledge from the force of objects to the dynamics of subjective consciousness, here Kant cedes effectivity to the object world, at least momentarily (until the contest of the faculties ensues and reason takes over where imagination is short-circuited). As I suggested, the dynamic of the contest of faculties sends the subject upward toward its reasoning ability, in contrast to Freud's perspective, which effectively reverses the direction of the Kantian version of the sublime. Instead of moving upward to a transcendent sphere of reason, the subject is sent downward, deep within its subconscious, a place (described in chapter 1) as "awash in psychic energy whose aims are unconscious." Arguably, the cinematic style of Delillo's prose, "reminiscent" of "the domestic anomie of the New Wave . . . [a] Resnais-like fogginess" sends the *reader* downward into the depths of her/his subconscious with its "oblique silences and enigmatic close-ups." It's an effect that (as a critic suggests), "lowers the reader into an inexorable rendezvous with raw terror."[47]

In sum, with emphasis on both the dynamics of intelligibility and affective impact, DeLillo's novel is a critical intervention into the collective negotiation of a historical event; it's a player in a rendezvous with political history. To locate how it works, rather than privileging either the Kantian or Freudian subject, my approach (as is the case with my treatment of other artistic texts) is on displacing the subject–object relationship as the locus of comprehension by focusing not on a contest of faculties nor on an intra-psychic struggle but on a discursive struggle carried on in a battle of texts, some artistic and some governmental or official. That displacement doesn't disqualify either Kantian or Freudian insights. The Kantian recognition that a sublime event initially disrupts the move from apprehension to compre-hension holds, and the Freudian insight that the trauma of the event creates a chain of associations in individual and collective subjects that shield them from what have been their ongoing preoccupations prior to the event (and continue to baffle them as those preoccupations surface after the event is coded in difficult-to-comprehend ways) holds as well. That said, the 9/11 event was both sublime (chez Kant) and uncanny (chez Freud), and DeLillo's novel captures both the philosophical and psychoanalytic dimensions of its impact as it enters the post-9/11 interpretive clash of texts, competing to locate the event's ongoing will-have-been (the unceasing historical negoti-ation of its significance).

A Kantian sublimity (with a Burkean inflection) is immediately evident in DeLillo's *Falling Man*. A terrorizing, incomprehensible world emerges in the novel's opening sentence: "It was not a street anymore but a world, a time and space of falling ash and near night," followed a few sentences later by specifics: "This was the world now. Smoke and ash came rolling down streets and turning corners, bursting around corners, seismic tides of smoke, with office paper flashing past, standard sheets with cutting edge, skimming, whipping past, otherworldy things in the morning pall."[48] It's an incomprehensible world for which people are unprepared. Once De-Lillo's varyingly traumatized characters emerge as describable individuals and begin their attempts to make sense of their lives in an altered world, DeLillo's rendering of the 9/11 sublimity becomes more Freudian as the novel's multiple narratives emphasize personal trauma, articulated through various experiences of the uncanny; he elaborates the secrets that his characters have been keeping from themselves. His first protagonist, Keith Neudecker, who emerges from one of the towers covered in ash and blood with glass particles embedded in his face and scalp, has his body headed somewhere that his conscious behavior had foreclosed; for reasons he cannot at the moment fathom, he headed to his former home where his estranged wife and son live. His journey is taking him through a formerly familiar urban scene (the area of lower Manhattan near the towers) that no longer retains its usual contours: "There was something critically missing from the things around him. They were unfinished, whatever that means."[49]

In a line that echoes DeLillo's opening section, Lyotard characterizes the traumatic nature of sublime experiences for such characters: "The event clears a vertiginous space and time, untethered from its context or perceptual environment, its discontinuity or hovering goes hand in hand with anxiety."[50] Opting explicitly for a Freudian rather than a Kantian emphasis, Lyotard locates the "truth" of sublime events in *figural* space rather than within a (Kantian) epistemological mental geography: "Truth is discordant . . . its possible *topos* cannot be determined by the coordinates of the geography of knowledge. Instead it makes itself felt on the surface of discourse through effects. . . . Freud gives us guidelines for discernment [not to] grab hold of truth itself [but to recognize that] deception and truth go hand in hand."[51] In addition, emphasizing "figural" rather than "textual space" (where the latter is the arena in which signifiers reign), Lyotard suggests that "the figural . . . will slow down the eye, and judgment, forcing the mind to take a position in front of the sensory [and] . . . leave behind communicable transparency."[52] As he heeds the dominance of the figural over the textual, Lyotard insists that it's an event's force (i.e., the way it is desire driven) rather than the signification(s) it acquires that must be appreciated. Rather than what is directly perceived or turned into a knowledge-related account, "The event [is a] disturbance [that] defies knowledge, either by challenging knowledge articulated in discourse or . . . by shattering the quasi-comprehension of the body itself, putting it out of tune. . . . The event cannot be situated elsewhere than in the space opened up by desire."[53]

That DeLillo appreciates the opening of that space is evident, for along with a narrative thread with a Kantian emphasis on various discursive encounters, as his characters attempt to move toward a shared sense of what has happened, is a parallel emphasis on how the bodies of his characters (especially Keith's) are "out of tune," causing them to rethink and recharge their intimacy and erotic networks after the event. His novel's narrative structure and motions effectively accord with the insight that "every discourse whether linguistic or plastic, has [both] textual and figurative aspects."[54] While DeLillo's sorting of his characters' attempts at shared sense-making take place in dialogues, like Lyotard he also turns to art to articulate the ways in which the event bypasses signification. To articulate that extra-discursive duration of the event, his *Falling Man* borrows its title (and thus foregrounds the event's most iconic moment) from the performance artist who continually replicates a man falling from the towers: "Suddenly and unannounced, the artist appears in public places transforming Manhattan into a stage for his performances. Secured only with an almost invisible harness, he jumps head on from buildings and remains, like the photo still in simulated free fall, evoking the memory of the photograph."[55]

However, the primary extra-discursive moments that DeLillo includes to bring back the deeper phenomenological force of the event summon the work of a painter. While Lyotard (influenced by Merleau-Ponty) turns for an example of the force of an event to Cézanne's Mount Sainte-Victoire canvases ("Cézanne," he writes, "desires nothing more than to have Mount Sainte-Victoire cease to be an object of sight to become an event in the visual field"), DeLillo turns to the still-life canvases of Giorgio Morandi (e.g., figure 5.2).[56]

Morandi first emerges in the novel when Lianne (the main protagonist, Keith's estranged wife) sees his work on a museum wall, two still lifes that "she loved most . . . groupings of bottles, jugs, biscuit tins" (12). Lianne is the character most attuned to the aesthetic comprehension that is central to the novel's approach to the event's sublimity. She is the one gathering information about the "falling man" (she does a Google search to gather information about his (David Janiak's) life and death, and she is the one most attentive to and affected by the Morandi paintings after spending a long time looking at them in an exhibition: "She was trying to absorb what she saw, take it home, wrap it around her, sleep in it. There was so much to see" (210).

Morandi, who shares the aesthetic space of the novel with the "falling man," shows up again, shortly after Lianne's exhibition excursion, on the wall in the apartment of Nina Bartos (Lianne's mother): two "beautiful still lifes," gifts from her lover, Martin (45). Later, as Martin looks at one of the paintings, he's carried into a different spatio-temporality, as one of the paintings evokes the uncanny, mimicking the post-9/11 disorientation that had ensued for him: "I'm looking at these objects, kitchen objects but

Figure 5.2 Giorgio Morandi, *Natura Morta* (Still Life)

removed from the kitchen. . . . I must be back in another time zone. I must
be more disoriented than usual. . . . Because I keep seeing the towers in this
still life" (49). Throughout the novel, the Morandi still lifes are irrepress-
ible. As chapter 7 opens, one of the still lifes, "two dark objects, the white
bottle, the huddled boxes," evokes the uncanny again, this time for Lianne,
who turned from looking at the painting and "saw the room itself as a still
life, briefly. Then human figures appear, Mother and lover" (111).

Later, Nina recalls the initial conversation about Morandi that she's had
with Martin as she showed him the still lifes in a book. Martin then traveled

to Bologna to see Morandi's work (in his house/studio), initially dismissing Morandi as a "minor artist" but ultimately able to "see form, color, depth, beauty" (145). And finally near the end of the novel, chapter 12 begins with Nina attending "a show of Morandi paintings in Chelsea, still lifes, six of them . . . and of course she went [despite] mixed feelings. . . . Because even this, bottles and jars, a vase, a glass, simple shapes in oil on canvas, pencil on paper, brought her back into the midst of it, thrust of arguments, perceptions, deadly politics." It is evident that Morandi serves DeLillo the way Cézanne serves Lyotard, as the power of the silent effectivity of the figural as it articulates what remains "unspeakable" about the 9/11 event. DeLillo makes that point explicitly with a conversation in which Nina is chiding Lianne about her husband's unexpected return home (after barely surviving the attack on the tower in which he worked), for having chosen a man who "doesn't paint, doesn't write poetry." She asks, would he "be allowed to behave unspeakably if he were 'a raging artist'?" (12). "Tell me this," Nina says, "What kind of painter is allowed to behave more unspeakably, figurative or abstract?" (13). One of W. J. T. Mitchell's insights is apropos here. What is "expressive" or "unspeakable" alerts us to those moments when "words fail" to "capture the density of signification in the image."[57]

That "density" has a duration that summons the novel's characters' pasts at the same time that their presents are vexed—for example, for "Rosellen S," an Alzheimer's patient who experiences "an elemental fear out of deepest childhood. She could not remember where she lived"; for her, "the world was receding, the simplest recognitions. . . . She began to lose her sense of clarity, of distinctiveness" (93–94). While the novel's American protagonists struggle to adapt to an altered world, the conspirators (and the U.S. agency officials) are reducing the world. In a conversation between DeLillo's versions of two of the conspirators, Hammad asks about those "others" who will die along with those on their suicidal mission (which they regard not as suicide but as destiny, as "finding the way already chosen for us" [175]). Amir responds, "There are no others. The others exist only to the degree that they fill the role we have designed for them. Those who will die have no claim to their lives outside the useful fact of their dying" (176). The "others" have been reduced to subjects whose existence is exhausted by their plan. Whatever thickness the others' lives involve is lost on those for whom their subjectivity is merely instrumental.

The official U.S. response to the "plot" is effectively a mirror image of the world- and subjectivity-reducing modes of the conspirators. It also reduces the world and its subjects. In terms of the "world," rather than recognizing the vast diversity of cultural, religious, and political system diversity throughout the world of Islam, Washington constructed (what I have elsewhere called) an "architecture of enmity" as it practiced its imaginary of the parts of the world it planned to denigrate and/or attack.[58] Thus, for example, Afghanistan is reduced to a venue of enemy-harboring terrorists, making it irrelevant that "thousands of Afghans, innocent Afghans were killed when we invaded the country," and Iran is merely a staging ground for Islamic militancy.[59] It takes little more than experiencing a critically reflective artistic production from within that denigrated world for one to enlarge it and thus render complex what has been reduced and simplified in U.S. policy discourses and practices. For example, in a film by the Iranian director Asghar Farhadi, *Beautiful City* (2004), a father, desiring revenge for his murdered daughter, refuses to issue the forgiveness that would spare the life of the perpetrator. When he confronts the imam in the mosque he attends, he asks, "Doesn't the Koran give me the right to revenge?" In response, the imam tells him that he will indeed find places in the Koran that give him that right, but he will also find *more* places in that sacred book that promote forgiveness.[60] As Farhadi's film suggests, parts of the world from which "terrorists" bent on deadly violence are recruited contain counter-forces that inhibit violence.

Although DeLillo's novel bypasses much of the complex world from which the 9/11 conspirators emerge, it nevertheless produces a deeper phenomenology of the conspiring subjects than is contained in the discourses in which they are reduced to the geopolitical antagonisms to which they are allegiant and/or to their deadly mission. DeLillo's strategy is to represent the complexities of their world *within* one of his characters. In contrast to the resolute Amir, Hammad struggles to overcome ambivalence toward their deadly mission and has to "fight against the need to be normal [and to] . . . struggle against himself first, and then against the injustice that haunted their lives" (83). Although DeLillo allocates some space to making sense of the way the conspirators must have struggled to stifle desires for interpersonal intimacy, most of his focus is on the complexities of the domestic lives in the venue of the attack and on the subsequent dynamic through which they (his American characters) seek to make the altered world intelligible—for example, as Martin puts it at one point, "this is not an attack on one country, one or two cities, we are all targets now" (47).

At the same time, they are trying to make that altered world congenial to a restoration of their interpersonal intimacies. And crucially, the characters' different modes of accommodation reflect their diverse approaches to sensing the world. Keith's tendency is to lower the volume on incoming sensations, reflected in, among other places, his affective connection with his deceased friend Rumsey: "The persistence of the man's needs had a kind of crippled appeal. . . . It opened Keith to dimmer things and odder angles, to something crouched and uncorrectable in people but also capable of stirring a warm feeling in him, a rare tinge of affinity" (123). In contrast, Lianne is hyperalert to the need to figure out what has become of her world. That she is very much tuned in (while Keith has hit the mute button) is reflected in how unable she is to tune out a neighbor's loudly blaring Middle Eastern music. And Martin becomes a conduit for some things DeLillo wants to say—for example, at a moment in which he acknowledges the variability of perceptual practices that the novel is articulating, he remarks to Nina, "'What you see is not what we see, what you see is distracted by memory, by being who you are, all this time, for all these years'" (114).

In short, DeLillo's main emphasis is on the dynamic through which his characters' initial experience of the sublime, a traumatic moment of apprehension, turns into a process of restoring (each according to his or her singularly shaped personal archives) an everyday comprehension in a world that requires radically altered premises. To manage a critical rendering of that dynamic, his novel proliferates layers of duration—historical and interpersonal—and intervenes in those durations with attentiveness to the nuances of lived temporal experience, one of which unfolds in the interval between the attacks on the first and second towers. Keith to his paramour, Florence: "By the time the second plane appears . . . we're all a little older and wiser" (135). That wisdom is not limited to the deadly event; it incorporates death in general, achieving its resonance through embodiment—for example, for Lianne, who cannot resist the videotape of the event: "Every time she saw a videotape of the planes she moved a finger toward the power button on the remote. Then she kept on watching. The second plane coming out of the ice blue sky, this was the footage that entered the body, that seemed to run beneath her skin, the fleeting sprint that carried lives and histories, theirs and hers, everyone's into some other distance, out beyond the towers. . . . They would all be dead, passengers and crew, and thousands in the towers dead, and she felt it in her body" (134).

DeLillo emphasizes the way the different bodies record the world around them as well as how they manage the temporal duration of their lives, from memory through attention to anticipation—for example, Lianne's late father, whose focus is primarily on the management of his personal biography. He commits suicide rather than "submit to the long course of senile dementia" (40). In contrast, the conspirators actively link their biographies to the way they want to intervene in the contemporary history of the world: "There was a feeling of lost history. They were too long in isolation. This is what they talked about, being crowded out by other cultures, other futures [specifically], the all-enfolding will of capital markets and foreign policies" (80). Thus, as the history of the event unfolds—from plotting to actualization to aftereffects (albeit not in a linear sequence)—the characters' management of their personal and interpersonal biographies proceeds. The novel's political reflection is therefore filtered through an array of experiential temporalities. Insofar as sense making is shared, it emerges through inconclusive encounters between individual wills, expressed through the linguistic and perceptual practices each has available. For example, Keith and Lianne's son Justin practice a recalcitrant temporality, "repositioning" events by locating them as future possibilities (102). "Kids," as Nina suggests, "have enormous gleaming worlds they don't share with their parents" (36). The suggestion is that unlike some who seek to reduce the world, "kids" tend to enlarge it because they have available an imagination that has yet to be stifled. DeLillo's has not been stifled. What he has available is the writer's imaginative craft. And in response to 9/11, "the writer," he says (to repeat his above remark) "wants to understand what this day has done to us."

There is another artist who also wants to "understand what this day has done to us," Art Spiegelman, who practices another kind of writing. Like DeLillo, he uses his craft (in his case the comic strip or graphic story, what he calls "commix") to make sense of the event. To review and reflect on his way of coming to terms with the 9/11 sublime, with a different artistic genre, I turn to his *In the Shadow of No Towers* (a "shadow" that has haunted New Yorkers especially but also all those for whom the image of the World Trade Center towers was iconic).[61]

Spiegelman's Approach to the Post-9/11 Trauma

Like DeLillo's novel, which combines text and imagery to complicate the problem of historical memory while highlighting perceptual difference within families (for example, that between Justin and his parents), Spiegelman's graphic stories have also manifested an image–language tension that articulates itself within families and renders ambiguous the hold of historical memory. As I put it elsewhere in a reading of his Holocaust stories, *Maus I* and *Maus II*, "The genre-assisted breakdown of narrative in *Maus* highlights what is at stake in a conflict among generations aiming to install an alternative politics of historical memory."[62] However, while DeLillo manages the tension through the different voices, the "heteroglossia" and perceptual styles of his characters, Spiegelman's genre strategy (what he calls "commix") is a method in which the visual part of the text can subvert the discursive part: "I prefer the word commix, to mix together, because to talk about comics is to talk about mixing together words and pictures to tell a story."[63] Moreover, the topology of a comic strip ambiguates narrative structure and breaks down imagery because it can be read horizontally, vertically, diagonally, or in separate iconic fragments.[64] "Unlike a more linear historical narrative, the commixture of words and images generates a triangulation of meaning—a kind of three-dimensional narrative—in the movement between words, images, and the reader's eye."[65]

To conceptualize the way Spiegelman's commix text disrupts narrativity, we can heed the way Claude Debussy's compositions disrupt the traditions of tonality. As I've put it elsewhere, "Claude Debussy's melodic ideas are not contingent on a rigid tonal structure . . . his compositions resist expectations of closure. Rejecting the authority of conventional tonality, his scales have no conventional points of beginning and ending. [He] . . . creates musical fragments, a multiplicity, a non-linear set of musical associations, and repetitive patterns that resist instead of moving toward a stable narrative or set of references."[66] Similarly, Spiegelman's fragment-composing, multidirectional form in his commix avoids a singular narrativity.

What prompts Spiegelman's text? His impressions begin with his sublime experience of the attack. Although he didn't witness the first plane hitting one of the towers, a short while afterward he saw in real time a vast and overwhelming scene while standing in a nearby street: "the looming north tower's glowing bones just before it vaporized."[67] That image has since haunted Spiegelman: "it still remains burned onto the inside of my eyelids several years later."[68] Seeing the event directly in real time instead of watching its many iterations on television contributed to the attack's sublimity and its subsequent traumatic aftereffects, because as the text in one of Spiegelman's panels (an image of Dan Rather reporting the event) suggests, the vast size of what is destroyed is imperceptible on the small screen: "Maybe it's just a question of scale. Even on a large TV, the towers aren't much bigger than, say, Dan Rather's head."[69] That observation fits well into Kant's speculation about aesthetic comprehension in reaction to sublime experiences. Noting that the subject must look for a unit of measure to try and comprehend the scope of the object or event, Kant suggests at one point that the unit can be found in the human body—for example, "A tree judged by the height of a man gives, at all events, a standard for a mountain."[70]

As for how the event's sublimity is articulated throughout Spiegelman's text, it's also a matter of scale. The very large format of *No Towers*, an "oversize picture-book" in which "the tower can frame the page, extending to the full twenty inches of the longer side of the opened book," repeats many times what Spiegelman saw as "awesome."[71] Katalin Orban suggests that "this treatment invokes the notion of the sublime even as it undermines its totality through the obsessive repetition of the traumatic image."[72] I would add that the undermining derives from Spiegelman's studied movement from apprehension to a traumatized comprehension (he refers to the book as his "slow motion diary") so that repetition is his way of indicating the space where the event sits.[73] What is that space? To repeat Lyotard's version of post-event trauma: "The event clears a vertiginous space and time, untethered from its context or perceptual environment, its discontinuity or hovering goes hand in hand with anxiety."[74] In accord with what Lyotard suggests about traumatic events, Spiegelman "locates the 'truth' of [this] sublime event" in *figural* space, which follows from the way the attack on the World Trade Center has been experienced; the destruction is "functionally visible."[75] What he undertakes is thus an aesthetic comprehension. However, inasmuch as his graphic account merges images of the event with his moment-to-moment personal experience of it, the process he evokes involves sense-memory, a dynamic that Jill Bennett captures; it's "a process experienced not as a remembering of the past but as a continuous negotiation of the present with indiscernible links to the past. The poetics of sense memory [which Spiegelman effects in his commix approach to the event] involve not so much *speaking of* but *speaking out of* a particular memory or experience . . . speaking from the body *sustaining sensation*."[76]

We must be clear, however, that aesthetic comprehension, which is constitutive of Kant's approach to the universalizing of the subjective knowledge process, is not part of the "synthesis of the imagination" required for coming to terms with experience. As Deleuze famously points out, "Aesthetic comprehension is not part of the synthesis"; rather, it is the basis for the synthesis, which, as Deleuze adds, "is fundamentally fragile, because the aesthetic comprehension of the unit of measure . . . can at each instant be overwhelmed."[77] It is overwhelmed, according to Deleuze, because as Kant confronted the problem of the synthesis in his Third Critique (which he initially undertook in the First Critique) he had to address the second aspect of estimating the scope of an experience. In addition to the question of the unit of measure was the issue of how to separate out the parts of experience to be measured. The vexing question that Kant never resolved is what counts as a part. The subject's imagination, involved in the process of coming to terms with the experience, requires, as Deleuze puts it, the "gathering of parts into a whole."[78] And crucially, the world is not complicit in supplying either the unit of measure or the boundaries that separate one part of an experience from another. Recognizing the radical contingency of how experience is partitioned locates us in Spiegelman's dilemma. Given the difficulty of creating coherence in reaction to the 9/11 sublime, he found himself with the task (in his words) of "sorting out the fragments."[79] That "sorting" is constitutive of the structure of his commix approach to the event, because a commix is a concatenation of fragments for which there is no singular synthesis. Christina Meyer summarizes the implications for the reader: "Spiegelman does not create *one* single truth, *one* single narrative about the events; nor does he mimetically represent what happened in 2001. Rather, Spiegelman offers a distinctively subjectivized and thus limited collection of impressions of the terrorist attacks—fragments—and the reader has to look through the equivalent of a narrative periscope . . . there is not one single story."[80]

Nevertheless, what *No Towers* does provide is a political challenge to the dominant narratives that the mainstream media and U.S. government were promoting. As Spiegelman states, he strove to maintain control over what he actually saw from "the media images that threatened to engulf" what he had seen.[81] He had to "distil and depict his own memories of the event and his government's unfolding response to it."[82] As a juxtaposition with the Bush administration's appropriation of the event, *No Towers*'s challenge works micropolitically by withdrawing from the larger geopolitical model that was officially imposed to a "near view" within which the reader is invited "to face the tableau with which Spiegelman's controlled chaos renders a sublime experience of the event."[83]

How then is *No Towers* organized? One version has it concisely: "Chaotic and dense in appearance these pages are intended to convey 'that all-at-onceness' that was the overwhelming feeling of September 11th. Through the use of a 'vivid kind of collaging,' [Spiegelman] sets four or five narratives into motion on a single page that simultaneously compete for the viewer's attention . . . what order should we read these sequences? . . . what are the spatial and temporal relations between different sections of the page?"[84] For example, on the book's first page (figure 5.3), the image fragments and sequences competing for the reader's attention include the many repetitions of the north tower disintegrating (which Spiegelman designates as his most sublime image), a large circle with frightened people running because they expect "that other shoe to drop" (a large shoe is suspended overhead), Dan Rather's head, and three separate cartoon strips, one at the top showing a family freaking out at what they see on television, and two strips below the title ("In the Shadow of No Towers") with characters gleaned from old comics but with altered scenarios involving shoe-dropping episodes. With all the images is a variety of spoken text, most of which convey Spiegelman's reactions to the images.

To locate the temporality of Spiegelman's commix construction of the event, we should recall that the uncanny, as Freud articulates it, involves a feeling in which something that has been familiar and has been domesticated by the subject (i.e., is located in a comfortable place) becomes strange and terrorizing. Articulating the Burkean notion of the terrorizing effect of the sublime with the Freudian uncanny, Anthony Vidler applies that feeling to architecture. He recounts instances in which an aesthetic vision of a domesticated place (specifically a building) emerges in an anxiety-producing disordered reality because the building contains a doubleness: it contains something familiar and something strange. The uncanny, Vidler suggests, is "aesthetically an outgrowth of the Burkean sublime. A domesticated version of absolute terror," which he applies to architectural spaces.[85] His emphasis is on designs in which a building's lighted areas are juxtaposed to darkened ones, even dungeon-like spaces in which the gaze cannot penetrate (recalling that for Burke the terror of the sublime is figured in terms of darkness)—for example, the designs of Étienne-Louis Boullée, whose designs incorporate "absolute light" and "absolute darkness," a terror-inducing juxtaposition.[86]

The building metaphor of the uncanny is especially apropos for Spiegelman's commix rendering of the event because he likens the structure of his commix to the windows of a building. However, Spiegelman provides a different version of an architectural uncanny. The terror of the sublime in this case is not a function of lightness versus darkness; it involves instead a

Figure 5.3 Page from Spiegelman's *No Towers*

shift in appearance. What was once an enduring solid and familiar presence has suddenly disintegrated before one's very eyes. The resulting void in what is both a material and symbolic order induces the terror that ensues when something whose familiar presence has become a sudden absence. That absence (implied in the title), along with a disturbing image, the falling bodies, which haunt Spiegelman although he did not see them in real time, constitutes what is endlessly repeated in Spiegelman's imagination. Unable to finish the story of the event by ending it in a comprehension-creating interpretation, Spiegelman supplies an enigmatic ending to his *No Towers* commix. The disintegrating towers, which in the last three panels begin to fade away, still "have come to loom larger than life . . . but they seem to get smaller every day . . . happy anniversary" (Spiegelman's captions in the last three panels).

Ultimately for Spiegelman, the event is an "ahistorical sublime" in that the initial apprehension endures; consummating comprehension is endlessly deferred, for Spiegelman provides repetition instead of consummation.[87] Oban has it right: "This treatment invokes the notion of the sublime even as it undermines its totality through the obsessive repetition of the traumatic image."[88] The event remains a difficult-to-conceive absence that cannot be definitively consummated as a single story. It is therefore appropriate that it is rendered in Spiegelman's commix as a chaotic pattern of static images, which represent the way the event has insinuated itself into his imagination. It's an imagination whose material basis is inscribed in Spiegelman's vocation as a graphic artist, hence "The Comic Supplement" at the end of *No Towers* in which a history of cartoon characters experience catastrophes and—ultimately in the last section—appear among New York's tall buildings, feeling lost.

Although Spiegelman's commix approach to the event is a concatenation of static images, his approach to the event's sublimity has a temporality nevertheless. "Static images," Oban points out, can express temporal processes in two ways: "as time sedimented in the making of the image . . . or by juxtaposition, often according to cultural convention of the visual equivalents of *before* and *after*. The logic of juxtaposition allows for the suturing of temporally discontinuous, even wildly discontinuous, elements without necessarily giving rise to a process-type connection between them."[89] Of course, cinema has an advantage in its capacity for articulating the temporality of events, using long takes and depth-of-focus shots to convey sedimented time and editing to manage what Deleuze refers to as direct time images—those constructed through editing as opposed to those involving the indirect temporality achieved when time is a function of the camera following action.⁹⁰ Therefore, to think the event through cinema, I turn to a textual approach, which anticipates the 9/11 event, Johan Grimonprez's film, *Dial H-I-S-T-O-R-Y*, a film (or more properly a video assemblage) about the history of airplane hijackings as portrayed by television media, interspersed with voice-over passages from DeLillo's novels, *White Noise* and *Mao II*, more pervasively the latter in which (as I note above) the writer laments the terrorists' hijacking of his cultural role as an arbiter of collective consciousness. Well before 9/11, cinematic and televisual media had prepared the public for comprehending the event. The immediacy of the catastrophe was effectively premediated by feature films about global terrorism and by television coverage of plane hijackings. "The public [was made somewhat] ready for the future [9/11 catastrophe] not as it emerge[d] immediately into the present but before it happene[d]."⁹¹ However, rather than reinforcing and anticipating the way the media will have narrativized the 9/11 events, Grimonprez's video contests and confounds its way of summoning receptive comprehension.

Dial H-I-S-T-O-R-Y

Although the ostensible object of his video is plane hijacking, Grimonprez's *Dial* is more about the way media, especially television, have appropriated/invented the meaning of plane hijacking. As Grimonprez remarks, "every technology invents its own catastrophe. TV technology has reinvented a way to look at the world and think about death."⁹² While DeLillo constructs himself as a writer competing with terrorists for an effect on public consciousness, Grimonprez is a filmmaker contending with television media. He sees the television medium as the main protagonist that hijacks the catastrophic sublime. Television journalism commands the gap between the initial apprehension that occurs when a plane is hijacked and the dominant comprehension that ensues. To challenge TV journalism's commanding position, he brings journalists into the film to demonstrate how what they do is turn a sublime event into a commodity for media consumption. He then decenters their role. To do so, like Spiegelman, he constructs a mixed-media narrative to oppose the way mainstream television media narrativize events. His hybrid cinematic text bears comparison with the genre-bending textual practice in the video film work of Péter Forgács, who supplies a collage of decades of footage from Hungarian and Dutch home movies, compiled and rearticulated with segments of news reports of historical events, music, and occasional voice-overs to renarrativize historical moments—in his case the "periods of extraordinary upheaval and cultural loss—World official history . . . [in order to have] us understand that time does not unfold through a [single] collective narrative."[93]

Similarly, Grimoprez rearticulates a history of plane hijackings, with that variety of archived film segments—in his case nonchronologically arranged television coverage of plane hijackings between 1931 and 1996, comprised of footage from CNN and ABC news archives, which he then intersperses with images from cartoons, advertisements, propaganda and Hollywood films, segments from didactic videos (which are reminiscent of the documentary film work of Harun Farocki) and his own home movies. While Spiegelman's commix is a concatenation of images arranged in a pattern that affords multiple ways of interconnecting the segments to challenge an attempt at a single narration of the event, Grimonprez's approach is more akin to the remixing of DJs working with turntables. Their cutting practices mix together disparate musical segments to rearticulate music history by reordering the prominence of alternative musical moments. Remixing challenges the control over the communication of sound by a small group of entrepreneurs who have dominated musical commerce. In the form understood as "regenerative remix," remixing disrupts traditional musical temporality, reordering the salience of historically developed musical moments. Instead of pandering to consumption, the regenerative impulse seeks with a practice of "cut/copy and paste" to elevate and add nuance to cultural forms that have been commoditized.[94] That remix effect as operated in literary responses to the 9/11 event—for example, in the edited collection *In the Shadow of the Towers*, in which twenty stories remix history to demonstrate the contingency of events—showing that "momentous events [that] shape our lives . . . could easily have been otherwise."[95]

Grimonprez's film responds to a different critical issue. He surveys and remixes the contexts of plane hijackings because from his point of view, "The plane is a metaphor for history. It is transgressive, always on the move between several countries, between several homes."[96] The artistic focus on the historical significance of the plane replaces the earlier historical focus on the train, which artists (noted in chapter 4) placed in that same, future-welcoming temporal role: the *train* as a metaphor for history. However, Grimonprez's main concern is not simply the plane's historical role as articulated in the genealogy of hijacking episodes; he is concerned rather with a different aspect of the events. His film video is primarily about the hijacking of the hijacking, i.e., about the media's capture of the events. Thus while DeLillo constructs a contention between the terrorist and the writer (both his character Bill Gray in *Mao II* and himself in his *Harper's* essay), Grimonprez's battle, as I have suggested, is between the filmmaker and television journalism. It is a contention over a history of a particular manifestation of a terror sublime, a cinematic challenge that "counter-actualizes" the way television journalism invents the meaning of plane hijacking.

The cinematic renarrativization that Grimonprez enacts comports with Deleuze's account of the way counter-actualization works. The film mimics the events, continually repeating them in different formats, making Grimonprez a "mime of what *effectively* occurs [in order, as Deleuze suggests] to double the actualization with a counter-actualization . . . to give the truth of the event the only chance of not being confused with its inevitable actualization."[97] Unlike the Kantian model in which the initial awe occasioned by an event yields understanding, as reason takes over from a disrupted imagination (moving within consciousness from apprehension to comprehension), Grimonprez creates a Deleuzian reaction in which one shows how an artistic mediation rather than a purely cognitive one can move from what is virtual in an event to one among alternative actualizations. In so doing (in the case of plane hijackings), he pluralizes what television journalism fixes as *the* event, opening it to continual rethinking.

What determines the way television closes in on and remediates an event? Television journalism's approach to closing events operates within a *dispositif* (an apparatus that includes desk editors, reporters, photographers, and so on) comprised of structured assignments, which are oriented toward commercial consumption. As a voice-over in the film says, "Nothing happens until it is consumed." What is produced is "news" that results from a process of time-pressured production and circulation, and what emerges therefore is "by no means the property of the event" but is a function of how news sources are organizationally managed to compete in a situation of a need for rapid production and circulation in order to hold its viewers.[98] In contrast, Grimonprez's splicing and zapping, which creates repeated moments within continually altered contexts, is organized to open the event to critical political reflection. His perspective is therefore attuned to a Deleuzian version of the sublime in which critique is concerned not with justification (as it is for Kant) but with providing the possibility of a different future, which involves "a different . . . sensibility."[99] To open the perspective of the viewer to that difference, Grimonprez curates a different way of having history while imposing a curatorial task on the viewer with a film that mimics the zapping practices of viewers with remotes in their hands. As a result, his film video conforms to the way television technology has (in his words) "replaced our conventional models of perception and experience."[100] The viewers are left to try to reorganize what Grimonprez's zapping disorganizes, as he throws back at them a work of rapid editing that mimics and thus contends with their editing/zapping role. However, at the same time, by emphasizing the way television journalism appropriates each hijacking event (for example, in scenes that cut from the footage of the event to swarms of television journalists and cameramen pursuing the hijackers), the film is a counter-actualization of definitive modes of the narrativized comprehension that television creates rather than merely an alternative object of commercial consumption meant to close the process of coming to terms with the event. In light of the subsequent catastrophic hijacking event ending in the attack on the Twin Towers of the World Trade Center, the film is a prescient "premeditation" that (like DeLillo's *Mao II*) prepares the way for modes of comprehension that challenge those of both official agencies and television (where television is the most influential medium through which the event's significance has been inscribed, in terms of both images and commentary). Grimonprez competes with the media within his film. For example, in his footage of the Lod Airport massacre in Jerusalem, 1972, we see the perpetrator, Kozo Okamoto, on trial in Tel Aviv, with media shots of his courtroom persona, wearing headphones and in handcuffs while guards manage his movements with restraining equipment—the typical media approach to the event, focusing on the implements of capture and control framed within the scene of the trial. What Grimonprez adds are Okamoto's words, which carry the event beyond the claustrophobic courtroom protocols; onscreen is his metaphorical rendering of his act in which he sees himself bound to his victims—a poesis of terrorism: "We Red Army soldiers wanted to become stars of Orion. It calms my heart to think that all the people we killed will be stars in the sky. As the revolution goes on how the stars will multiply."

Ultimately, Grimonprez's film video is shaped by a politically nuanced "chronotope," M. M. Bakhtin's term for the way literary genres articulate temporality.[101] Suggesting that "history is always happening between places. . . . It is only afterwards that the structures of power consolidate it into a text, an image, a TV series, a narrative," Grimonprez puts a particular history of terrorism—plane hijacking—on the move again in order to allow for different readings and show that no one version can ultimately capture an event. "History," he states, "is read differently by different people."[102] The temporality of Grimonprez's video reenactments, with their incessant interruptions that create thinking spaces, presents viewers with a situation in which what is available to cognition is "continually breached," forcing them to think, because the signposts that encourage familiar forms of recognition are destabilized.[103]

While films and literature will doubtless continue to reflect on the 9/11 event, the primary medium with which the 9/11 attack on the Twin Towers of the World Trade Center will be continuously recalled is architecture. Architecture was the terrorists' target, and architecture—as actualized in the National September 11 Memorial and Museum—constitutes the institutionalized remembrance of the attack. It is the medium with which comprehension of the event will be enjoined for generations. Although in comparison with the more dynamic art of moving images, architecture manifests a material fixity, it nevertheless articulates a temporality that allows for continual rethinking. To conclude this chapter, I reflect on the way the architectural response to 9/11 will continually insert itself in the gap between the initial apprehension of the event and its ongoing comprehension.

Architecture: Violence, Sublimity, Temporality

Two forms of violence met when the planes crashed into the Twin Towers; one was sudden and one was slow. The latter "slow violence" was a violence of erasure:

> Twelve blocks of downtown Manhattan were obliterated to provide the sixteen-acre site for the series of buildings that constituted the World Trade Center . . . the most extensive erasure in the site's volatile human history. . . . It took out an area known as the Syrian Quarter. [It was] a diverse Middle Eastern neighborhood, including Arabic people from Egypt, Iraq, Lebanon, Palestine, and elsewhere . . . an internationally known thriving bazaar.[104]

As the architect Bernard Tschumi insists, "There is no architecture without action, no architecture without events, no architecture without program. By extension, there is no architecture without violence." With respect to the latter remark, Tschumi refers to that violence as a function of architecture's intervention in spatio-temporality: "Architecture's violence is fundamental and unavoidable, for architecture is linked to events in the same way that the guard is linked to the prisoner, the police to the criminal, the doctor to the patient, order to chaos. . . . Actions qualify spaces as much as spaces qualify actions."[105] Of course, the attack on the World Trade Center was far more violent, as it caused the deaths of more than three thousand innocent victims, a result that continues to weigh heavily on America's understanding of its vulnerability and has, as a result of the "war on terror" that followed, created other vulnerabilities (of thousands of innocents as well as hostile forces), as America's reaction to the event was to go to war on (some of) the states that were said to harbor the conspirators behind the attack.

Here my concern is with the way the architecture of aftermath, which effaces architecture's prior effects (violent and otherwise), participates in the public negotiation of the meaning and implications of the 9/11 terrorist attack. To appreciate such a role for architecture, we need to distinguish the awe-inspiring and perspective-subjugating effects of architectural monumentalism with forms of architectural design that enfranchise a thinking/perceiving subject. Irwin Panofsky has captured that distinction in his comparison of Gothic and Romanesque cathedral designs. Referring to the "old mental habit" (in which "faith is insulated from reason by an impenetrable barrier") built into the Romanesque cathedral, he refers to the way the design "conveys the impression of a space determinate and impenetrable, whether we find ourselves inside or outside of the edifice."[106] In contrast with the Romanesque cathedral's materialization of an enigmatic objectness, the Gothic cathedral materializes an "aesthetic [i.e., Kantian] subjectivism," as the architectural details liberate thinking subjects because the architectural details of the Gothic cathedral accommodate forms of vision that accord with the tenets of scholastic thought.[107]

The city of Berlin provides the appropriate historical setting for a more contemporary contrast, which emerges when we examine the difference between the monumentalism of the designs of Hitler's architect, Albert Speer, and the postwar architecture of the "New Berlin." As Andreas Huyssen puts it, Berlin's postwar architecture is self-consciously "anti-monumental"—exemplified by Norman Forster's new Reichstag, which is designed to provide visibility and ease of access (with its glass dome and spiraling ramps that make the inside accessible) in contradistinction to Speer's architectural sublime, a monumentalism whose opacity (dauntingly impenetrable façades) reflected an unaccountable authority structure.[108] The design impetus in the buildings comprising "the New Berlin" was reanimated by an architectural event that alerted Berliners to the relationship between its rebuilt monuments and the need to think about its continually renegotiated community of sense, Christo's 1995 wrapping of the Reichstag. In Huyssen's words, that event "dissolved [the Reichstag's] spatial monumentality . . . and accentuated [its historical impression with] a lightness of being that was a stark contrast with the visual memory of the heavy-set, now veiled architecture."[109] That veiling, he adds, "muted the voice of politics as usual [and] . . . opened a space for reflection and contemplation as well as for memory . . . a genuinely popular event . . . celebrating a symbol of German democracy in all its fragility and transitoriness."[110]

As an architecture of aftermath, the architecture of the New Berlin features a series of elaborate materialized thought gestures aimed at filling symbolic and material voids—Berlin's "ruptured history . . . as symbolic space of the East-West confrontation" and subsequently as a city that had to fill in the voids owed to the catastrophic events of the hot and cold wars (the destruction of much of the city from Allied bombing at the end of World War II, and the end of the cold war, which featured the tearing down of the Berlin Wall).[111] That filling is constituted through the way a comprehension of the past and hopes for a different future are materialized in the city's buildings, which are aimed at inventing a new national community of sense, a collective allegiance to a democratic future.

Similarly, another "ruptured history," an event involving a catastrophic loss of life and a resulting symbolic and material void in New York, the legacies of the destruction of the World Trade Center, will be perpetually (re)negotiated through the way the post-event architecture has filled the void at ground zero. Inspired by the design orientation of Daniel Libeskind, whose original vision for the architecture of the 9/11 memorial was to resist narrative closure (as is the case with his design of the Jewish Museum in Berlin), the design for the new World Trade Center is aimed at filling the void not only by "knitting the memorial site back into the fabric of the city [while also] marking with two large voids the enormous absence [some] continue to feel"[112] but also by creating positive space—for example, "an interpretive center, where artifacts of 9/11 would return to the World Trade Center site and be placed alongside narrative historical exhibits" (as indeed they have been in the new memorial museum).[113] Moreover, in contrast with the rapid and noisy commercial activities within and outside the new

World Trade Center, the section with the memorial pools has waterfalls with a muted sound designed to "provide tranquility . . . and add to the feeling of a contemplative space distinct from the bustle of lower Manhattan," a "heterotopia" or other space that (in Foucault's terms) is "incompatible" and functions as "a space of compensation" for those concerned with a memorial rather than a commercial activity.[114] By constructing a place for solitude, an "aesthetic place," the memorial architecture of the new World Trade Center will be fulfilling what Jacques Rancière refers to as the "task for engaged art, . . . a form of art that tries to create new forms of social bonds," which is characteristic of art involved in "intervention."[115] Ultimately, the architecture of the World Trade Center memorial will bring together two communities of sense: "the 'community of sense' constituting the work [and] the community that is supposed to result from it."[116] Heeding the art–"community of sense" relationship that Rancière helps us recognize, I turn in a brief afterword to a reflection on that relationship, along with an emphasis on how duration has invested the critical work that is central to an appreciation of the book's approach to the "political sublime."

AFTERWORD   IT'S ALL ABOUT DURATION

In the introduction I referred approvingly to Jacques Rancière's perspective that politics is sublime, sublime in the sense that politics is an event based on "an aesthetic break." The political sublime as I have been conceiving it emerges from events and experiences that disrupt usual sense-making practices and summon, shape, and render visible and voluble oppositional communities of sense. They provoke aesthetic breaks that intervene in duration and as a consequence precipitate another duration, a negotiation process in which new interactions and alternative sense-making possibilities emerge. In this afterword I want to pursue the notion of the aesthetic break as a disruption and initiator of duration, because duration resonates importantly throughout my investigations of the political sublime. Events don't happen to quiescent subjects. After Bergson, we must recognize that *subjects* are durations upon which external durations impact. The apprehension of events is suffused with recollection; "the body *is* something other than a mathematical point . . . it is the recollections of memory that link . . . instants to each other and interpolate the past in the present. . . . It is therefore memory that makes the body something other than instantaneous and gives it a duration in time."[1] Thus, for example, conceiving bodies as durations, DeLillo's *Falling Man* (treated in chapters 1 and 5) has characters bring different pasts to their engagements with the 9/11 event. And importantly, my reading of his text and the others I engage throughout this investigation brings a duration to the readings, a recollection of the historical trajectory of critical theoretical frames, which I apply to intervene in the texts on which I work.

Recalling my suggestion that for purposes of critical analysis a "text" (following Roland Barthes) is a "methodological field" rather than a mere literary object, I want to illustrate the disruption and subsequent remediation of duration one's critical engagement with a text involves by rehearsing briefly two readings of Gus Van Sant's 1998 remake of Alfred Hitchcock's 1960 classic film, *Psycho*.[2] The first reading is William Rothman's critique of the film in which he judges Van Sant's remake with resort to its content. Among his complaints are that the actor "Vince Vaughan pales in comparison to Anthony Perkin's 'boy next door quality'" and that "'the dialogue doesn't adhere to the original screenplay at several quintessential moments.'"[3] The second reading is Chelsey Crawford's response to Rothman (reviewed briefly in chapter 1) in which she invokes Mikhail Iampolski's concept of cinematic quotation: "'The quote is a fragment of the text that violates its linear development and derives the motivation that integrates it into the text from outside the text itself'" and adds, "The quotation interrupts the linearity of the text because it fractures the mind of the viewer—causing her or him to enact an alternate, yet simultaneous, mode of thought."[4]

Crawford's intervention, in which she remediates the film by treating the cinematic text as a methodological field rather than as a simple container of content, correlates well with several aspects of my investigations in the preceding chapters. Attributing a cinematic sublime to Van Sant's remake, she gives that sublime the kind of critical duration I have emphasized; she sees the initial imagination-challenging experience of the film as an occasion for subsequent creative thinking, liberated by a disruption of the original narrative sequences. To appreciate Crawford's emphasis on the critical mind-fracturing shift of the viewer's anticipation of the narrative sequence in Van Sant's *Psycho*, we have to reprise the way the fracture is effected in Hitchcock's original version, which was an "aesthetic break" in film history.

"The moment of *Psycho*" is David Thomson's expression for Hitchcock's cinematic event, which shocked film audiences with its murder scene, an arbitrary and very graphic slaying of the victim, Marion Crane (Janet Leigh), by a psychotic killer, Norman Bates (Anthony Perkins). As Thomson describes the scene, it comes across as terrifyingly sublime, as a challenge to the imagination in which (as is typical of Hitchcock) "the imaginary triumphs over the actual":

The audience is left to make sense of the gap between the ordinary and the absurd (the life on the road versus life in the Bates house). There's no doubt about the cinematic quality of the shower sequence. This is an old-fashioned montage, an impression of a lethal attack to which has been added the utmost expressiveness of Herrmann's music and the soundtrack in which it is embedded. The total effect is delirium. . . . The question that remains [as the audience seeks comprehension] is not just who has killed Marion Crane, but what tempest has felt bound to overtake the film?[5]

Thomson goes on to point out that the "measure of the breakthrough that had occurred . . . is in the bloodletting, sadism, and slaughter that are now taken for granted,"[6] evident in *Psycho*'s cinematic legacy, which is articulated in such films as Roman Polanski's *Repulsion* (1965), "a clever replay of the lovely blonde under duress,"[7] and David Lynch's *Blue Velvet*, in which the audience is invited into "the soaring inwardness of a dream," after "a boy finds an ear and wonders where the rest of the body is [and comes to] realize that evil lurks in his hometown."[8]

Throughout his film corpus Hitchcock delivers imagination-challenging moments with shocking sequences. For example (as I note in chapter 3), there are scenes in which his camera begins by surveying a seemingly innocent landscape, which suddenly becomes perverse. Exemplary is the sudden disturbance of a pastoral setting in his *North by Northwest* (1959), when what was a distant small plane, seeming to be crop dusting, suddenly fills the frame and attacks the protagonist, Roger Thornhill (Cary Grant). Through the innovative development of a new kind of cinematic shock effect, the temporal consequence of the Hitchcock moment has been its effect on a subsequent cinematic history. Since Hitchcock, a cinematic genre has developed to reinforce and popularize a terror-inducing Gothic uncanny, opening thinking to recognition of the dark underside of seemingly benign settings in diverse parts of the lifeworld.[9] After Hitchcock everyday life's façade of innocence has become suspect. The more recent event, featured in chapter 5, has had a similar durational impact. After 9/11 a Hitchcockian gothic uncanny prevails. As Mike Davis puts it, the consequence of the 9/11 event is "a permanent foreboding about urban space as potential Ground Zero."[10]

I want to add, finally, that in Crawford's reading of Van Sant's remake of Hitchcock's *Psycho*, a different kind of duration is enjoined. Rather than creating the kind of duration associated with the uncanny, the film's imagination-challenging impact (identified in Iampolski's perspective on cinematic quotation that she uses) is attributable to the critical effects of repetition.[11] Repetition, which mimics an event within an altered moment, reveals the contingencies of experience and makes possible critical thinking as opposed to mere "recognition." Repetition, in the form of new temporal rhythms, imperils "opinion . . . a thought that is closely molded on the form of recognition [a form of thought mired in] orthodoxy."[12]

In order to move beyond the institutionalized forms of opinion that have owned historical events, I have enlisted post-Kantian versions of sublime experiences that defer the movement from initial apprehension to comprehension and look to the way aesthetic practices mediate what can or will be comprehended. Accordingly, to exemplify and investigate those deferrals, I have turned to texts (mainly artistic ones) that reengage both sudden and long-term catastrophic events in order to resist event-closing orthodoxies—that open them to a political negotiation about how they can be (re)thought. Moreover and crucially, the genres (the form and dynamics of their compositions) to which I have turned challenge the Kantian assumption that sublime experience will ultimately validate the existence of a universal *sensus communis*. They introduce dissonance and disjuncture that break down walls. They lay siege to the institutionalized forms of quiescence and passivity that turn events into impregnable monuments. Critical political thinking comes about through an intervention in duration, a rethinking of events that reveal, redistribute, and thus create the conditions of possibility for the divided modes of political comprehension that emerge from oppositional communities of sense.

INTRODUCTION

1 Shapiro, "The Sublime Today," 699.

2 See Shapiro, *Politics and Time*.

3 Pease, "Sublime Politics," 275.

4 Pease, "Sublime Politics," 276.

5 See, for example, Panagia, *The Poetics of Political Thinking* and *The Political Life of Sensation*.

6 For a review of alternative politics of aesthetics that compares the three thinkers, see Zepke, "Contemporary Art—Beautiful or Sublime?"

7 The phrase "politics *is* sublime" is the title of an analysis of the ways a Kant-influenced politics of aesthetics emerges in the thinking of Hannah Arendt and Jacques Rancière; emphasis added. See Dikeç, "Politics Is Sublime." The term "aesthetic break" is from Rancière, "Aesthetic Separation, Aesthetic Community."

8 Rancière, "The Thinking of Dissensus," 6.

9 See Deleuze, "The Method of Dramatization."

10 *Longinus.*

11 Hertz, "A Reading of Longinus," 1–2.

12 Hertz, "A Reading of Longinus," 8.

13 Benjamin, *The Arcades Project*, 460.

14 Barthes, "From Work to Text," 156–157.

15 Barthes, "From Work to Text," 157.

16 Barthes, "From Work to Text," 158.

17 Mowitt, *Text.*

18 Mowitt, *Text*, 44, 45.

19 Mowitt, *Text*, 46.

20 Rancière, "Thinking between Disciplines," 7.

21 Rancière, "Thinking between Disciplines," 9.

22 Christine Battersby draws similar inspiration from Kant's ambivalence, finding it "politically useful" because of how it opens a way to "rethink the subject in modernity and postmodernity": Battersby, *The Sublime, Terror, and Human Difference*, 193.

23 Mowitt, *Text*, 84.

24 On the "interference" that philosophy enacts in artistic texts, applied by Deleuze to cinema, see Deleuze, *Cinema 2*, 280. The concept is applied to literature in Casarino, *Modernity at Sea*.

25 Elsewhere I have theorized aesthetics subjects as characters (primarily those in artistic texts) who "are invented less to reveal their psychic or attitudinal orientations than to reveal the forces at work in the spaces within which they move and to display the multiplicity of subject positions historically created within those spaces": Shapiro, *The Time of the City*, 7, or as characters "whose movements and actions (both purposive and non purposive) map and often alter experiential, politically relevant terrains": Shapiro, *Studies in Trans-Disciplinary Method*, ix.

One. Toward a Political Sublime

1 Kant, *The Critique of Judgement*, 97.

2 Kant, *The Critique of Judgement*, 106, 99.

3 Kant, *The Critique of Judgement*, 101.

4 The quotation is from Zepke, "Contemporary Art—Beautiful or Sublime?," 14.

5 Kant, *The Critique of Judgement*, 115.

6 Kant, *The Critique of Judgement*, 120.

7 Lindner, "The Passagen-Werk, the Berlin Kindheit, and the Archaeology of the 'Recent Past,'" 26.

8 Deleuze and Guattari, *A Thousand Plateaus*, 179.

9 Lacan, "On a Question Preliminary to Any Possible Treatment of Psychosis," 217.

10 Lacan, "On a Question Preliminary to Any Possible Treatment of Psychosis," 217.

11 Lacan, "Desire and the Interpretation of Desire in *Hamlet*," 12.

12 Lacan, "On a Question Preliminary to Any Possible Treatment of Psychosis," 219.

13 Wolff, "Winter Light."

14 Foucault, "The Father's No," 82.

15 The quotation is from Stone, "Split Subjects, Not Atoms," 189.

16 Stone, "Split Subjects, Not Atoms," 179.

17 Stone, "Split Subjects, Not Atoms," 186.

18 The quotations are from *Longinus on the Sublime*, 8–9.

19 *Longinus on the Sublime*, 42.

20 *Longinus on the Sublime*, 104–105.

21 Sartre, *The Family Idiot*, 127.

22 Sartre, *The Family Idiot*, 128.

23 Shaw, *The Sublime*, 2.

24 The quoted expression of Kant's is taken from Klein, "Kant's Sunshine," 28.

25 *Longinus on the Sublime*, 46.

26 *Longinus on the Sublime*, 75.

27 Deleuze and Guattari, *What Is Philosophy?*, 28.

28 *Longinus on the Sublime*, 64–65.

29   Deleuze and Guattari, *What Is Philosophy?*, 192.

30   The overall quotation is from Shaw, *The Sublime*, while the inner quotation is from Milbank, "Sublimity," 212.

31   Didi-Huberman, "The Art of Not Describing," 135.

32   Crawford, "The Permeable Self," 107–108.

33   See Heidegger, *What Is a Thing?*

34   Milbank, "Sublimity," 212.

35   Kant, *The Critique of Judgement*, 91.

36   Kant, *The Critique of Judgement*, 106.

37   Kant, *The Critique of Judgement*, 115.

38   Deleuze, "The Idea of Genesis in Kant's Esthetics," 70.

39   Kant, *The Critique of Judgement*, 115.

40   Shapiro, "The Sublime Today," 666.

41   Burke, *A Philosophical Inquiry into the Origin of Our Ideas of the Sublime*, 33.

42   The quotations are from Paul Guyer's introduction to Burke, *A Philosophical Inquiry into the Origin of Our Ideas of the Sublime*, 7.

43   Burke, *A Philosophical Inquiry into the Origin of Our Ideas of the Sublime*, 109.

44   See section 14, on "The Effects of Sympathy in the Distresses of Others," in Burke, *A Philosophical Inquiry into the Origin of Our Ideas of the Sublime*.

45   The quotation is from Shapiro, "From the Sublime to the Political," 219.

46   Shapiro, "From the Sublime to the Political," 219.

47   The quotation is from Hinnant, "Schiller and the Political Sublime," 121.

48   Schiller, "Of the Sublime," 90–91.

49   Schiller, "Of the Sublime," 91.

50   Schiller, "On the Sublime (1801)."

51   Schiller, "On the Sublime (1801)."

52   White, "The Politics of Historical Interpretation," 68–69; "mastery" quotation from Hinnant, "Schiller and the Political Sublime," 133.

53   Schiller, "On the Sublime (1801)."

54   Foucault, "Nietzsche, Genealogy, History," 153.

55   The quotations belong to Shaviro, "The 'Wrenching Duality' of Aesthetics," 4. See Deleuze on Leibnitz for the articulation of that position: Deleuze, *The Fold*.

56   See Hegel, *Lectures on Aesthetics Part II*, www.marxists.org/reference/archive/hegel/works/ae/ch02.htm. For a good explication of Hegel on the sublime, see Pillow, *Sublime Understanding*, 197–230.

57   Rancière, "The Method of Equality," 278.

58   Deleuze, *Kant's Critical Philosophy*, 17.

59   Lyotard, "After the Sublime," 137.

60   The quotation belongs to Shaviro, "Beauty Lies in the Eye," 9.

61   Shapiro, "The Sublime Today," 666–667.

62   Lyotard, "After the Sublime," 138.

63   Lyotard, "After the Sublime," 141–142.

64   The quotations are from David Carroll's discerning review of Lyotard's *Le differend*: Carroll, "Rephrasing the Political with Kant and Lyotard," 83.

65　See Deleuze, *The Logic of Sense*, 147.

66　This apt expression belongs to Zourabichvili, *Deleuze*, 97.

67　See Shapiro, "Hiroshima Temporalities."

68　The quotation is from Ziarek, *The Force of Art*, 19.

69　DeLillo, "In the Ruins of the Future," 33.

70　DeLillo, "In the Ruins of the Future," 33.

71　DeLillo, "In the Ruins of the Future," 34. For Deleuze on counter-actualization, see his *The Logic of Sense*, 150.

72　The expression belongs to Gilles Deleuze in his analysis of the canvases of Francis Bacon: Deleuze, *Francis Bacon*.

73　DeLillo, "In the Ruins of the Future," 39.

74　DeLillo, *Falling Man*, 135.

75　The "effect that seems to exceed its causes" quotation is from Žižek, *Event*, ebook, loc. 114. The "framework" quote is from Bakhtin, *Problems of Dostoevsky's Poetic*, 57.

76　The remark belongs to Julia Apitzsch, quoted in Schweighauser and Schneck, "Introduction," in *Terrorism, Media, and the Ethics of Fiction*, 6.

77　Lyotard, *Discourse, Figure*, 129.

78　On the "unpresentable" within presentation, see Lyotard, *The Postmodern Condition*, 81.

79　The quotation is from Fassin and Rechtman, *The Empire of Trauma*, 39.

80　Fassin and Rechtman, *The Empire of Trauma*, 104.

81　The quoted expression is in a DVD review by Anaya, 129.

82　The quotations are from Rainer, "Candid Camera."

83　May, "Reading the Short Story."

84　Caruth, *Unclaimed Experience*, 3–4.

85　The report is on the web at www.britannica.com/event/Kobe-earthquake-of-1995.

86　"The City Isn't Quaking, but Maybe It Should Be," *New York Times*, October 30, 2000, www.nytimes.com/2000/10/30/world/30JAPA.html.

87　For an analysis that connects Heidegger's "story of being" with Freud's uncanny, see Withy, *Heidegger on Being Uncanny*.

88　Martin Heidegger, *What Is Called Thinking*, 27.

89　As Heidegger suggests, "In defining the essence of a thing . . . Perhaps . . . what we call feeling or mood . . . is more intelligently perceptive . . . more open to Being than all that reason which, having become *ratio* [the Roman refiguring of what the Greeks meant by thinking], was misinterpreted as being rational." See his "The Origin of a Work of Art," 25.

90　Haruki Murakami, quoted in the *Jerusalem Post*, February 15, 2009, available at www.goodreads.com/quotes/140477-if-there-is-a-hard-high-wall-and-an-egg.

91　Murakami, *After the Quake*, 3.

92　Murakami, *After the Quake*, 4–5.

93　I am quoting from my reading of the novel: Shapiro, *Deforming American Political Thought*, 37.

94   Hammett, *The Maltese Falcon*, 63.

95   Hammett, *The Maltese Falcon*, 64.

96   The quotation is from Shapiro, *Deforming American Political Thought*, 39.

97   The "emotional aftershocks" quote is from Giles's review of *After the Quake*, "A Shock to the System."

98   The quotations are from Boulter, *Melancholy and the Archive*, 94.

99   Murakami, *After the Quake*, 20.

100 Murakami, "A Walk to Kobe."

101 Murakami, *Underground*, 234.

102 The quotation is from Seats, *Murakami Haruki*, 19.

103 The quotation belongs to Bloom, "Freud and Beyond," 145.

104 Bloom sees Freud's essay on the uncanny as his theory of the sublime: Bloom, "Freud and the Poetic Sublime," 218.

105 The quotations belong to Santner's reflections on Freud. See his *On the Psychotheology of Everyday Life*, ebook loc. 316.

106 In his article, "The Uncanny" (first published in *Image* Bd. V., 1919), Freud writes, "the 'uncanny' is that class of the terrifying which leads back to something long known to us, once very familiar." As a result, he adds, "what is novel can easily become frightening and uncanny," 1–2.

107 Quotations in Santner, *On the Psychotheology of Everyday Life*, loc. 291.

108 Rancière, "Contemporary Art and the Politics of Aesthetics," 31.

109 Murakami, "A Walk to Kobe."

110 Murakami, *After the Quake*, 36.

111 Murakami, *After the Quake*, 37.

112 The apt expression belongs to Redfield, "Pynchon's Postmodern Sublime," 155.

113 The quotation is from a report, "Haruki Murakami's Passion for Jazz," July 2014, www.openculture.com/2014/07/haruki-murakamis-passion-for-jazz.html.

114 Murakami, *After the Quake*, 74.

115 Murakami, *After the Quake*, 90.

116 Bloom, "Freud and Beyond," 145.

117 Guattari, *Schizoanalytic Cartographies*, 222.

118 The quotations are from Seats, *Murakami Haruki*, 114. See Murakami, *After the Quake*, 97.

119 Mackey, *Atet* A.D., 4–5.

120 Mackey, *Atet* A.D., 7.

121 Clark, *Civic Jazz*, 150.

122 Murakami, *After the Quake*, 145.

123 Murakami, *After the Quake*, 147.

124 Lyotard, "The Sublime and the Avant Garde," 93. Jacques Rancière puts it similarly: "Fiction invents new communities of sense . . . new trajectories between what can be seen, what can be said, and what can be done." Rancière, "Contemporary Art and the Politics of Aesthetics," 49.

Two. The Racial Sublime

1 Jones, *The Known World*, 14.

2 Jones, *The Known World*, 16.

3 Shapiro, *Deforming American Political Thought*, xiii–xiv.

4 Wittenberg, "Paton's Sublime," 3.

5 Wittenberg, "Paton's Sublime," 7.

6 Wittenberg, "Paton's Sublime," 5; Burke, *A Philosophical Inquiry into the Origins of Our Ideas of the Sublime and Beautiful*, 49.

7 Burke, *A Philosophical Inquiry into the Origins of Our Ideas of the Sublime and Beautiful*, 116.

8 Kant, *Observations of the Feeling of the Beautiful and Sublime*, 110.

9 Quotations from Wittenberg, *Paton's Sublime*, 7.

10 Shapiro, "Hurricane Katrina's Bio-Temporalities," in *Politics and Time*. The inner quotation refers to Dyson, "Racial Terror, Fast and Slow."

11 Shapiro, *Deforming American Political Thought*, 195.

12 This version of Gramsci's concept of "organic intellectuals" (explicated in his *Prison Notebooks*) is an adequate account: "'Traditional' intellectuals are thought to be disinterested and to rise in the name of reason and truth above sectarian or topical interests. 'Organic' intellectuals, on the other hand, speak for the interests of a specific class. Moreover, traditional intellectuals are bound to the institutions of the previous hegemonic order while organic intellectuals seek to win consent to counter-hegemonic ideas and ambitions."

13 The phrase "believing themselves white" belongs to Ta-Nehisi Coates, who uses it continually (mimicking a similar phrase found in much of Baldwin's writing). See his *Between the World and Me*. See Baldwin, *The Fire Next Time*, 5.

14 Baldwin, *The Fire Next Time*, 101.

15 The quotation is from the Amazon.com page on which the Vintage International edition of Baldwin's book is advertised: www.amazon.com/gp/product/B00EGMV00W?ie=UTF8&isInIframe=1&n=133140011&redirect=true&ref_=dp_proddesc_0&s=digital-text&showDetailProductDesc=1#iframe-wrapper, accessed July 21, 2017.

16 Jones, "Introduction" to James Baldwin, *Notes of a Native Son*, xiv.

17 Coates, *Between the World and Me*, 17–18.

18 I am quoting from Du Bois, *The Souls of Black Folk*.

19 Coates, "The Black Family in the Age of Mass Incarceration."

20 Coates, "The Black Family in the Age of Mass Incarceration."

21 See Kristof, "When Whites Just Don't Get It."

22 Du Bois, *Black Reconstruction*, 350.

23 Du Bois, *Black Reconstruction*, 353, 352.

24 Du Bois, *The Souls of Black Folk*.

25 Crooks, "From the Far Side of the Urban Frontier," 68.

26 Borneman, "American Anthropology as Foreign Policy," 668.

27 Borneman, "American Anthropology as Foreign Policy," 667. The internal quotations are from Hinsley, "Ethnographic Charisma and Scientific Routine," 53.

28 An interview with Alexie about his novel *Indian Killer*, quoted in Van Stylesdall, "The Trans/Historicity of Trauma in Jeannette Armstrong's *Slash* and Sherman Alexie's *Indian Killer*," 210.

29 See Ellison, *Invisible Man*.

30 I am quoting from IFL Science, "What Causes Brazil's Bizarre 'Meeting of the Waters?," www.iflscience.com/environment/what-causes-brazil%E2%80%99s -bizarre-meeting-waters, accessed July 21, 2017.

31 I am quoting Gilroy, *Darker Than Blue*, 10.

32 Kempton, *Boogaloo*, 17.

33 Kempton, *Boogaloo*, 30.

34 Gussow, *It Seems like Murder Here*, 161.

35 The expression "ethnic dissonance" is from Moore, *Yankee Blues*, 67. The quotation is from one of my earlier studies: Shapiro, *Deforming American Political Thought*, 150.

36 Quoted in Denning, *The Cultural Front*, 313.

37 Quoted in Swain, *The Broadway Musical*, 56.

38 Clark, *Civic Jazz*, 150.

39 The quotation is from Price, "Bluegrass Nation," 8.

40 Price, "Bluegrass Nation," 9.

41 Price, "Bluegrass Nation," 10.

42 The quotation is from Gooding-Williams, "Du Bois's Counter-Sublime," 207.

43 Powers, *The Time of Our Singing*.

44 The quoted phrase is from Peter Dempsey's review of the novel in the *Guardian*, March 29, 2003, www.theguardian.com/books/2003/mar/29/featuresreviews .guardianreview13.

45 Powers, *The Time of Our Singing*, 12–13.

46 The "contrapuntal interludes" quotation is from my earlier analysis of the novel in Shapiro, *Deforming American Political Thought*, 146.

47 See Moskowitz, "The Enduring Importance of Richard Wright."

48 Spillers, "Mama's Baby, Papa's Maybe," 60.

49 Asking "What then is Time?," Augustine ponders the problem of reconciling the nonpresence of past and future states with the unity of one's existence. How, he asks, can "these two kinds of time, the past and the future, be, when the past no longer is and the future as yet does not be?" St. Augustine, *The Confessions*, 288.

50 Powers, *The Time of Our Singing*, 93.

51 The quotations are from Mendelsohn's insightful review of the novel, "A Dance to the Music of Time."

52 Powers, *The Time of Our Singing*, 92.

53 The quotation is from Deleuze, *The Logic of Sense*, 161.

54 Bourdieu, *Photography, a Middle-brow Art*, 19, 26.

55 Bourdieu, *Photography, a Middle-brow Art*, 29.

56 Deleuze, *Cinema 1*, 121.

57 Pérez-Peña, "Upbeat Interracial Ad for Old Navy Leads to a Backlash. Twice."

58 The quotations are from Rancière, "Fictions of Time."

59 Lelyveld, "Introduction," in *How Race Is Lived in America*, xv.

60 Ojito, "Best of Friends, Worlds Apart," 26.

61 Ojito, "Best of Friends, Worlds Apart," 29.

62 Ojito, "Best of Friends, Worlds Apart," 23.

63 "Epidermalization" is Frantz Fanon's expression for absorbing identity totally into skin tone: Fanon, *Black Skin, White Masks*.

64 Fiske, *Media Matters*, 165.

65 Ojito, "Best of Friends, Worlds Apart," 28.

66 Ojito, "Best of Friends, Worlds Apart," 31–32.

67 Lewin, "Growing Up, Growing Apart," 151.

68 Lewin, "Growing Up, Growing Apart," 155.

69 Lewin, "Growing Up, Growing Apart," 161.

70 Lewin, "Growing Up, Growing Apart," 169.

71 Lewin, "Growing Up, Growing Apart," 160.

72 Lewin, "Growing Up, Growing Apart," 167.

73 Sack, "Shared Prayers, Mixed Blessings," 5.

74 Ojito, "Best of Friends, Worlds Apart," 27.

75 Woods, "Katrina's World," 428.

76 Brumfield, "New Orleans Officers Convicted in Post Katrina Shooting Get New Trial."

77 Herbert Marcuse famously uses the concept of repressive desublimation to refer to how arts become banal everyday phenomena that have lost their oppositional critique of reality. I am using the concept in a reverse way, to refer to how what is repressed can be activated and revealed. For the Marcuse version, see *One-Dimensional Man*.

78 Dixon, "New Orleans' Racial Divide."

79 The quotation is from Jones-Deweever, "The Forgotten Ones," ebook loc. 4142.

80 As I've put it elsewhere, "Lee's soundtrack . . . stages a contrapuntal encounter between the exemplary musical scores of two alternative American thought-worlds, connected with alternative American experiences." Shapiro, *Deforming American Political Thought*, 146.

81 Deleuze and Guattari, *A Thousand Plateaus*, 179.

82 The long quotation is from Shapiro, *Studies in Trans-Disciplinary Method*, 67, and the inner quotation is from Gilroy, *Darker Than Blue*, 59.

83 An interview with Spike Lee on NPR: "Spike Lee on Race, Politics and Broken Levees."

84 On the film–affective map relationship, see Shaviro, *Post-Cinematic Affect*, 6.

85 "Spike Lee on Race, Politics and Broken Levees."

86 Cole, "Death in the Browser Tab," 20.

87 Cobb, "What I Saw in Ferguson."

88 Kundera, *Slowness*, 79.

89 For a review of the pervasiveness of the social media response, see Bonilla and Rosa, "#Ferguson."

90 On "truth weapons," see Foucault, *Fearless Speech*.

91   Schiappa, "#IfTheyGunnedMeDown," 49.

92   See Brown, "Quilts with a Sense of Place, Stitched in Oakland."

93   See Ratcliffe, "To Be a Witness."

94   Coates, *Between the World and Me*, 83.

95   Coates, *Between the World and Me*, 15.

96   For "ungrievable," see Butler, *Frames of War*; Coates, *Between the World and Me*, 44.

97   Nancy, *The Inoperative Community*, 77.

98   Nancy, *The Inoperative Community*, 76; Shapiro, *For Moral Ambiguity*, 120.

99   Coates, *Between the World and Me*, 38.

100 Coates, *Between the World and Me*, 44.

101 Baker, *Modernism and the Harlem Renaissance*, 33–36.

102 Baker, *Modernism and the Harlem Renaissance*, 50–51.

103 Coates, *Between the World and Me*, 44, 45; Baker, *Modernism and the Harlem Renaissance*, 56.

104 Coates, *Between the World and Me*, 137.

105 Coates, *Between the World and Me*, 145.

106 Coates, *Between the World and Me*, 145–146.

107 The quotation is from Turner, *Awakening to Race*, 48.

108 Douglas, "Parties Were Made for Men, Not Men for Parties."

Three. The Nuclear Sublime

1   That summary is quoted from Rubin, *Haruki Murakami and the Music of Words*, 257.

2   The quotation is from Unger, *The Rise and Fall of Nuclearism*, 68.

3   The quotation is from a commentary on the film by the writer Tobias Wolff, "Winter Light."

4   Brown, *The Making of Late Antiquity*, 12.

5   Brown, *The Making of Late Antiquity*, 13.

6   See James, "The Will to Believe."

7   DeLillo, *White Noise*, 175.

8   DeLillo, *White Noise*, 199–120.

9   DeLillo, *White Noise*, 121.

10   Shapiro, *Reading the Postmodern Polity*, 128–129.

11   See Heidegger, *What Is Called Thinking?*

12   The quotations are in Heidegger, *What Is Called Thinking?*, 25.

13   Heidegger, *What Is Called Thinking?*

14   On the initiation of the concept of a textual community, see Stock, *The Implications of Literacy*.

15   The expression belongs to Menand, "Fat Man."

16   Kahn, *Thinking about the Unthinkable*, 19.

17   Quotation from Menand, "Fat Man."

18   See Kahn, *On Thermonuclear War*.

19   Kahn, *On Thermonuclear War*, 41.

20 Menand, "Fat Man."

21 Quoted in Menand, "Fat Man."

22 Menand, "Fat Man."

23 Menand, "Fat Man."

24 Derrida, "No Apocalypse, Not Now."

25 For an ethnography that demonstrates the influence of nuclear laboratories on weapons development and testing, see Gusterson, *People of the Bomb*.

26 Derrida, "No Apocalypse, Not Now," 21, 20.

27 Derrida, "No Apocalypse, Not Now," 22.

28 Derrida, "No Apocalypse, Not Now," 23.

29 Derrida, "No Apocalypse, Not Now," 23, 30.

30 Rancière, "Fictions of Time."

31 Derrida, "No Apocalypse, Not Now," 21.

32 Derrida, "No Apocalypse, Not Now," 29.

33 Derrida, "No Apocalypse, Not Now," 30.

34 Schell, "Introduction," in Tredici, *At Work in the Fields of the Bomb*, x.

35 The quotations are from Chaloupka, *Knowing Nukes*, 7.

36 Quoted in Chaloupka, *Knowing Nukes*, 8.

37 Kramer, "Hiroshima," 535.

38 Ibuse, *Black Rain*, 171.

39 DeLillo, "Human Moments in World War III."

40 DeLillo, "Human Moments in World War III."

41 DeLillo, "Human Moments in World War III."

42 Spivak, *An Aesthetic Education in the Era of Globalization*, 317.

43 Ray, *Terror and the Sublime in Art and Critical Theory*, 5.

44 Brown, "The First American Sublime," 147.

45 The concept belongs to Boelhower, *Through a Glass Darkly*.

46 The quotations are from Brown, "The First American Sublime," 148.

47 Shapiro, *Deforming American Political Thought*, 111–112 (the inner quotations are from Jefferson's *Notes on the State of Virginia*).

48 Shapiro, *Deforming American Political Thought*, 112.

49 I am quoting from my chapter "Landscape and Nationhood" in Shapiro, *Methods and Nations*, 127. The inner quotation references Boime, *The Magisterial Gaze*.

50 The quotations are from Wilton, "The Sublime in the Old World and the New," 23.

51 The quotations are from Barringer, "The Course of Empires," 49.

52 Mitchell, "Imperial Landscape," 10.

53 See my treatment of the painting in Shapiro, *Methods and Nations*, 129.

54 Ziff, *Writing in the New Nation*, 172.

55 Ziff, *Writing in the New Nation*, 165.

56 The quotation from Boelhower, "Stories of Foundation, Scenes of Origin," 391.

57 See Cooper, "American and European Scenery Compared," 52.

58 I am quoting from my earlier analysis of Cooper's American sublime: Shapiro, *Methods and Nations*, 109.

59 See Dennis, *Cultivating a Landscape of Peace*, 17ff.

60 Reported in Basso, *Wisdom Sits in Places*, 34.

61 Scheckel, *The Insistence of the Indian*, 17.

62 Scheckel, *The Insistence of the Indian*, 22.

63 Scheckel, *The Insistence of the Indian*, 25.

64 Scheckel, *The Insistence of the Indian*, 39.

65 Shapiro, *Methods and Nations*, 112 (the internal quotations are from Seed, "Mapping the Course of Empire in the New World," 87.

66 Boime, *The Magisterial Gaze*, 137.

67 The quotation is from Shapiro, *Deforming American Political Thought*, 12, and the internal quotes are from Pynchon, *Mason & Dixon*, 608.

68 Shapiro, *Violent Cartographies*.

69 I am quoting Wilson, "Towards the Nuclear Sublime," in his *American Sublime*, 228.

70 I am quoting from Wilson's article version: Wilson, "Towards the Nuclear Sublime," 408.

71 Cohn, "Sex and Death in the Rational World of Defense Intellectuals," 701.

72 The quotations are from Hale, "The Atomic Sublime," 9.

73 Hale, "The Atomic Sublime."

74 Hale, "The Atomic Sublime."

75 For a treatment of the details of the film and its delayed release, see Deamer, *Deleuze, Cinema, and the Atom Bomb*. "Slow violence," as Rob Nixon has rendered it, involves the long-term deadly attrition that receives little or no coverage in mainstream media (the environmental degradation caused by unregulated capitalism, starvation owed to both structures of inequality and violent conflicts that destroy food sources, and the lethal zones left with toxicities, mines, and other unexploded military ordnance in the aftermath of wars: Nixon, *Slow Violence and the Environmentalism of the Poor*.

76 The quotation is from my chapter, "Landscape and Nationhood," in Shapiro, *Methods and Nations*, 132.

77 Solnit, *Savage Dreams*, 4.

78 See Alexie, "Indian Country."

79 That analysis is in Shapiro, *Methods and Nations*, 132–135.

80 Shapiro, *Methods and Nations*, 132.

81 Silko, *Ceremony*, 245.

82 Shapiro, *Methods and Nations*, 134; Silko, *Ceremony*, 246.

83 Kuletz, *The Tainted Desert*, 19.

84 Kuletz, *The Tainted Desert*, 7, 13. That wasteland designation operated during the first American sublime as well. For example, it was articulated in Theodore Roosevelt's popular nineteenth-century history, *The Winning of the West*, in which he justifies the Euro-American ethnogenesis (Euro-American westward expansion) suggesting that Native Americans occupied "waste spaces," which they visited only occasionally: Roosevelt, *The Winning of the West*.

85 The quotation is from Sehgal, "Fighting 'Erasure.'"

86 Kuletz, *The Tainted Desert*, 33.

87 Shapiro, "Introduction," in Campbell and Shapiro, *Moral Spaces*, xvi.

88 Hau'ofa, "Our Sea of Islands," 3.

89 The quotations are from Hau'ofa, "Our Sea of Islands."

90 Goin, *Nuclear Landscapes*, 8.

91 Hau'ofa, "Our Sea of Islands," 8.

92 As I noted in chapter 1, Edmund Burke's version of the sublime emphasizes the terror associated with a sublime experience, e.g., "Whatever is fitted in any sort to excite the ideas of pain and danger . . . whatever is in any sort terrible, or is conversant about terrible objects, or operates in manner analogous to terror, is a source of the *sublime*": Burke, *A Philosophical Enquiry into the Origin of Our Ideas of the Sublime and Beautiful*, 33.

93 See Eichenberger et al., "Nuclear Stewardship."

94 Eichenberger et al., "Nuclear Stewardship."

95 The long quotation is from Wagner, "Globalizing Discourses," 230. Other quotations are from Eperjesi, *The Imperialist Imaginary*, 52.

96 Lindstrom, "Images of Islanders in Pacific War Photographs," 108, 110.

97 Lindstrom, "Images of Islanders in Pacific War Photographs," 107.

98 Lindstrom, "Images of Islanders in Pacific War Photographs," 110.

99 Lindstrom, "Images of Islanders in Pacific War Photographs." The internal quotations are from Edwards, "Introduction," in Edwards, *Anthropology and Photography, 1860–1920*, 6.

100 Lindstrom, "Images of Islanders in Pacific War Photographs," 108.

101 The quoted passage is Foucault's explication of the concept of the *dispositif*. See Foucault, "The Confession of the Flesh," 194.

102 The quotation is from Schneider, "Foreword," in Gallagher, *American Ground Zero*, xvi.

103 Schneider, "Foreword" in Gallagher, *American Ground Zero*, xxiii.

104 Deleuze, *Cinema 1*, 24.

105 For the former, see Lefebvre, "Introduction," in *Landscape and Film*, xii, and for the latter, Lefebvre, "Between Setting and Landscape in Cinema."

106 Lefebvre, "Between Setting and Landscape," 28.

107 Lefebvre, "Between Setting and Landscape," 22.

108 Lefebvre, "Between Setting and Landscape," 23.

109 See Landy, *Cinema and Counter-History*, 2.

110 I am quoting Morris, "From a Chomskian Couch," 685.

111 Shapiro, *Deforming American Political Thought*, 71.

112 Deleuze, *Cinema 1*, 121.

113 The quotation is from my earlier analysis of the film: Shapiro, *Deforming American Political Thought*, 74.

114 The expression "image facts" belongs to the film theorist Andre Bazin, whose concept I analyze in Shapiro, *Cinematic Geopolitics*, 154.

115 Population data are available at http://dmla.clanlib.nv.us/docs/nsla/archives/political/historical/hist18.htm, accessed May 15, 2017.

116 The first quotation is from Lukinbeal, "Cinematic Landscapes," 8. The second quotation is from Gillian Rose, who states that a landscape's "visuality is seen as looking back . . . and having an effect in itself": "Afterwords," 167.

117   Regarding "who the landscape thinks it is," here I am adapting Deleuze and Guattari's heading "Who Does the Earth Think It Is?," in *A Thousand Plateaus*, 39.

118   See Bersani and Dutoit, *Forms of Being*, 136.

119   I am borrowing from Martin Scorsese's observation about the films of Michelangelo Antonio, because it fits Malick so well. See Scorsese, "The Man Who Set Film Free."

120   The quotation is from Dillon, "'Some Magic Land.'"

121   Benitez-Rojo, *The Repeating Island*, 16–17.

122   That attribution belongs to Flanagan, "'Everything a Lie,'" 123.

123   I am quoting my earlier reading of the film: Shapiro, *Cinematic Geopolitics*, 139.

124   Shapiro, *Cinematic Geopolitics*, 141.

125   Bersani and Dutoit, *Forms of Being*, 163.

126   See Bennett, *Empathic Vision*. I am adapting the expression "ethical weight" from Slavoj Žižek's reading of the novels of Henry James. See Žižek, "Kate's Choice," 290.

Four. The Industrial Sublime

1   The quotation is from Greenhouse, "On the Fringes," 40.

2   Greenhouse, "On the Fringes," 43.

3   Greenhouse, "On the Fringes," 78.

4   The quotation is from Jensen, "Picturing Manhatta," 73.

5   Mitchell, "Imperial Landscape," 10.

6   The quotation is from Trachtenberg, *The Incorporation of America*, 46.

7   Lefebvre, "Between Setting and Landscape in the Cinema," 23.

8   See Landy, *Cinema and Counter-History*.

9   Jones, review of *Dead Man* in *Cineaste* 22, no. 2 (1996): 45.

10   The quotation is from Shapiro, *The Time of the City*, 7. I develop more aspect of aesthetic subjects in Shapiro, *Studies in Trans-Disciplinary Method*.

11   On the way the rule of the gun shaped the American West, see Slotkin, *Gunfighter Nation*.

12   Quoted in Chiapello, "Accounting and the Birth of the Notion of Capitalism."

13   Marx, *The Machine in the Garden*, 15–16.

14   Marx, *The Machine in the Garden*, 155, 156.

15   See Nabokov and Easton, *Native American Architecture*, 39.

16   Berardi, *The Uprising*, 17, 22.

17   Berardi, *The Uprising*, 36–37.

18   The quotation is from Nieland, "Graphic Violence," 190.

19   Nye, *The American Technological Sublime*.

20   Quoted in Trachtenberg, *The Incorporation of America*, 45.

21   The expression "imperial we" is from Nye, *The American Technological Sublime*, 235.

22   Nye, *The American Technological Sublime*, 46.

23   Despotopoulou, "'Running on Lines,'" 48.

24   The quotations are from Wolf, "A Grammar of the Sublime, or Intertextuality Triumphant in Church, Turner, and Cole," 324.

25 The quotations are from Le Fanu, "In This World," 9.

26 Pasolini, "The Cinema of Poetry," 178.

27 Pasolini, "The Cinema of Poetry," 179.

28 The quoted reference to Chirico belongs to Matthew Gandy, "Landscapes of Deliquescence in Michelangelo Antonioni's 'Red Desert,'" 227.

29 Burke, *A Philosophical Inquiry into the Origin of Our Ideas of the Sublime*, 100.

30 Burke, *A Philosophical Inquiry into the Origin of Our Ideas of the Sublime*, 102.

31 Gandy, "Landscapes of Deliquescence in Michelangelo Antonioni's 'Red Desert,'" 221.

32 Antonioni, "Interview with Francois Mauzin," 253 (quoted in Gandy, "Landscapes of Deliquescence in Michelangelo Antonioni's 'Red Desert,'" 220); Antonioni, "Il Bosco bianco," 83 (also quoted in Gandy, "Landscapes of Deliquescence in Michelangelo Antonioni's 'Red Desert,'" 222).

33 Antonioni, "Il Bosco bianco."

34 Antonioni, "Il Bosco bianco," 184.

35 The expression "obsessive framing" is from Antonioni, "Il Bosco bianco," 179.

36 The quotation belongs to Forgacs, who provides a frame-by-frame commentary on the film.

37 Farocki, "Workers Leaving the Factory."

38 See Handke's novella "The Lesson of Mont Sainte-Victoire," in *Slow Homecoming*, 155.

39 Antonioni, cited in Gandy, "Landscapes of Deliquescence," 225.

40 Antonioni, cited in Gandy, "Landscapes of Deliquescence," 225.

41 The quotation is from Gandy, "Landscapes of Deliquescence," 221.

42 Gandy, "Landscapes of Deliquescence," 222.

43 Gandy, "Landscapes of Deliquescence," 224.

44 Forgacs, *Red Desert* commentary, 18.

45 See Cox, "Introduction," 10.

46 See Cox, "Introduction," 15.

47 Cox, "Introduction," 16.

48 Quoted in Joseph Thompson, "Unrecoverable Spin," in Maisel, *Black Maps*, 158.

49 Bell, *Scrapper*, 1.

50 Bell, *Scrapper*, 1. The expression "urban stones of memory" is from Beatriz Jaguaribe, in her analysis of ruins in Rio de Janeiro: Jaguaribe, "Nostalgia for the Future," 369.

51 Jaguaribe, "Nostalgia for the Future," 369.

52 Jaguaribe, "Nostalgia for the Future," 386.

53 See Edensor, *Industrial Ruins*, 13.

54 For an explication of "sign function value" (value conferred on people through the objects with which they are associated), see Baudrillard, "Sign Function and Class Logic."

55 Edensor, *Industrial Ruins*, 67.

56 Edensor, *Industrial Ruins*, 101.

57 Edensor, *Industrial Ruins*, 164.

58 The quotation belongs to Connolly, *The Fragility of Things*, 31.

59 See Ben Wojdyla, "The Ruins of Detroit Industry: Five Former Factories," December 16, 2008, Jalopnik.com/5110995/the-ruins-of-five-former-factories.

60 Harney, "Hapticality in the Undercommons, or from Operations Management to Black Ops."

61 Robbins, "The Sweatshop Sublime."

62 Robbins, "The Sweatshop Sublime." There is a more elaborate engagement with Robbins's analysis in my chapter "Keeping Time: The Rhythms of Work and the Arts of Resistance," in Shapiro, *Politics and Time*, 117–119.

63 Reported in Ross, *No Sweat*, 97.

64 Ross, *No Sweat*, 98.

65 Hapke, *Sweatshop*, 4.

66 Hapke, *Sweatshop*, 21.

67 See Hapke, *Sweatshop*, 29.

68 Hapke, *Sweatshop*, 99.

69 See Hapke, *Sweatshop*, 100.

70 See Shapiro, *Politics and Time*, 105.

71 Shapiro, *Politics and Time*, 105. The quotations are from "Blood and Exhaustion behind Bargain."

72 "Blood and Exhaustion behind Bargain."

73 Stabile, "Nike, Social Responsibility, and the Hidden Abode of Production," 197.

74 Stabile, "Nike, Social Responsibility, and the Hidden Abode of Production," 188.

75 See Keady, "When Will Nike 'Just Do It' on the Sweatshop Issue?"

76 See Geertz, "Thick Description."

77 See Abel, *Violent Affect*, 189.

78 I am quoting Wahlberg's *Documentary Time*, 8.

79 DeLillo, "In the Ruins of the Future," 19.

80 Benjamin, "The Work of Art in the Age of Mechanical Reproduction," 238.

Five. The 9/11 Terror Sublime

1 See Shapiro, "Wanted Dead or Alive." In the internal quotation, DeLillo was commenting through one of his novelistic characters on an earlier imagination-challenging event, the assassination of President John F. Kennedy. See DeLillo, *Libra*, 8.

2 Nair, "Plummeting to the Pavement," loc. 368.

3 For a treatment of pre- and remediation, see Grusin, *Premediation*.

4 Shulevitz, "Chasing after Conrad's Secret Agent."

5 The quotation is from Snauwaert's "Introduction," in *Stan Douglas, the Secret Agent*.

6 Quotations and paraphrasing from Snauwaert, "Introduction," 5.

7 Rodowick, *Reading the Figural*, 173, 174–175.

8 See Braudel, *Afterthoughts on Material Civilization and Capitalism*.

9 Ray, *Terror and the Sublime in Art and Critical Theory*, ix.

10 Stock, *The Implications of Literacy*, 89.

11 Stock, *The Implications of Literacy*, 152.

12 The Marxist thinker Ernst Bloch famously quipped, "The best thing about religion is that it makes for heretics": Bloch, *Atheism in Christianity*, 1.

13 Miller, *Time Bends*, 175.

14 On the perversion of the original spirit of the tragedies by Euripides, see Nietzsche, *The Birth of Tragedy*. I treat the dilemma of justice aspect of Greek tragedies in Shapiro, *For Moral Ambiguity*, 17–21.

15 Bauman, "Performance and Honor in 13th-Century Iceland," 145.

16 Magnuson, "Introduction," in *Njal's Saga*, 25.

17 Quotations from Magnuson, "Introduction," 26.

18 Bauman, "Performance and Honor in 13th-Century Iceland," 145.

19 Ouaknin, *The Burnt Book*, 282.

20 Ouaknin, *The Burnt Book*, 159, 282, 285.

21 Ouaknin, *The Burnt Book*, 294.

22 Shapiro, *Cinematic Political Thought*, 53.

23 Brown, *Authority and the Sacred*, 69.

24 See Sand, *The Invention of the Jewish People*.

25 Rasmussen, *Queequeg's Coffin*, 1.

26 Rasmussen, *Queequeg's Coffin*, 2.

27 Marcus, "A Broad(er) Side to the Canon," 405.

28 Marcus, "A Broad(er) Side to the Canon," 396.

29 Marcus, "A Broad(er) Side to the Canon," 403.

30 Smock, "Translator's Introduction," in Maurice Blanchot, *The Space of Literature*, 3.

31 Clift, *Committing the Future to Memory*, 199.

32 DeLillo, "In the Ruins of the Future," 33.

33 Burgin, *The Remembered Film*, 21.

34 Mills, "Review of Franz Neumann's *Behemoth*."

35 DeLillo, "In the Ruins of the Future," 34. For a review of the mainstream security-oriented responses, see Allen, *Blinking Red*, and for an example of the standard international relations–oriented response, see Lebovic, *Deterring International Terrorism and Rogue States*.

36 DeLillo, "In the Ruins of the Future," 34.

37 DeLillo, "In the Ruins of the Future," 39.

38 The concept of a paradigmatic event belongs to Karl Mannheim, who refers to "paradigmatic experiences," which serve as a "measuring rod for human conduct." See Mannheim, *Diagnoses of Our Time*, 136. DeLillo, *Falling Man*, 138.

39 DeLillo, "In the Ruins of the Future," 34.

40 He repeats that remark in his novel: DeLillo, *Falling Man*, 174.

41 DeLillo, *Players*, 107.

42 DeLillo, "In the Ruins of the Future," 34.

43 DeLillo, *Mao II*, 41.

44 Caruth, *Unclaimed Experience*, 3–4.

45 Gray, "Open Doors, Closed Minds," 131. For family drama, see, for example, Ragussis, *Acts of Naming*.

46 Kant, *Critique of Judgement*, 101.

47 The quotations are from a review of the novel: Rich, "The Clear Blue Sky."

48 DeLillo, *Falling Man*, 3.

49 DeLillo, *Falling Man*, 5.

50 Lyotard, *Discourse, Figure*, 129.

51 Lyotard, *Discourse, Figure*, 12.

52 Lyotard, *Discourse, Figure*, 212.

53 Lyotard, *Discourse, Figure*, 12.

54 The quotation is from Rodowick's application of Lyotard's argument: *Reading the Figural*, 10.

55 DeLillo, *Falling Man*, 32.

56 Lyotard, *Discourse, Figure*, 155.

57 Mitchell, "The Unspeakable and the Unimaginable," 291.

58 Shapiro, *Cinematic Geopolitics*, 19.

59 Medea Benjamin, interviewed in Jhally and Earp, eds., *Hijacking Catastrophe*, 27.

60 For details on the film, see Shapiro, *Cinematic Geopolitics*, 1–2 (I was a juror on a "peace film" jury at the 2005 *Tromso International Film Festival*, in which we awarded the Peace Film Prize to Fahradi for that film).

61 Spiegelman, *In the Shadow of No Towers*.

62 Shapiro, *For Moral Ambiguity*, 33.

63 The concept of heteroglossia (translated from a Russian expression that means "many contending voices") belongs to Bakhtin, "Discourse and the Novel," 259–422. Spiegelman, quoted in James E. Young, "The Holocaust as Vicarious Past," 672.

64 For commentaries on the "commix" strategy, see Spiegelman, *Breakdowns*; Young, "The Holocaust as Vicarious Past."

65 Young, "The Holocaust as Vicarious Past."

66 Shapiro, *Deforming American Political Thought*, 152–153.

67 Spiegelman, "The Sky Is Falling," his preface to the images in *In the Shadow of No Towers*.

68 Spiegelman, "The Sky Is Falling."

69 Spiegelman, *In the Shadow of No Towers*, 1.

70 Kant, "Analytic of the Sublime," para. 256, sec. 26.

71 The quotations are from Orban, "Trauma and Visuality," 81.

72 Orban, "Trauma and Visuality," 81.

73 Spiegelman, "The Sky Is Falling."

74 Lyotard, *Discourse, Figure*, 129.

75 Orban, "Trauma and Visuality," 59.

76 Bennett, "The Aesthetics of Sense-Memory," 33.

77 Deleuze, "Lecture on Kant."

78 Deleuze, "Lecture on Kant."

79 Spiegelman, "The Sky Is Falling."

80 Meyer, "'Putting It into Boxes,'" 485.

81 Spiegelman, "The Sky Is Falling."

82 The quotation is from Aili McConnon's review of *In the Shadow of No Towers*, "The Glowing Bones," *The Guardian*, September 11, 2004, www.theguardian.com/books/2004/sep/11/comics.politics.

83 The quotations are from Oban, "Trauma and Visuality," 82.

84 Kuhlman, "The Traumatic Temporality of Art," 850.

85 Vidler, *The Architectural Uncanny*, 3.

86 Vidler, *The Architectural Uncanny*, 172.

87 The expression "ahistorical sublime" is from Oban, "Trauma and Visuality," 81.

88 Oban, "Trauma and Visuality," 81.

89 Oban, "Trauma and Visuality," 84.

90 On the "time image" as a direct approach to time, see Deleuze, *Cinema 2*.

91 I am quoting Nair, "Plummeting to the Pavement," loc. 264. He is quoting Grusin, *Premediation*, 12.

92 Catherine Bernard, "Supermarket History: An Interview with Johan Grimonprez," 1998, www.johangrimonprez.be/main/interviews_DH_st4.html, accessed July 21, 2017.

93 The quotation is from Silverman, "Waiting, Hoping, among the Ruins of All the Rest," 96.

94 The quotation (and much of my understanding of remix as method) is from Navas, *Remix Theory*, 65.

95 See Lain, *In the Shadow of the Towers*. The quotation is from Rothman, "The Unsettling Arrival of Speculative 9/11 Fiction."

96 See Bernard, "Supermarket History."

97 The quotation is from Deleuze, *The Logic of Sense*.

98 See Smith, "On Sociological Description," 332.

99 The quotations are from Zepke, "The Sublime Conditions of Contemporary Art." For Deleuze's full version of the sublime, see his *Difference and Repetition*.

100 Obrist, "Interview with Johan Grimonprez."

101 See Bakhtin, "Forms of Time and of the Chronotope in the Novel," 84–258.

102 Bernard, "Supermarket History."

103 I am borrowing the phrase "continually breached" from Wood, "Grimonprez's Remix."

104 On slow violence, see Nixon, *Slow Violence and the Environmentalism of the Poor*. The long quotation is from Smith, *The Architecture of Aftermath*, 99.

105 Tschumi, "Violence of Architecture."

106 The quotation is from my reading of Irwin Panofsky's treatise on Gothic cathedrals: Shapiro, *Deforming American Political Thought*, 121. See Panofsky, *Gothic Architecture and Scholasticism*, 43.

107 Panofsky, *Gothic Architecture and Scholasticism*, 13.

108 For "anti-monumental," see Huyssen, *Presents Past*, 51.

109 Huyssen, "Monumental Seduction," 186.

110 Huyssen, "Monumental Seduction," 187.

111 Huyssen, *Presents Past*, 53.

112 The quotation is from *A Place of Remembrance*, 153.

113 *A Place of Remembrance*, 141.

114 See Foucault, "Of Other Spaces."

115 The quotations are from Rancière, "Aesthetic Separation, Aesthetic Community."

116 Rancière, "Aesthetic Separation, Aesthetic Community."

Afterword

1 The quotation is from Deleuze, *Bergsonism*, 25–26.

2 My examples are drawn from Chelsey Crawford's analysis: Crawford, "The Permeable Self."

3 Crawford, "The Permeable Self," 106, quoting Rothman, "Some Thoughts on Hitchcock's Authorship," 30.

4 Crawford, "The Permeable Self," 107, quoting Iampolski, *The Memory of Tiresias*.

5 Thomson, *The Moment of Psycho*, 63.

6 Thomson, *The Moment of Psycho*, 67.

7 Thomson, *The Moment of Psycho*, 120.

8 Thomson, *The Moment of Psycho*, 130.

9 See Morris, "Gothic Sublimity," for an elaboration of the effects.

10 Davis, "The Flames of New York."

11 The critical effects of repetition are elaborated in Deleuze, *Difference and Repetition*.

12 The quotation is from Deleuze and Guattari, *What Is Philosophy?*, 107–108.

Abel, Marco. *Violent Affect: Literature, Cinema, and Critique after Representation*. Lincoln: University of Nebraska Press, 2007.

Alexie, Sherman. "Indian Country." *New Yorker*, March 13, 2000, 76–84.

Allen, Michael. *Blinking Red: Compromise in American Intelligence after 9/11*. Washington, DC: Potomac Books, 2013.

Anaya, Ella Ruth. Review of the DVD of "Eleven Short Films about 9/11." *Global Media Journal—Canadian* 4, no. 2 (2011): 129–131.

Antonioni, Michelangelo. "Interview with Francois Mauzin." *Humanite Dimanche* 23 (September 1964).

Augustine, Saint. *The Confessions*. Translated by John K. Ryan. New York: Doubleday, 1960.

Baker, Houston A., Jr. *Modernism and the Harlem Renaissance*. Chicago: University of Chicago Press, 1987.

Bakhtin, M. M. *The Dialogic Imagination*. Translated by Caryl Emerson and Michael Holquist. Austin: University of Texas Press, 1981.

———. "Discourse and the Novel." In *The Dialogic Imagination*, 259–422.

———. "Forms of Time and of the Chronotope in the Novel." In *The Dialogic Imagination*, 84–258.

———. *Problems of Dostoevsky's Poetic*. Translated by Caryl Emerson. Minneapolis: University of Minnesota Press, 1984.

Baldwin, James. *The Fire Next Time*. New York: Vintage, 2013.

———. *Notes of a Native Son*. Boston: Beacon, 2012.

Banks, Russell. *Cloudsplitter*. New York: Harper, 1999.

Barringer, Tim. "The Course of Empires: Landscape and Identity in America and Britain 1820–1880." In Andrew Wilton and Tim Barringer, *American Sublime: Landscape Painting in the United States 1820–1880*. Princeton, NJ: Princeton University Press, 2002.

Barthes, Roland. "From Work to Text." In *Image, Music, Text*, translated by Stephen Heath, 55–164. New York: Hill and Wang, 1977.

Basso, Keith. *Wisdom Sits in Places: Landscape and Language among the Western Apache*. Albuquerque: University of New Mexico Press, 1996.

Battersby, Christine. *The Sublime, Terror, and Human Difference*. New York: Routledge, 2007.

Baudrillard, Jean. "Sign Function and Class Logic." In *For a Critique of the Political Economy of the Sign*. Translated by Charles Levin. St. Louis: Telos, 1981.

Bauman, Richard. "Performance and Honor in 13th-Century Iceland." *Journal of American Folklore* 99, no. 392 (April–June 1986): 131–150.

Bell, Matt. *Scrapper*. New York: Soho, 2015.

Benitez-Rojo, Antonio. *The Repeating Island: The Caribbean and the Postmodern Perspective*. Durham, NC: Duke University Press, 1992.

Benjamin, Walter. *The Arcades Project*. Translated by Howard Eiland and Kevin McLaughlin. Cambridge, MA: Harvard University Press, 2002.

———. "The Work of Art in the Age of Mechanical Reproduction." In *Illuminations*, edited by Hannah Arendt, translated by Harry Zohn, 217–251. New York: Schocken, 1969.

Bennett, Jill. "The Aesthetics of Sense-Memory: Theorising Trauma through the Visual Arts." In *Regimes of Memory*, edited by Susannah Radstone and Katharine Hodgkin, 27–39. New York: Routledge, 2003.

———. *Empathic Vision: Affect, Trauma, and Contemporary Art*. Stanford, CA: Stanford University Press, 2005.

Berardi, Franco ("Bifo"). *The Uprising: On Poetry and Finance*. Los Angeles: Semiotext(e), 2007.

Bernard, Catherine. "Supermarket History: An Interview with Johan Grimonprez." In *Parkett*, no. 53 (1998): 6–18. www.johangrimonprez.be/main/interviews_DH_st4.html.

Bersani, Leo, and Dutoit, Ulysse. *Forms of Being: Cinema, Aesthetics, Subjectivity*. London: BFI, 2004.

Blanchot, Maurice. *The Space of Literature*. Lincoln: University of Nebraska Press, 1982.

———. *The Unavowable Community*. Translated by Pierre Joris. Barrytown, NY: Station Hill, 1988.

Bloch, Ernst. *Atheism in Christianity: The Religion of the Exodus and the Kingdom*. 2nd ed. New York: Verso, 2009.

"Blood and Exhaustion behind Bargain: Toys Made in China for Wal-Mart and Dollar General." China Labor Watch, June 29, 2011. http://digitalcommons.ilr.cornell.edu/cgi/viewcontent.cgi?article=1908&context=globaldocs.

Bloom, Harold. "Freud and Beyond." In *Ruin the Sacred Truths: Poetry and Belief from the Bible to the Present*, 143–157. Cambridge, MA: Harvard University Press, 1989.

———. "Freud and the Poetic Sublime: A Catastrophe Theory of Creativity." In *Freud: A Collection of Critical Essays*, edited by Perry Meisel. Englewood Cliffs, NJ: Prentice Hall, 1991.

Boelhower, William. "Stories of Foundation, Scenes of Origin." *American Literary History* 5, no. 3 (fall 1993): 391–428.

———. *Through a Glass Darkly: Ethnic Semiosis in American Literature*. New York: Oxford University Press, 1987.

Boime, Albert. *The Magisterial Gaze: Manifest Destiny and American Landscape Painting c. 1830–1865*. Washington, DC: Smithsonian Institution, 1991.

Bonilla, Yarimar, and Rosa, Jonathan. "#Ferguson: Digital Protest, Hashtag Ethnography, and the Racial Politics of Social Media in the United States." *American Ethnologist* 42, no. 1 (January 2015): 4–17.

Bonitzer, Pascal. "Hitchcockian Suspense." In *Everything You Always Wanted to Know about Lacan (But Were Afraid to Ask Hitchcock)*, edited by Slavoj Žižek, 21–31. New York: Verso, 1992.

Borneman, John. "American Anthropology as Foreign Policy." *American Ethnologist* 97, no. 4 (December 1995): 663–672.

Boulter, Jonathan. *Melancholy and the Archive: Trauma, History and Memory in the Contemporary Novel*. New York: Bloomsbury, 2011.

Bourdieu, Pierre. *Photography, a Middle-brow Art*. Translated by Shaun Whiteside. Stanford, CA: Stanford University Press, 1990.

Braudel, Fernand. *Afterthoughts on Material Civilization and Capitalism*. Baltimore, MD: Johns Hopkins University Press, 1979.

Brown, Chandos Michael. "The First American Sublime." In *The Sublime: From Antiquity to the Present*, edited by Timothy M. Costello. New York: Cambridge University Press, 2012.

Brown, Patricia Leigh. "Quilts with a Sense of Place, Stitched in Oakland." *New York Times*, February 3, 2016. www.nytimes.com/2016/02/03/arts/design/quilts-with-a-sense-of-place-stitched-in-oakland.html?_r=0.

Brown, Peter. *Authority and the Sacred*. New York: Cambridge University Press, 1995.
———. *The Making of Late Antiquity*. Cambridge, MA: Harvard University Press, 1978.

Brumfield, Ben. "New Orleans Officers Convicted in Post Katrina Shooting Get New Trial." CNN, August 19, 2015. www.cnn.com/2015/08/19/us/new-orleans-trial-danziger-bridge-police-shootings/.

Burgin, Victor. *The Remembered Film*. London: Reaktion, 2004.

Burke, Edmund. *A Philosophical Inquiry into the Origin of Our Ideas of the Sublime and Beautiful*. Oxford: Oxford University Press, 2015.

Butler, Judith. *Frames of War: When Life Is Grievable*. New York: Verso, 2010.

Campbell, David, and Michael J. Shapiro, eds. *Moral Spaces: Rethinking Ethics and World Politics*. Minneapolis: University of Minnesota Press, 1999.

Carroll, David. "Rephrasing the Political with Kant and Lyotard: From Aesthetic to Political Judgments." *Diacritics* 14, no. 3 (autumn 1984): 73–88.

Caruth, Cathy. *Unclaimed Experience*. Baltimore: Johns Hopkins University Press, 1996.

Casarino, Cesare. *Modernity at Sea: Melville, Marx, Conrad in Crisis*. Minneapolis: University of Minnesota Press, 2002.

Chaloupka, William. *Knowing Nukes: The Politics and Culture of the Atom*. Minneapolis: University of Minnesota Press, 1992.

Chiapello, Eve. "Accounting and the Birth of the Notion of Capitalism." Accessed July 20, 2017. www.mngt.waikato.ac.nz/ejrot/cmsconference/2003/proceedings/proceedings_criticalaccounting.asp.

Clark, Gregory. *Civic Jazz: American Music and Kenneth Burke on the Art of Getting Along*. Chicago: University of Chicago Press, 2015.

Clift, Sarah. *Committing the Future to Memory: History, Experience, Trauma*. New York: Fordham University Press, 2014.

Coates, Ta-Nehisi. *Between the World and Me*. New York: Spiegel and Grau, 2015.

———. "The Black Family in the Age of Mass Incarceration." *Atlantic*, October 2015. http://theatlantic.com/magazine/archives/2015/10/the-black-family-in-the-age-of -mass-incarceration/4032/46/.

Cobb, Jelani. "What I Saw in Ferguson." *New Yorker*, August 14, 2014, www.newyorker .com/news/news-desk/saw-ferguson.

Cohn, Carol. "Sex and Death in the Rational World of Defense Intellectuals." *Signs* 12, no. 4 (summer 1987): 687–718.

Cole, Teju. "Death in the Browser Tab." *New York Times Magazine*, May 21, 2015, 19–21.

Connolly, William E. *The Fragility of Things: Self-Organizing Processes, Neoliberal Fantasies, and Democratic Activism*. Durham, NC: Duke University Press, 2013.

Cooper, James Fenimore. "American and European Scenery Compared." In Motley F. Deakin, *The Home Book of the Picturesque*, 51–70. Gainesville, FL: Scholars' Facsimiles & Reprints, 1967.

Correspondents of the *New York Times*. *How Race Is Lived in America: Pulling Together, Pulling Apart*. New York: Times Books, 2001.

Cox, Julian. "Introduction: An Exquisite Problem." In David Maisel, *Black Maps: American Landscape and the Apocalyptic Sublime*. Göttingen, Germany: Steidl, 2003.

Crawford, Chelsey. "The Permeable Self: A Theory of Cinematic Quotation." *Film—Philosophy* 19 (2015): 105–123.

Crooks, Robert. "From the Far Side of the Urban Frontier: The Detective Fiction of Chester Himes and Walter Mosley." *College Literature* 22, no. 3 (October 1995): 68–90.

Davis, Mike. "The Flames of New York." *New Left Review* 12 (November–December 2001). https://newleftreview.org/II/12/mike-davis-the-flames-of-new-york.

Deamer, David. *Deleuze, Cinema, and the Atom Bomb*. New York: Bloomsbury, 2014.

Deleuze, Gilles. *Bergsonism*. Translated by Hugh Tomlinson and Barbara Habberjam. New York: Zone Books, 1991.

———. *Cinema 1: The Movement-Image*. Translated by Hugh Tomlinson and Barbara Habberjam. Minneapolis: University of Minnesota Press, 1986.

———. *Cinema 2: The Time Image*. Translated by Hugh Tomlinson and Robert Galeta. Minneapolis: University of Minnesota Press, 1989.

———. *Desert Islands and Other Texts, 1953–1974*. Edited by David Lapoujade, translated by Michael Taormina. New York: Semiotext(e), 2004.

———. *Difference and Repetition*. Translated by Paul Patton. New York: Columbia University Press, 1994.

———. *The Fold: Leibnitz and the Baroque*. Translated by Tom Conley. Minneapolis: University of Minnesota Press, 1992.

———. *Francis Bacon: The Logic of Sensation*. Minneapolis: University of Minnesota Press, 2003.

———. "The Idea of Genesis in Kant's Esthetics." In *Desert Islands and Other Texts, 1953–1974*, 56–71.

———. *Kant's Critical Philosophy: The Doctrine of the Faculties*. Translated by Hugh Tomlinson and Barbara Habberjam. Minneapolis: University of Minnesota Press, 1984.

———. "Lecture on Kant." March 14, 1978. www.webdeleuze.com/php/texte.php?cle =66&groupe=Kant&langue=2.

———. *The Logic of Sense*. Translated by Mark Lester and Charles Stivale. New York: Columbia University Press, 1990.

———. "The Method of Dramatization." In *Desert Islands and Other Texts, 1953–1974*, 94–116.

Deleuze, Gilles, and Guattari, Félix. *A Thousand Plateaus*. Translated by Brian Massumi. Minneapolis: University of Minnesota Press, 1987.

———. *What Is Philosophy?* Translated by Hugh Tomlinson and Graham Burchell. New York: Columbia University Press, 1994.

DeLillo, Don. *Falling Man*. New York: Scribner, 2008.

———. "Human Moments in World War III." *Granta*, March 1, 1984. http://granta.com /human-moments-in-world-war-iii/.

———. "In the Ruins of the Future: Reflections on Terror and Loss in the Shadow of September." *Harper's Magazine* (December 2001): 33–40.

———. *Libra*. New York: Viking, 1988.

———. *Players*. New York: Vintage, 1977.

———. *White Noise*. New York: Viking Penguin, 1985.

Denning, Michael. *The Cultural Front: The Laboring of American Culture in the Twentieth Century*. New York: Verso, 1996.

Dennis, Matthew. *Cultivating a Landscape of Peace*. Ithaca, NY: Cornell University Press, 1993.

Derrida, Jacques. "No Apocalypse, Not Now (Full Speed Ahead, Seven Missiles, Seven Missives)." *Diacritics* 14, no. 2 (summer 1984): 20–31.

Despotopoulou, Anna. "'Running on Lines': Women and the Railway in Victorian and Early Modernist Culture." In *Women in Transit through Literary Liminal Spaces*, edited by Teresa Gomez Reus and Terry Gifford, 47–60. New York: Palgrave Macmillan, 2013.

Didi-Huberman, Georges. "The Art of Not Describing: Vermeer—The Detail and the Patch." *History of the Human Sciences* 2 (1989): 135–169.

Dikeç, Mustapha. "Politics Is Sublime." *Environment and Planning D: Society and Space* 30 (2012): 262–279.

Dillon, Sarah. "'Some Magic Land': Terrence Malick's Sublime Vision of America." Film489: Research Project, Victoria University of Wellington, October 30, 2014. www .academia.edu/11749650/Honours_Dissertation_Some_Magical_Land_Terrence _Malicks_Sublime_Visions_of_America.

Dixon, Emma. "New Orleans' Racial Divide; An Unnatural Disaster." CommonDreams .org, November 16, 2005. www.commondreams.org/views05/1116-34.htm.

Douglass, Frederick. "Parties Were Made for Men, Not Men for Parties: An Address Delivered in Louisville, Kentucky on 25 September 1883." In *The Frederick Douglass Papers, Series One: Speeches, Debates, and Interviews*, edited by John W. Blassingame, John R. McKivigan, and Gerald W. Fulkerson, 5:91–92. New Haven, CT: Yale University Press, 1992.

Du Bois, W. E. B. *Black Reconstruction: An Essay toward a History of the Part Which Black Folk Played in the Attempt to Reconstruct Democracy in America: 1860–1880*. New York: Harcourt, Brace and Company, 1935.

———. *The Souls of Black Folk*. www.gutenberg.org/files/408/408-h/408-h.htm.

Dyson, Michael Eric. "Racial Terror, Fast and Slow." *New York Times*, April 17, 2015. www.nytimes.com/2015/04/17/opinion/racial-terror-fast-and-slow.html?_r=0.

Edensor, Tim. *Industrial Ruins: Spaces, Aesthetics and Materiality.* New York: Berg, 2005, 13.

Edwards, Elizabeth. "Introduction." In *Anthropology and Photography, 1860–1920,* edited by Elizabeth Edwards. New Haven, CT: Yale University Press, 1992.

Eichenberger, John, Freymueller, Jeff, Hill, Graham, and Patrick, Matt. "Nuclear Steward-ship: Lessons from a Not-So-Remote Island." *Geotimes* (March 2002). www.geotimes .org/mar02/feature_amchitka.html.

Ellison, Ralph. *Invisible Man.* New York: Vintage, 1995.

Eperjesi, John R. *The Imperialist Imaginary: Visions of Asia and the Pacific in American Culture.* Hanover, NH: Dartmouth College Press, 2005.

Fanon, Frantz. *Black Skin, White Masks.* New York: Grove, 2008.

Farocki, Harun. "Workers Leaving the Factory." *Senses of Cinema* 21 (July 19, 2002). http://sensesofcinema.com/2002/harun-farocki/farocki_workers/.

Fassin, Didier, and Rechtman, Richard. *The Empire of Trauma.* Translated by Rachel Gomme. Princeton, NJ: Princeton University Press, 2009.

Fiske, John. *Media Matters: Everyday Culture and Political Change.* Minneapolis: University of Minnesota Press, 1994.

Flanagan, Martin. "'Everything a Lie': The Critical and Commercial Reception of Ter-rence Malick's *The Thin Red Line*." In *The Cinema of Terrence Malick: Poetic Visions of America,* edited by Hannah Patterson, 123–136. New York: Wallflower, 2003.

Forgacs, David. *Red Desert* commentary. Accessed July 20, 2017. www.academia.edu/ 7619181/Red_Desert_Michelangelo_Antonioni_1964.

Foucault, Michel. *The Birth of Biopolitics.* Translated by Graham Burchell. New York: Palgrave, 2008.

———. "The Confession of the Flesh." In *Power/Knowledge,* edited by Colin Gordon, 194–228. New York: Pantheon, 1980.

———. "The Father's No." In *Language, Counter-Memory, Practice,* 68–86.

———. *Fearless Speech.* New York: Semiotext(e), 2001.

———. *Language, Counter-Memory, Practice.* Edited by Donald F. Bouchard, translated by Donald Bouchard and Sherry Simon. Ithaca, NY: Cornell University Press, 1977.

———. "Nietzsche, Genealogy, History." In *Language, Counter-Memory, Practice,* 139–164.

———. "Of Other Spaces: Utopias and Heterotopies." Translated by Jay Miskowiec. *Architecture, Mouvement, Continuité* 5 (1984): 46–49. http://web.mit.edu/allanmc/ www/foucault1.pdf.

Freud, Sigmund. "The Uncanny." First published in *Image,* bd. 5, 1919. In *The Standard Edition of the Complete Psychological Works of Sigmund Freud,* vol. 17 (1917–1919), edited by James Strachey, 217–256. London: Hogarth, 1955.

Gandy, Matthew. "Landscapes of Deliquescence in Michelangelo Antonioni's 'Red Des-ert.'" *Transactions of the Institute of British Geographers* 28, no. 2 (June 2003): 218–237.

Geertz, Clifford. "Thick Description: Toward an Interpretive Theory of Culture." In *The Interpretation of Cultures: Selected Essays.* New York: Basic Books, 1973. www .sociosite.net/topics/texts/Geertz_Thick_Description.php.

Giles, Jeff. Review of *After the Quake*: "A Shock to the System." *New York Times*, August 18, 2002. www.nytimes.com/2002/08/18/books/a-shock-to-the-system.html.

Gilroy, Paul. *Darker Than Blue*. Cambridge, MA: Harvard University Press, 2010.

Gooding-Williams, Robert. "Du Bois's Counter-Sublime." *Massachusetts Review* 35, no. 2 (summer 1994): 202–224.

Gramsci, Antonio. *Selections from the Prison Notebooks*. London: Electric Book Company, 1999. http://abahlali.org/files/gramsci.pdf.

Gray, Richard. "Open Doors, Closed Minds: American Prose Writing in a Time of Crisis." *American Literary History* 2, no. 1 (spring 2009): 128–151.

Greenhouse, Wendy. "On the Fringes: Picturing New York's Waterways, Bridges, and Docklands, 1890–1913." In *Industrial Sublime: Modernism and the Transformation of New York's Rivers, 1900–1940*, 33–47. New York: Hudson River Museum, 2013.

Grusin, Richard. *Premediation: Affect and Mediality after 9/11*. New York: Palgrave/Macmillan, 2010.

Guattari, Felix. *Schizoanalytic Cartographies*. Translated by Andrew Goffey. New York: Bloomsbury, 2013.

Gussow, Adam. *It Seems like Murder Here*. Chicago: University of Chicago Press, 2002.

Gusterson, Hugh. *People of the Bomb*. Minneapolis: University of Minnesota Press, 2004.

Hale, Peter B. "The Atomic Sublime." *American Studies* 32, no. 1 (spring 1991): 1–27.

Hammett, Dashiell. *The Maltese Falcon*. New York: Vintage, 1992.

Handke, Peter. "The Lesson of Mont Sainte-Victoire." In *Slow Homecoming*, translated by Ralph Mannheim, 139–211. New York: Macmillan, 1988.

Hapke, Laura. *Sweatshop: The History of an Idea*. New Brunswick, NJ: Rutgers University Press, 2004.

Harney, Stefano. "Hapticality in the Undercommons, or from Operations Management to Black Ops." Cumma papers no. 9, August 2013. https://cummastudies.files.wordpress.com/2013/08/cumma-papers-9.pdf.

Hau'ofa, Epeli. "Our Sea of Islands." Accessed July 20, 2017. http://savageminds.org/wp-content/image-upload/our-sea-of-islands-epeli-hauofa.pdf.

Hegel, G. W. F. *Lectures on Aesthetics Part II: Of the Ideal of Classic Art*. Accessed July 20, 2017. www.marxists.org/reference/archive/hegel/works/ae/ch02.htm.

Heidegger, Martin. "The Origin of a Work of Art." In *Poetry, Language, Thought*, translated by Albert Hofstadter. New York: Harper & Row, 1971.

———. *What Is a Thing?* Translated by Vera Deutsch and W. B. Barton. South Bend, IN: Gateway, 1967.

———. *What Is Called Thinking?* Translated by J. Glen Gray. New York: Harper & Row, 1968.

Hertz, Neil. "A Reading of Longinus." In *The End of the Line: Essays in Psychoanalysis and the Sublime*. New York: Columbia University Press, 1985.

Hinnant, Charles H. "Schiller and the Political Sublime: Two Perspectives." *Criticism* 44, no. 2 (spring 2002): 121–138.

Hinsley, Curtis. "Ethnographic Charisma and Scientific Routine." In *Observers Observed: Essays on Ethnographic Fieldwork*, edited by George Stocking, 14–53. Madison: University of Wisconsin Press, 1983.

Huyssen, Andreas. "Monumental Seduction." *New German Critique* 69 (autumn 1996): 181–200.

———. *Presents Past: Urban Palimpsests and the Politics of Memory*. Stanford, CA: Stanford University Press, 2003.

Iampolski, Mikhail. *The Memory of Tiresias: Intertextuality and Cinema*. Translated by Harsha Ram. Berkeley: University of California Press, 1998.

Ibuse, Masuji. *Black Rain*. Translated by John Bester. 1969. Reprint, New York: Kodansha, 2012.

Jaguaribe, Beatriz. "Nostalgia for the Future: Monument, Ruin and the New in the City." In *Collective Imagination: Limits and Beyond*, edited by Enrique Rodriguez Laretta. Rio de Janeiro: UNESCO.ISSC.EDUCAM, 2001.

James, William. "The Will to Believe." An Address to the Philosophical Clubs of Yale and Brown Universities. Published in *New World*, June 1896. http://educ.jmu .edu//~omearawm/ph101willtobelieve.html.

Jensen, Kirsten M. "Picturing Manhatta: Modernism, Urban Planning, and New York, 1920–1940." In *Industrial Sublime: Modernism and the Transformation of New York's Rivers, 1900–1940*, 71–91. New York: Fordham University Press, 2013.

Jhally, Sut, and Earp, Jeremy, eds. *Hijacking Catastrophe*. Northampton, MA: Olive Branch Press, 2004.

Jones, Edward P. "Introduction." In Baldwin, *Notes of a Native Son*.

———. *The Known World*. New York: HarperCollins, 2003.

Jones-Deweever, Avis. "The Forgotten Ones: Black Women in the Wake of Katrina." In *The Neoliberal Deluge: Hurricane Katrina and the Remaking of New Orleans*, edited by Cedric Johnson. Minneapolis: University of Minnesota Press, 2011.

Kahn, Herman. *On Thermonuclear War*. Princeton, NJ: Princeton University Press, 1962.

———. *Thinking about the Unthinkable*. New York: Avon, 1962.

Kant, Immanuel. *The Critique of Judgement*. Translated by James Creed Meredith. Oxford, UK: Clarendon, 1952.

———. *Observations of the Feeling of the Beautiful and Sublime*. Translated by John Goldthwait. 1790. Reprint, Berkeley: University of California Press, 1991.

Keady, Jim. "When Will Nike 'Just Do It' on the Sweatshop Issue?" *Huffington Post*, December 2, 2009. www.huffingtonpost.com/jim-keady/when-will-nike-just-do-it -it_b_308448.html.

Kempton, Arthur. *Boogaloo*. New York: Pantheon, 2003.

Klein, Richard. "Kant's Sunshine." *Diacritics* 11, no. 2 (summer 1981): 26–41.

Kramer, Aaron. "Hiroshima: A 37-Year Failure to Respond." *New England Review and Broadleaf Quarterly* 5, no. 4 (summer 1983): 534–548.

Kristof, Nicholas. "When Whites Just Don't Get It, Part 6." *New York Times*, Sunday Review (April 2, 2006). www.nytimes.com/2016/04/03/opinion/sunday/when-whites -just-dont-get-it-part-6.html?_r=0.

Kuhlman, Martha. "The Traumatic Temporality of Art: Spiegelman's *In the Shadow of No Towers*." *Journal of Popular Culture* 40, no. 5 (2007): 849–866.

Kuletz, Valerie L. *The Tainted Desert*. New York: Routledge, 1998.

Kundera, Milan. *Slowness*. London: Faber and Faber, 1996.

Lacan, Jacques. "Desire and the Interpretation of Desire in *Hamlet*." Translated by James Hulbert. *Yale French Studies* no. 55/56 (1977): 11–52.

———. "On a Question Preliminary to Any Possible Treatment of Psychosis." In *Écrits: A Selection*, translated by Alan Sheridan, 179–221. New York: W. W. Norton, 1977.

Lain, Douglas, ed. *In the Shadows of the Towers*. New York: Night Shade, 2015.

Landy, Marcia. *Cinema and Counter-History*. Bloomington: Indiana University Press, 2015.

Lebovic, James H. *Deterring International Terrorism and Rogue States: US Security Policy after 9/11*. London: Routledge, 2006.

Lee, Spike. "Spike Lee on Race, Politics and Broken Levees." *All Things Considered*, NPR, August 13, 2006. www.npr.org/templates/story/story.php?storyId=5641453.

Le Fanu, Mark. "In This World." Published with the Criterion Collection DVD version of *Red Desert* (2010).

Lefebvre, Martin. "Between Setting and Landscape in the Cinema." In *Landscape and Film*, edited by Lefebvre, 19–59. New York: Routledge, 2006.

Lelyveld, Joseph. "Introduction." In Correspondents of the *New York Times, How Race Is Lived in America*, ix–xix.

Lewin, Tamar. "Growing Up, Growing Apart." In Correspondents of the *New York Times, How Race Is Lived in America*, 151–170.

Lindner, Burkhardt. "The Passagen-Werk, the Berlin Kindheit, and the Archaeology of the 'Recent Past.'" *New German Critique* 39 (fall 1986): 25–46.

Lindstrom, Lamont. "Images of Islanders in Pacific War Photographs." In *Perilous Memories: The Asia-Pacific War(s)*, edited by T. Fugitani, Geoffrey White, and Lisa Yoneyama, 107–128. Durham, NC: Duke University Press, 2001.

Longinus. Translated by W. Rhys Roberts. Web edition, eBooks@Adelaide. https://ebooks.adelaide.edu.au/l/longinus/on_the_sublime/.

Longinus on the Sublime. Translated by James A. Arieti and John M. Crossett. New York: Edwin Mellen Press, 1985.

Lowell, Robert. "Fall 1961." www.blueridgejournal.com/poems/rl—fall.htm.

Lukinbeal, Chris. "Cinematic Landscapes." *Journal of Cultural Geography* 23, no. 1 (fall/winter 2005): 3–22.

Lyotard, Jean-François. "After the Sublime, the State of Aesthetics." In *The Inhuman*, 135–143.

———. *Discourse, Figure*. Translated by Antony Hudek and Mary Lydon. Minneapolis: University of Minnesota Press, 2011.

———. *The Inhuman*. Translated by Geoffrey Bennington and Rachel Bowlby. Stanford, CA: Stanford University Press, 1991.

———. *The Postmodern Condition: A Report on Knowledge*. Translated by Geoffrey Bennington and Brian Massumi. Minneapolis: University of Minnesota Press, 1984.

———. "The Sublime and the Avant Garde." In *The Inhuman*, 135–143.

Mackey, Nathaniel. *Atet A.D.* San Francisco, CA: City Lights Books, 2001.

Magnuson, Magnus. "Introduction." In *Njal's Saga*, translated by Hermann Palsson, 9–35. New York: Penguin, 1960.

Maisel, David. *Black Maps: American Landscape and the Apocalyptic Sublime*. Göttingen, Germany: Steidl, 2003.

Mannheim, Karl. *Diagnoses of Our Time*. London: Kegan Paul, Trench, Trubner & Co., 1943.

Marcus, George. "A Broad(er) Side to the Canon." *Cultural Anthropology* 6, no. 3 (1991): 385–405.

Marcuse, Herbert. *One-Dimensional Man: Studies in the Ideology of Advanced Industrial Society*. 2nd ed. Boston: Beacon, 1991.

Martin, Colin. "Haruki Murakami's Passion for Jazz." OpenCulture.com, July 2014. www.openculture.com/2014/07/haruki-murakamis-passion-for-jazz.html.

Marx, Leo. *The Machine in the Garden: Technology and the Pastoral Ideal in America*. New York: Oxford University Press, 1964.

May, Charles. "Reading the Short Story." *May on the Short Story* (blog), January 2011. http://may-on-the-short-story.blogspot/2011/01/Haruki-murakami-after-quake.html.

Menand, Louis. "Fat Man: Herman Kahn and the Nuclear Age." *New Yorker*, June 27, 2005. www.newyorker.com/magazine/2005/06/27/fat-man.

Mendelsohn, Daniel. "A Dance to the Music of Time." *New York Times*, January 26, 2003. www.nytimes.com/2003/01/26/books/a-dance-to-the-music-of-time.html.

Meyer, Christina. "'Putting It into Boxes': Framing Art Spiegelman's 'In the Shadow of No Towers.'" *Amerikastudien/American Studies* 55, no. 3 (2010): 479–494.

Milbank, John. "Sublimity: The Modern Transcendent." In *Transcendence: Philosophy, Theology, and Literature Approach the Beyond*, edited by Regina Schartz. New York: Routledge, 2004.

Miller, Arthur. *Time Bends: A Life*. New York: Grove, 1987.

Mills, C. Wright. "Review of Franz Neumann's *Behemoth: The Structure and Function of National Socialism 1933–1944*." Accessed July 20, 2017. www.wbenjamin.org/Behemoth.html.

Mitchell, W. J. T. "Imperial Landscape." In *Landscape and Power*, 5–34. Chicago: University of Chicago Press, 2002.

———. "The Unspeakable and the Unimaginable: Word and Image in a Time of Terror." *ELH* 72 (summer 2005): 291–308.

Moore, Macdonald Smith. *Yankee Blues: Musical Culture and American Identity*. Bloomington: Indiana University Press, 1985.

Morris, David B. "Gothic Sublimity." *New Literary History* 16, no. 2 (winter 1985): 299–319.

Morris, Robert. "From a Chomskian Couch: The Imperialistic Unconscious." *Critical Inquiry* 29, no. 4 (summer 2003): 678–694.

Moskowitz, Milton. "The Enduring Importance of Richard Wright." *Journal of Blacks in Higher Education*, April 1, 2008. www.jbhe.com/features/59_richardwright.html.

Mowitt, John. *Text: The Genealogy of an Anti-Disciplinary Object*. Durham, NC: Duke University Press, 1992.

Murakami, Haruki. *After the Quake*. Translated by Jay Rubin. New York: Vintage, 2000.

———. Interview. *Jerusalem Post*, February 15, 2009. www.goodreads.com/quotes/140477-if-there-is-a-hard-high-wall-and-an-egg.

———. *Underground: The Tokyo Gas Attack and the Japanese Psyche*. Translated by Alfred Birnbaum and Philip Gabriel. New York: Vintage, 2001.

———. "A Walk to Kobe." *Granta* 124 (summer 2013). https://granta.com/a-walk-to-kobe/.

Nabokov, Peter, and Easton, Robert. *Native American Architecture*. New York: Oxford University Press, 1989.

Nair, Kartak. "Plummeting to the Pavement: The Fall of the Body in *Spider-Man*." In *Terror and the Cinematic Sublime*, edited by Todd A. Comer and Lloyd Isaac Vayo. Jefferson, NC: McFarland, 2013.

Nancy, Jean-Luc. *The Inoperative Community*. Translated by Peter Connor and Lisa Garbus. Minneapolis: University of Minnesota Press, 1991.

Navas, Eduardo, *Remix Theory: The Aesthetics of Sampling*. New York: Springer, 2012.

Nieland, Justus. "Graphic Violence: Native Americans and the Western Archive in *Dead Man*." *CR: The New Centennial Review* 1, no. 2 (fall 2001): 171–200.

Nietzsche, Friedrich. *The Birth of Tragedy*. Translated by M. Tanner. New York: Penguin, 1994.

Nixon, Rob. *Slow Violence and the Environmentalism of the Poor*. Cambridge, MA: Harvard University Press, 2011.

Nye, David E. *The American Technological Sublime*. Cambridge, MA: MIT Press, 1994.

Obrist, Hans. "Interview with Johan Grimonprez." Accessed July 20, 2017. http://archive.constantvzw.org/events/e11/en/jg.html.

Ojito, Mirta. "Best of Friends, Worlds Apart." In Correspondents of the *New York Times*, *How Race Is Lived in America*.

Orban, Katalin. "Trauma and Visuality: Art Spiegelman's *Maus* and *In the Shadow of No Towers*." *Representations* 92, no. 1 (winter 2007): 57–89.

Ouaknin, Marc-Alain. *The Burnt Book*. Translated by L. Brown. Princeton, NJ: Princeton University Press, 1995.

Panagia, Davide. *The Poetics of Political Thinking*. Durham, NC: Duke University Press, 2006.

———. *The Political Life of Sensation*. Durham, NC: Duke University Press, 2009.

Panofsky, Irwin. *Gothic Architecture and Scholasticism*. New York: Meridian, 1958.

Pasolini, Pier Paolo. "The Cinema of Poetry." In *Heretical Empiricism*, edited by Louise K. Barnett, translated by Ben Lawton and Louise K. Barnett. Bloomington: Indiana University Press, 1988.

Pease, Donald E. "Sublime Politics." *boundary 2* 12, no. 3 / 13, no. 1 (spring–autumn 1984): 259–279.

Pérez-Peña, Richard. "Upbeat Ad for Old Navy Leads to a Backlash. Twice." *New York Times*, May 5, 2016. www.nytimes.com/2016/05/05/us/upbeat-interracial-ad-for-old-navy-leads-to-backlash-twice.html?_r=0.

Pillow, Kirk. *Sublime Understanding: Aesthetic Reflection in Kant and Hegel*. Cambridge, MA: MIT Press, 2000.

Powers, Richard. *The Time of Our Singing*. New York: Farrar, Straus and Giroux, 2003.

Price, Leslie Blake. "Bluegrass Nation: A Historical and Cultural Analysis of America's Truest Music." Honors thesis, University of Tennessee, 2011. http://trace.tennessee.edu/cgi/viewcontent.cgi?article=2472&context=utk_chanhonoproj.

Pynchon, Thomas. *Mason & Dixon*. New York: Picador, 2004.

Ragussis, Michael. *Acts of Naming: The Family Plot in Fiction*. New York: Oxford University Press, 1986.

Rancière, Jacques. "Aesthetic Separation, Aesthetic Community: Scenes from the Aesthetic Regime of Art." *Art & Research* 2, no. 1 (summer 2008). www.artandresearch .og.uk/v2n1/ranciere.html.

———. "Contemporary Art and the Politics of Aesthetics." In *Communities of Sense: Rethinking Aesthetics and Politics*, edited by Beth Hinderliter et al., 31–50. Durham, NC: Duke University Press, 2009.

———. "Fictions of Time." In *Rancière and Literature*, edited by Grace Hellyer and Julian Murphet. Edinburgh: Edinburgh University Press, 2016.

———. "The Method of Equality: An Answer to Some Questions." In *Jacques Ranciere: History, Politics, Aesthetics*, edited by Gabriel Rockhill and Philip Watts, 258–272. Durham, NC: Duke University Press, 2009.

———. "Thinking between Disciplines: An Aesthetics of Knowledge." *Parrhesia* no. 1 (2006): 1–12.

———. "The Thinking of Dissensus: Politics and Aesthetics." In *Reading Rancière*, edited by Paul Bowman and Richard Stamp. New York: Continuum, 2011.

Rainer, Peter. "Candid Camera." *New York Magazine*, October 21, 2002. http://nymag .com/nymetro/movies/reviews/n_8955/.

Rasmussen, Birgit Brander. *Queequeg's Coffin: Indigenous Literacies and Early American Literature*. Durham, NC: Duke University Press, 2012.

Ratcliffe, Viola. "To Be a Witness: Lynching and Postmemory in LaShawnda Crowe Storm's "Her Name Was Laura Nelson." Accessed July 20, 2017. https://etd.ohiolink .edu/pg_10?0::NO:10:P10_ACCESSION_NUM:bgsu1435789289.

Ray, Gene. *Terror and the Sublime in Art and Critical Theory: From Auschwitz to Hiroshima to September 11 and Beyond*. New York: Palgrave Macmillan, 2005.

Redfield, Marc W. "Pynchon's Postmodern Sublime." *PMLA* 104, no. 2 (March 1989): 152–162.

Rich, Frank. "The Clear Blue Sky" (book review). *New York Times*, May 27, 2007. www .nytimes.com/2007/05/27/books/review/Rich-t.html?_r=0.

Robbins, Bruce. "The Sweatshop Sublime." *PMLA* 117, no. 1 (January 2002): 84–97. www.columbia.edu/-bwr2001/papers/sweatshop.pdf.

Rodowick, D. N. *Reading the Figural, or, Philosophy after the New Media*. Durham, NC: Duke University Press, 2001.

Roosevelt, Theodore. *The Winning of the West*. New York: J. P. Putnam's Sons, 1889.

Rose, Gillian. "Afterwords: Gazes, Glances and Shadows." In *Cultural Landscapes*, edited by I. Robertson and P. Richards. London: Arnold, 2003.

Ross, Andrew, ed. *No Sweat: Fashion, Free Trade, and the Rights of Garment Workers*. New York: Verso, 1997.

Rothman, Joshua. "The Unsettling Arrival of Speculative 9/11 Fiction." *New Yorker*, September 11, 2015. www.newyorker.com/culture/cultural-comment/the-creepy -power-of-speculative-911-fiction.

Rothman, William. "Some Thoughts on Hitchcock's Authorship." In *Alfred Hitchcock: Centenary Essays*, edited by Richard Allen and S. Ishii Gonzales, 29–44. London: BFI, 1999.

Rubin, Jay. *Haruki Murakami and the Music of Words*. London: Vintage, 2012.

Sack, Kevin. "Shared Prayers, Mixed Blessings." In Correspondents of the *New York Times*, *How Race Is Lived in America*, 3–22.

Sand, Shlomo. *The Invention of the Jewish People*. New York: Verso, 2009.

Santner, Eric. *On the Psychotheology of Everyday Life: Reflections on Freud and Rosenzweig*. Chicago: University of Chicago Press, 2001.

Sartre, Jean-Paul. *The Family Idiot: Gustave Flaubert 1821–1857*. Translated by Carol Cosman. Chicago: University of Chicago Press, 1987.

Scheckel, Susan. *The Insistence of the Indian: Race and Nationalism in Nineteenth-Century American Culture*. Princeton, NJ: Princeton University Press, 1999.

Schell, Jonathan. "Introduction." In Robert Del Tredici, *At Work in the Fields of the Bomb*, iii–xi. New York: Harper & Row, 1987.

Schiappa, Jacqueline. "#IfTheyGunnedMeDown: The Necessity of 'Black Twitter' and Hashtags in the Age of Ferguson." *ProudFlesh: New Afrikan Journal of Culture and Consciousness* 10 (2014). www.africaknowledgeproject.org/index.php/proudflesh/article/view/2144.

Schiller, Friedrich. "Of the Sublime: Towards the Further Realization of Some Kantian Ideas." *Fidelio* 13, nos. 1–2 (spring–summer 2004): 90–99.

———. "On the Sublime (1801)." Translated by William F. Wertz Jr. philosophyproject.org/wp-content/uploads/2013.09/on-the-sublime.pdf.

Schley, Jim, ed. *Writing in a Nuclear Age*. Hanover, NH: University Press of New England, 1985.

Schneider, Keith. "Foreword." In Carole Gallagher, *American Ground Zero: The Secret Nuclear War*. Cambridge, MA: MIT Press, 1993.

Schweighauser, Philipp, and Peter Schneck. "Introduction." In *Terrorism, Media, and the Ethics of Fiction*. New York: Bloomsbury, 2012.

Scorsese, Martin. "The Man Who Set Film Free." *New York Times*, August 12, 2007. www.nytimes.com/2007/08/12/movies/12scor.html?_r=0.

Seats, Michael Robert. *Murakami Haruki: The Simulacrum in Contemporary Japanese Culture*. Lanham, MD: Lexington Books, 2009.

Seed, David. "Mapping the Course of Empire in the New World." In *Pynchon and Mason & Dixon*, edited by Brooke Horvath and Irving Malin. Newark: University of Delaware Press, 2000.

Sehgal, Parul. "Fighting 'Erasure.'" *New York Times Magazine*, February 7, 2016. www.nytimes.com/2016/02/07/magazine/the-painful-consequences-of-erasure.html?_r=0.

Shapiro, Gary. "From the Sublime to the Political: Some Historical Notes." *New Literary History* 16, no. 2 (winter 1985): 213–235.

Shapiro, Michael J. *Cinematic Geopolitics*. New York: Routledge, 2009.

———. *Cinematic Political Thought: Narrating Race, Nation and Gender*. Edinburgh: Edinburgh University Press, 1999.

———. *Deforming American Political Thought: Challenging the Jeffersonian Legacy*. 2nd ed. New York: Routledge, 2016.

———. *For Moral Ambiguity: National Culture and the Politics of the Family*. Minneapolis: University of Minnesota Press, 2001.

———. "Hiroshima Temporalities." *Thesis Eleven* 129, no. 1 (August 2015): 40–56.

———. "Introduction." In *Moral Spaces: Rethinking Ethics and World Politics*, edited by David Campbell and Michael J. Shapiro. Minneapolis: University of Minnesota Press, 1999.

———. "The Light of Reason: Reading the *Leviathan* with 'The Werckmeister Harmonies.'" *Political Theory* 45 (2017): 385–415.

———. *Methods and Nations: Cultural Governance and the Indigenous Subject.* London: Routledge, 2004.

———. *Politics and Time.* Cambridge, UK: Polity, 2016.

———. *Reading the Postmodern Polity: Political Theory as Textual Practice.* Minneapolis: University of Minnesota Press, 1992.

———. *Studies in Trans-Disciplinary Method: After the Aesthetic Turn.* New York: Routledge, 2012.

———. "The Sublime Today: Re-Partitioning the Global Sensible." *Millennium* 34, no. 3 (August 2006): 657–681.

———. *The Time of the City: Politics, Philosophy and Genre.* New York: Routledge, 2010.

———. *Violent Cartographies: Mapping Cultures of War.* Minneapolis: University of Minnesota Press, 1997.

———. "Wanted Dead or Alive." *Theory and Event* 5, no. 4 (2001).

———. *War Crimes, Atrocity, and Justice.* Cambridge, UK: Polity, 2015.

Shaviro, Steven. "Beauty Lies in the Eye." In *A Shock to Thought*, edited by Brian Massumi, 9–19. New York: Routledge, 2002.

———. *Post-Cinematic Affect.* Washington, DC: Zero Books, 2010.

———. "The 'Wrenching Duality' of Aesthetics: Kant, Deleuze, and the 'Theory of the Sensible.'" Shaviro.com, November 10, 2007. www.shaviro.com/Othertexts/SPEP.pdf.

Shaw, Philip. *The Sublime.* New York: Routledge, 2006.

Shulevitz, Judith. "Chasing after Conrad's Secret Agent." *Slate*, September 2001. www .slate.com/articles/arts/culturebox/2001/09/chasing_after_conrads_secret_agent.html.

Silko, Leslie Marmon. *Ceremony.* New York: Penguin, 1986.

Silverman, Kaja. "Waiting, Hoping, among the Ruins of All the Rest." In *Cinema's Alchemist: The Films of Péter Forgács*, edited by Bill Nichols and Michael Renov, 96–118. Minneapolis: University of Minnesota Press, 2011.

Slotkin, Richard. *Gunfighter Nation: The Myth of the Frontier in Twentieth-Century America.* Norman: University of Oklahoma Press, 1998.

Smith, Dorothy. "On Sociological Description: A Method from Marx." *Human Studies* 4 (1981): 313–337.

Smith, Terry. *The Architecture of Aftermath.* Chicago: University of Chicago Press, 2006.

Snauwaert, Dirk. "Introduction." In *Stan Douglas, the Secret Agent.* Brussels: Ludion, 2015.

Solnit, Rebecca. *Savage Dreams: A Journey in the Hidden Wars of the American West.* Berkeley: University of California Press, 2014.

Spiegelman, Art. *Breakdowns: From "Maus" to Now: Anthology of Strips by Art Spiegelman.* New York: Belier, 1977.

———. *In the Shadow of No Towers.* New York: Pantheon, 2004.

Spillers, Hortense. "Mama's Baby, Papa's Maybe: An American Grammar Book." *Diacritics* 17, no. 2 (summer 1987): 64–81.

Spivak, Gayatri. *An Aesthetic Education in the Era of Globalization.* Cambridge, MA: Harvard University Press, 2012.

Stabile, Carol A. "Nike, Social Responsibility, and the Hidden Abode of Production." *Critical Studies in Media Communication* 17, no. 2 (June 2000): 186–204.

Stock, Brian. *The Implications of Literacy: Written Language and the Models of Interpretation in the 11th and 12th Centuries.* Princeton, NJ: Princeton University Press, 1983.

Stone, Allucquére Rosanne. "Split Subjects, Not Atoms; or How I Fell in Love with My Prosthesis." *Configurations* 2, no. 1 (1994): 173–190.

Swain, Joseph P. *The Broadway Musical.* New York: Oxford University Press, 1990.

Thomson, David. *The Moment of Psycho: How Alfred Hitchcock Taught America to Love Murder.* New York: Basic Books, 2009.

Trachtenberg, Alan. *The Incorporation of America: Culture and Society in the Gilded Age.* New York: Hill and Wang, 1982.

Tredici, Robert Del. *At Work in the Fields of the Bomb.* New York: HarperCollins, 1987.

Tschumi, Bernard. "Violence of Architecture." In *Architecture and Disjunction.* Cambridge, MA: MIT Press, 1996. http://th3.fr/theme.php?id=YUYI1&PHPSESSID =fvtkroupr85hv7a126dvbf2a85.

Turner, Jack. *Awakening to Race: Individual and Social Consequences in America.* Chicago: University of Chicago Press, 2012.

Unger, Sheldon. *The Rise and Fall of Nuclearism.* University Park: Pennsylvania State University Press, 1992.

Van Stylesdall, Nancy. "The Trans/Historicity of Trauma in Jeannette Armstrong's *Slash* and Sherman Alexie's *Indian Killer.*" *Studies in the Novel* 40, nos. 1 and 2 (summer 2008): 203–223.

Vidler, Anthony. *The Architectural Uncanny: Essays in the Modern Unhomely.* Cambridge, MA: MIT Press, 1992.

Wagner, Keith B. "Globalizing Discourses: Literature and Film in the Age of Google." *Globalizations* 12, no. 2 (2015): 229–243.

Wahlberg, Malin. *Documentary Time: Film and Phenomenology.* Minneapolis: University of Minnesota Press, 2008.

White, Hayden. "The Politics of Historical Interpretation." In *The Content of Form: Narrative, Discourse and Historical Representation*, 58–82. Baltimore: Johns Hopkins University Press, 1987.

Wideman, John Edgar. *Brothers and Keepers.* New York: Houghton Mifflin, 2005.

Wilson, Rob. "Towards the Nuclear Sublime: Representations of Technological Vastness in Postmodern American Poetry." *Prospects* 14 (1989): 407–439.

———. "Towards the Nuclear Sublime: Representations of Technological Vastness in Post Nuclear America." In *American Sublime.* Madison: University of Wisconsin Press, 1991.

Wilton, Andrew. "The Sublime in the Old World and the New." In Andrew Wilton and Tim Barringer, *American Sublime: Landscape Painting in the United States 1820–1880.* Princeton, NJ: Princeton University Press, 2002.

Withy, Katherine. *Heidegger on Being Uncanny.* Cambridge, MA: Harvard University Press, 2009.

Wittenberg, Hermann. "Paton's Sublime: Race, Landscape and the Transcendence of the Liberal Imagination." *Current Writing: Text and Reception in Southern Africa* 17, no. 2 (2005): 3–23.

Wolf, Bryan J. "A Grammar of the Sublime, or Intertextuality Triumphant in Church, Turner, and Cole." *New Literary History* 16, no. 2 (winter 1985): 321–341.

Wolff, Tobias. "Winter Light." *New Yorker*, June 9, 2008. www.newyorker.com/magazine/2008/06/09/winter-light.

Wood, Eben. "Grimonprez's Remix." December 2010. www.johangrimonprez.be/main/Film_DIALHISTORY_Story_6.html.

Woods, Clyde. "Katrina's World: Blues, Bourbon, and the Return to the Source." *American Quarterly* 61, no. 3 (September 2009): 427–453.

Young, James E. "The Holocaust as Vicarious Past: Art Spiegelman's *Maus* and the Afterimages of History." *Critical Inquiry* 24, no. 3 (spring 1998): 666–699.

Zepke, Stephen. "Contemporary Art—Beautiful or Sublime? Kant in Rancière, Lyotard and Deleuze." *Avello Publishing Journal* 1, no. 1 (2011): 1–21.

———. "The Sublime Conditions of Contemporary Art." *Deleuze Studies* 5, no. 1 (2011): 73–83.

Ziarek, Krzysztof. *The Force of Art.* Stanford, CA: Stanford University Press, 2004.

Ziff, Larzer. *Writing in the New Nation.* New Haven, CT: Yale University Press, 1991.

Žižek, Slavoj. *Event: A Philosophical Journey through a Concept.* Brooklyn, NY: Melville House, 2014.

———. "Kate's Choice, or The Materialism of Henry James." In *Lacan: The Silent Partners*, edited by Slavoj Žižek. New York: Verso, 2006.

Zourabichvili, François. *Deleuze: A Philosophy of the Event.* Translated by Kieran Aarons. Edinburgh: Edinburgh University Press, 2012.